CHILDHOOD DISORDERS

D0207343

Childhood Disorders

Philip C. Kendall
Temple University, Philadelphia, USA

Psychology Press
a member of the Taylor & Francis group

Copyright © 2000 by Psychology Press Ltd (a member of the Taylor & Francis group) and Philip C. Kendall.

All rights reserved. No part of this book may be reproduced in any form by photostat, microform, retrieval system, or any other means without the prior written permission of the publisher.

Psychology Press Ltd, Publishers
27 Church Road
Hove
East Sussex, BN3 2FA
UK

British Library Cataloguing-in-Publication Data

A catalogue record for this book is available from the British Library

ISBN 0-86377-608-6 (hbk)
ISBN 0-86377-609-4 (pbk)
ISSN 1368-454X (Clinical Psychology: A Modular Course)

Cover Illustration:
A Family of Fish, a watercolour by Peter J. Mikulka, PhD.
Although biology sets boundaries (e.g. the patterns of color), environmental factors (quality of water, access to food, social behavior) play a crucial role in development and adjustment.

Typeset by Facing Pages, Southwick, West Sussex
Printed and bound in the UK by TJ International Ltd, Padstow, Cornwall, UK

Contents

Series preface   ix

1. **Getting to know the children**   **1**
   Introducing some of the children   2
   Introducing some of the questions   8

2. **Models of childhood disorders**   **11**
   Biological models   11
   Behaviorism: The learning models   15
   Cognitive model   20
   Psychodynamic model   23
   Systems models   28
   Diathesis-stress model   30
   Changing times   30
   Summary   31

3. **Issues facing the disorders of childhood**   **33**
   Developmental psychopathology   34
   Parenting and family factors   35
   Assessing and classifying childhood disorders   39
   Treating disorders of childhood   47
   Summary   49

4. **Conduct disorders**   **51**
   Phenomenology and classification   51
   Causes   55
   The course of conduct disorder   59
   Treatments   60
   Summary   64

5. **Attention-deficit hyperactivity disorder   65**
    Phenomenology and classification   65
    Causes   70
    The course of ADHD   73
    Medications and psychosocial programs for ADHD   76
    Summary   81

6. **Anxiety disorders   83**
    Normal emotional development   83
    Phenomenology and classification   85
    Causal forces   90
    Treatment   92
    Summary   94

7. **Depression   95**
    Phenomenology and classification   95
    Causal forces   98
    The course of childhood depression   100
    Treatment   101
    Summary   102

8. **Eating disorders   103**
    Feeding disorders of infancy or early childhood   103
    Anorexia nervosa   104
    Bulimia nervosa   109
    Treatment   112
    Summary   114

9. **Mental retardation and learning disabilities   115**
    Mental retardation   115
    Learning disabilities   128
    Summary   132

10. **Pervasive developmental disorders   135**
    Autism   136
    What can be done about self-injury?   150
    Other pervasive developmental disorders   152
    Summary   154

11. **Tics and elimination disorders   155**
    Tic disorders   155
    Enuresis and encopresis   157
    Summary   159

12. Questions for your consideration   161
    What would you do?   162
    Summary   169

Suggested readings   171

References   173

Author index   211

Subject index   223

Series preface

Clinical Psychology: A Modular Course was designed to overcome the problems faced by the traditional textbook in conveying what psychological disorders are really like. All the books in the series, written by leading scholars and practitioners in the field, can be read as stand-alone texts, but they will also integrate with the other modules to form a comprehensive resource in clinical psychology. Students of psychology, medicine, nursing and social work, as well as busy practitioners in many professions, often need an accessible but thorough introduction to how people experience anxiety, depression, addiction, or other disorders, how common they are, and who is most likely to suffer from them, as well as up-to-date research evidence on the causes and available treatments. The series will appeal to those who want to go deeper into the subject than the traditional textbook will allow, and base their examination answers, research, projects, assignments, or practical decisions on a clearer and more rounded appreciation of the clinical and research evidence.

Chris R. Brewin

Other titles in this series:

Depression
Constance Hammen

Anxiety
S. Rachman

Getting to know the children 1

One unassuming fact is true of all of us—we have all been children. However unwittingly, each of us has completed the journey from newborn to young adult or beyond. Whether it is easy to recall the memories of favorable or unfavorable emotional experiences or barely remember going through several years of elementary school, all adolescents and adults have successfully charted the ever-changing waters of childhood.

For many reasons, although we can learn from retrospective reports of childhood experiences (Brewin, Andrews, & Gotlib, 1993), a complete understanding of childhood and the psychological disorders of childhood can not rely *solely* on children's own reports or on retrospective self-reports of adults about their childhood. Memories of past childhood experiences can be useful, but may not always be accurate or complete. Also, children are not consistently aware of the psychological difficulties associated with their behavior or with the reality that their behavior is aberrant.

A third simple fact: Although some of the disorders of childhood are severe and difficult to treat, many of the childhood disorders represent extensions or extremes of behavior and emotion that all of us have done or felt at some time in our lives. What can under some circumstances be considered a disorder when it is extreme and interfering with the adjustment of the child may, under other circumstances, be a routine struggle within normal development.

These several simple facts aside, the causes, nature, course, and treatments of childhood disorders are highly complex. The complexities of clinical work with children are evident when considering the following questions: Is it optimal to work with the child or should the treatment include members of the child's family? Under what circumstances is it best to work with the child alone and when is it best to work solely with the child's parents? What role should be played by the child's peers, by the school? Should treatment be provided in a mental health setting, or as part of the routine school day?

What I hope to accomplish in this book is not to fashion you into an expert or a professional, but instead to provide you, the reader, with the current information about childhood disorders and a discussion and evaluation of the major models that guide psychological thinking about these disorders. To do this, I provide a description of each of the major childhood disorders, a detailed consideration of the criteria used to make the diagnoses, a presentation of the latest research findings on the nature of the disorder, and an overview of the methods used and evaluations conducted for the treatment of the disorders. Throughout, the range of normal behavioral variations is set as the backdrop against which to make judgments about psychological disorders. Within the coverage of the treatments of childhood disorders, emphasis is placed upon those treatments that have been empirically evaluated and found to be effective in producing beneficial change for the children. Treatments that have been proffered but not supported by empirical research will be mentioned only minimally if at all.

Introducing some of the children

Plainly, and to the great satisfaction of many parents, not all children have psychological disorders. The pleasing truth is that although there are large numbers of disordered youngsters, many children experience and enjoy their childhood without serious psychological distress and mature into reasonably well-adjusted adults. For present purposes, however, we need to pay attention to those children whose psychological conditions are not satisfactory. To this end select cases of children with psychological difficulties will be submitted and described. Although some of the behavior that is described may seem familiar or even commonplace, you will, once you are accustomed to and familiar with the diagnostic criteria, recognize why these youngsters are outside the acceptable range of behavior.

Consider the following examples of children—pay special attention to their behavior, their emotional well-being, and the quality of their adjustment. The children are merely introduced here— brief descriptions to excite your curiosity and whet your interest. In the later chapters I provide more detailed information and offer insights into the children and their situation as well as hypotheses about the etiology of the problems and strategies for their remediation.

Jamie lives nears you. You don't know him well but you have seen him "hanging out" and playing with other kids in the neighborhood.

As you sit with a friend and talk with neighbors, the police race by and a fire alarm sounds. Your concern mounts and you begin to sweat as you notice that the police cars have stopped and the fire trucks have arrived at a house just two doors from where you live. You and your friend start to walk quickly toward your home. Jamie, a tough and troublesome 11-year-old, lives with his mother in the house that is now ablaze. You know that Jamie has been in trouble for excessive fighting and temper outbursts at school, and for vandalism at the park. You also recall seeing him being searched by the police at the shopping mall, and you recall seeing the police bringing him home very late one night during the summer. Although you have no evidence in the present case, you begin to wonder, might Jamie have intentionally started the fire? You think to yourself "I wouldn't be at all surprised if this fire is Jamie's doing." You don't want to blame him, and you feel disappointed in yourself for rashly thinking him responsible, yet you also trust your initial judgment. Again you wonder … might an 11-year-old intentionally start a fire?

Sarah was a relatively young and once-attractive woman. Presently, she works as a waitress and appears older than her years. You met her last summer while you were working a part-time job at a local restaurant. Although both you and Sarah were busy most of the time, there were quiet hours after work when the staff would share a bite to eat and a bit of conversation. It was during these after-hours calming conversations that you got to know personal information about several of the other staff, including Sarah. For example, you have heard Sarah describe her two young children. Her tone and manner disclose her genuine love for the children. Even when they upset her, her manner betrays her true maternal care. You have also heard her complaining, almost constantly, about her conflictive marriage. She often comes to work angry following her husband's outbursts, she has missed days off work because she is too upset to show her tearful eyes, and she has lied to cover-up incidents where it was suspected that she might have been physically beaten. Secretly, she has been seeking and planning a divorce.

Today, Sarah reports that her divorce is complete. Moreover, she discloses that she is both very worried and very hopeful—worried about keeping her ex-husband away from her and the children and hopeful that the fighting will end and that things will be better for her children. Will divorce be a solution to the conflictive marriage, or will the divorce add to the children's emotional turmoil? What effect does marital dissolution have on children? Are the effects different for children of different ages? Of different gender?

Not long ago, for a brief period, you volunteered at a community mental health center, answering the telephone of the "Hot Line." You met and got to know several of the professional staff and bonded with a few of the youthful callers.

The hot-line was set up for anyone in the community to call in whenever they feel troubled. Ads in businesses and schools, on the radio, and at concerts and athletic events were successful in bringing the service to the attention of members of the community. Recent calls had to do with suicide attempts, child abuse, and run-aways. On one otherwise quiet weekend morning, you answer the phone and a woman states that her daughter is having troubles. Without much introduction, she puts her daughter, Nora, on the phone. Nora speaks haltingly, "Uh, can I like talk to somebody who knows about being crazy." You reply "Perhaps I can help you." Nora stumbles "I need to talk to somebody because … well, because I don't think straight. But I really do. Nobody understands. I don't know, I just don't fit."

Nora—a lonely and depressed youngster who is seeking relief from the psychological pain of feeling useless, alone, and unloved—reports that she is 12 years old. She recognized that she had a problem but did not know what to do … did not know where to turn.

Most parents in your community are in favor of providing social gatherings for young teenagers. There is some question, however, about just when—at what age—children should have unsupervised dances at school or at community centers.

One evening, when the 13-year-olds are having a social dance, the loud music and dancing can be heard at several nearby homes and stores. It isn't deafening, but it does annoy some of the members of the neighborhood. Those who were in attendance at the event reported that the event was great—and that the loud music contributed to a lively and engaging party. The loudness is annoying but not the source of psychological concern.

As the hour gets late the party-goers get hungry, and pizzas are ordered and delivered. The food is wolfed down by everyone, especially Sheila. Soon after the food, you notice Sheila, who has told you that she doesn't want to gain weight, in the bathroom making herself vomit. She says other kids do it too, and that it helps her not to gain weight. Her parents do not know about the vomiting, and her girlfriends help her keep it a secret. Is her behavior putting her health at risk?

At the nursery in the hospital, when relatives and friends gather for the birth of a child, everyone wishes for the good health of the mother and of the newborn. Often, the child and mother are healthy and the parents emerge to begin to fill their roles as parents of the newborn. Such a preferred outcome is, unfortunately, not always the case.

When you met your new neighbors, and got to chat with them about their family, you learned about one of the children: David, a 4-year-old. David's mother apologetically stated that he "was late to walk and slow to learn." She added that his preschool teacher reported that he appeared to be unable to organize and plan his work. "He isn't a contrary child," the teacher said, "he just doesn't understand the lessons." David's mom didn't suggest that he had a disorder, and she seemed to describe him in euphemistic terms—using mild terms to describe behaviors that seem severe even to you. What was David's situation? He was noticeably impaired, but did he have a specific disorder? How will he adjust in adulthood? Psychological testing conducted at the time he entered preschool indicated that David's IQ score was 62. What does all of this mean?

Everyone seemed to know that Bernie was a "disturbed" child. He was variously described as "different," "stiff," and "nonresponsive."

Bernie never seemed to hear or respond to other people—not even when you looked him in the eye and spoke to him directly. He didn't socialize with other children, he didn't show interest in group activities, and he didn't seem to want to be near his parents.

Bernie was playing at the park and seeing him sparked you to ask some questions. Your mom knew Bernie's mother and his history and she was able to answer some of your queries. She stated that Bernie wasn't "cuddly" as an infant, and she recalled that he didn't enjoy playing with other children. She said that Bernie's mom told her that, as a baby and infant, he hadn't developed normal communication. You also learned that although Bernie's parents once thought he was deaf, he was recently tested and found to have normal hearing. Testing also revealed that Bernie was identified as having a pervasive developmental disorder called autism. What is autism?

The various cases that you have just read illustrate several of the psychological disorders that cause anguish in the lives of children and their parents around the globe. But do specific child behaviors automatically mean that a child has a disorder? Do nondisordered children display troubled behavior on occasion? Consider the following example, where no one specific disorder is being illustrated, but the behavior pattern is disturbed nonetheless.

Ginger, like most of the girls in her neighborhood, went to a summer camp organized by the local community athletic program. The girls had various likes and dislikes about the camp, but on average, they felt that it was one of the great fun activities of their summer. The adults who ran the camp had been given special instructions regarding Ginger. All sharp objects, especially pins, paper-clips, and needles had to be kept away from her. It wasn't to protect others from harm, but because Ginger would "stick" herself. During the Spring just before this year's camp, inch-long pins were found in her thumb. One needle had entered a vein in her leg and required that she be taken to the emergency room. Besides keeping pins and needles away from Ginger, what else can be done about such self-injurious behavior?

Childhood disorders are widespread, and examples of children with psychological problems are easy for me to recall and recount. Indeed, after over 20 years in the field—providing psychological assessment, diagnosis, and therapy for children in private practice and clinic settings, and conducting research on childhood disorders—and after 15 years of volunteering as a coach with community youth sports programs, it would be easy to provide many more illustrations of both mild and extreme maladaptive child behavior. It would also be easy to provide examples of what might appear to be a disturbing behavior but which, on closer inspection, is merely a transient adjustment issue for an otherwise *non*disturbed child. Indeed, it is one of the themes of this book that, although there are many disorders of childhood and many children who suffer from these disorders, there are many more youngsters who may temporarily experience emotional distress, display defiant behavior only on occasion, evidence transient scattered and impulsive thinking, or otherwise disturb teachers and parents only quite intermittently. It is essential to note that not all of these transient outbursts reflect psychological disorders—it is part of normal development to face and wrestle with emotional and social demands. To label all distress as a disorder is to over-pathologize normal variations in behavior and normal struggles with developmental challenges. Consider this one last example.

> Steve, a 12-year-old basketball player, sat on the bench while his teammates struggled to try to come from behind. His team was losing the important playoff game by 12 points, with only 3 minutes left to play. On any given day, it would be unanimous among the coaches that Steve should be in the game, playing guard. He is one of the best defensive players with a knack for stealing the ball and making the breakaway lay-up. His teammates, too, wanted to have him in the game for the last 3 minutes. This day, however, was different. He had received two technical fouls and was therefore ineligible to play. In the first quarter, when he was called for a foul, he turned to the referee and chided him with a comment and a "face." Referees may tolerate such acts in the professional sports, especially from the stars, but the referees in youth sports try to build good sportsmanship and they do not tolerate such antics. At halftime, in front of many spectators, Steve yelled to his coach that "That ref hates me, 'cause I made his kid look bad in a game a few weeks ago … The ref stinks, we should protest." A spectator who saw only this game might think that Steve is a "hot head" or that he has a problem controlling his anger. In fact, the spectator would

be wrong. Steve plays aggressively, as one should in the game of basketball. He also plays "smart"—he knows the rules and works within them to give his team an advantage. For the entire season, he had a total of zero technical fouls and had not previously fouled out of a game. Today, unlike other days, Steve was frustrated and tired. He was at a sleep-over the evening before the game, had been teased mercilessly by his friend's older brother, and, missing his mother's cooking, he didn't eat well. Steve's behavior on this day was not a model of ideal adjustment, but neither was it a sign or signal of serious disturbance.

Introducing some of the questions

Our journey through the psychological disorders of childhood provides information about what such disorders may look like to observers or feel like for the child, about the possible causes of the problems, the course of the disorders across the lifespan, as well as the treatments that are used to help rectify the childhood disorders. Some of the topics that we will address will help to clarify and answer some of the questions that may have come to mind as you read the examples just presented. If you haven't yet made a list of questions, you may want to do so. The following may spark your thinking. Perhaps some of these questions will sound familiar to you.

- Do children act out their psychological problems? Does their behavior reflect the quality of their inner psychological adjustment?
- Does divorce typically reduce the distress of a troubled marriage and will it help the children? Does divorce have differential effects for children at different ages?
- Can children become depressed; how do they display dysphoria; and how do they handle feelings of sadness?
- Are psychological disorders the product of genetics, without concern for the quality of their parenting or living environments? Stated simply, are children with disorders born that way?
- To what extent are the child-rearing practices of care-givers responsible for the psychological well-being of their children?
- Unlike adults, children do not seek psychological help for themselves. What brings them to treatment?
- Can someone really lose weight by vomiting after eating? Is it safe? Is it healthy?

- What level of psychological adjustment can children with low IQs attain as they grow older?
- What is autism, and what causes it?
- To what length can caregivers go to prevent a child from hurting him- or herself?
- Many troublesome behaviors or outbursts are transient—part of mastering the challenges of development. How do we differentiate between genuine disorders and routine struggles with adjustment?

Our discussion of the psychological disorders of youth is divided into several chapters. In the next chapter we overview the models that are offered to help organize and understand psychological disorder. We then examine several of the issues that impinge on our study of the disorders of childhood (Chapter 3). In the next two chapters we consider separately two behavior disorders—conduct disorder and attention-deficit hyperactivity disorder. The chapters that come after these behavior disorders address, separately, the emotional disorders of anxiety (Chapter 6) and depression (Chapter 7). Eating disorders, due to their initial appearance in the early years, are considered disorders of youth and are addressed in Chapter 8. The disorders associated with intellectual and learning performance are examined in Chapter 9; the pervasive developmental disorders are considered in Chapter 10; and a discussion of tics and the elimination disorders is presented in Chapter 11. Challenging questions are posed in the closing chapter, where you are asked to consider not only the questions and their potential answers, but also the implications of the various possible answers for you in particular and for society in general.

There are a few emphases that will be evident as you progress through this book. First, it is important that we use knowledge about normal development to make decisions about the presence of abnormality. The description of the disorders provide a sense of the disturbance, but judgments of disorder require comparisons against normal variations in behavior.

Second, the role of the family will be given emphasis. The family is the child's most powerful social context and as such plays an important role in the onset and course of psychological difficulties. Third, there is a strong emphasis on the empirical research literature: the studies that have been conducted and published are the basis for the information provided. This holds true for the descriptions of the nature of the disorders as well as the presentation of the interventions used to treat the disorders (Hibbs & Jensen, 1996; Kazdin & Weisz, 1998; Ollendick & King, 1998). Although the research base will be apparent, it does not take away from the fact that the children we are discussing are real people with real lives—numerous cases are presented to communicate the needed sensitivity to human struggle often associated with psychological distress. The names have been changed, but the authenticity of the struggles remains.

Models of childhood disorders 2

The psychological literature abounds with studies of the nature of the various childhood disorders. How can we organize our information about childhood disorders to guide future studies and applications? What is needed is a guiding framework—a model—to help conceptualize and organize the data about the onset and development of maladaptive behavior. Models stimulate hypotheses, and research tests the validity of the model's assumptions.

In this chapter several models pertinent to the study of the childhood disorders will be overviewed: the biological, behavioral, cognitive, psychodynamic, and systems models (see also Sonuga-Barke, 1998). No one grand model will explain all child psychopathology. However, focused versions of the models often do provide a satisfactory framework for understanding a specific disorder, and models that integrate features of these models are most promising. For example, a cognitive-behavioral model integrates learning theory with human information processing, and a diathesis-stress model involves the interaction of biological predispositions and environmental stressors. Integrative models, especially those focused on specific disorders, offer useful frameworks for understanding many of the child disorders.

Biological models

Biological models suggest that the symptoms of psychological disorders are caused by biological factors. Such models are variously referred to as medical, organic, biomedical, or disease models. Biological models may identify or suggest brain defects, infectious transmission, biochemical imbalances, and genetic predispositions as possible sources of psychological disorders.

The brain
The brain plays an important role within the biological model. Two major ways that the brain is suspected of producing abnormalities

concern the *structure* of the brain and *communication* between the brain structures.

Consisting of billions of cells, the brain is the most complex of all body parts. Different collections of neurons, in different regions of the brain are responsible for certain functions. For example, the cerebral cortex is primarily responsible for sensory processing, motor control, and higher mental functioning involving complex information processing, learning, memory, planning, and judgment. The brain has three sections: the forebrain, the midbrain, and the hindbrain. The forebrain consists of the two cerebral hemispheres, the thalamus, and the hypothalamus. The thalamus, for instance, is important in the processing and relaying of information between other regions of the central nervous system and the cerebral cortex, and the hypothalamus regulates hunger, thirst, sex drive, and body temperature. The limbic system, which includes parts of the cortex, the thalamus, and hypothalamus, provides homeostasis, or constancy of the internal environment, by regulating the activity of endocrine glands and the autonomic nervous system. These structures all play critical roles in emotions and drives (Kalat, 1995).

Below the forebrain is the midbrain, a way station that coordinates communications between the forebrain and the region just below it called the hindbrain. The hindbrain contains the pons, medulla, and reticular activating system and is connected to the spinal cord. The pons is involved in sleeping, waking, and dreaming; the medulla regulates breathing and heart rate. The pathways from other regions of the brain pass through the pons and medulla. The reticular activating system is a network of neurons that screens incoming information and arouses other areas of the brain.

Biological abnormalities in these structures can arise in numerous ways. A child might be born with an inordinately small or oddly formed brain structure. An injury resulting from complications at birth or a severe blow to the head might disturb a part of the brain and/or disrupt its development. More subtle processes such as prenatal exposure to toxins (e.g. drugs, alcohol, pollutants, viruses) can also alter the growth and development of the brain. Whatever their source, anatomical abnormalities have been linked to some psychological disorders. Recent interest in the biological model of psychopathology has focused not only on abnormalities in the structure of neurons, but also in how these neurons communicate (Rosenzweig, Leiman, & Breedlove, 1996).

For human behavior to take place, there must be communication in the brain. Neurons transmit electrical impulses to other neurons by means of neurotransmitters (Dunant & Israel, 1985). Neurotransmitters send signals within the brain (Sejnowski, Koch, & Churchland, 1988). A neuron receives a chemical signal or message in the form of a neurotransmitter and transforms it to an electrical impulse. When a signal reaches the end of the neuron, it prompts neurotransmitters to be released; they cross the synaptic cleft at the synapse and thereby pass on the signal to the next cell. Neurotransmitter substances are hot topics for research and scientists have so far discovered more than 50 different types of neurotransmitters in the brain—and these different neurotransmitters serve different regions of the brain.

Neurotransmission is not an elementary process. It can go awry in many ways because the processes governing both the release and reabsorption of a particular neurotransmitter substance are highly complex. Neurotransmission problems can involve the amount of the neurotransmitter, the neurotransmitter receptors, the presence or absence of neurons that inhibit neural connections, and the interrelationships between the different neurotransmitters. These neurotransmitter problems can contribute to psychopathology. Moreover, the effects on behavior can emerge when environmental forces such as stress inhibit synaptic transmission, or when medications used to treat the symptoms of certain mental disorders affect the neurotransmitter process.

Genetics

The idea that mental disorders might be inherited is a very old one. Currently, there are investigators who argue that certain traits, temperaments, and even specific disorders can have a genetic component (Bouchard, Lykken, McGue, Segal, & Tellegen, 1990; Lombroso, Pauls, & Leckman, 1994).

Chromosomes carry codes for the potential expression of characteristics in their basic units, genes. Each human cell normally contains 23 pairs of chromosomes. Genes control innumerable characteristics such as eye color, hair color, male baldness, and color-blindness. Do genes carry a code for psychological disorders?

Clinicians have been noted to have observed that some forms of psychological disorder run in families. Researchers have also noticed and quantified that monozygotic (identical) twins who share the same genetic makeup are more likely to share the same disorder than are dizygotic (fraternal) twins who share only 50% of their genes—like any other sibling pairs. For example, consider the data on the typically adult disorder schizophrenia (see Chapter 10). The average rate for adult schizophrenia in the full population is 1%. Yet studies have shown that when one monozygotic twin has schizophrenia, in about 40–50% of cases the other twin will also have schizophrenia. In comparison, under these same circumstances only 5–15% of dizygotic twins will have the disorder (Gottesman, McGuffin, & Farmer, 1987; Gottesman & Shields, 1972). Although not all of the childhood disorders show such a conspicuous genetic contribution, schizophrenia is a sound illustration that genetics does play a meaningful role in psychological disorders. But genes are not autonomous over behavior: Genes are influenced by other factors and, often, these factors are environmental (Nelson & Bloom, 1997).

Evaluating the biological model

Proponents of the biological model have identified how infectious agents, structural abnormalities, biochemical imbalances, and genetic predispositions might contribute to or produce psychological disorders. Schizophrenia, for example, has a genetic component. In addition, the biological model of psychological disorder has stimulated advances in medical treatments that have had positive effects. Psychoactive medications have helped countless thousands of youngsters to better manage their conditions.

As biological influences are identified, however, it is important that they are not automatically deemed to be the sole cause of disorder. Instead, they should be recognized and placed among the several causal factors. An attempt is made throughout this book to stipulate the need for integrated models linking biological vulnerability with social and psychological factors that lead to disorder in some individuals but not in others.

The biological model also has several potential shortcomings. First, it appears to be relevant to some problems but not others. A widespread and exclusive focus on biological processes might lead us to ignore or downplay the contributions of personal learning histories, ongoing interpersonal conflicts, or cognitive misperceptions of interpersonal events in the search for defective genes.

A second area of concern is gender differences. From the biological perspective, there is little information about gender differences in psychopathology. There are gender differences in several disorders, yet limited information on biological gender differences. To what degree do cultural values and social pressures contribute to these differences?

Third, the scientific status of biological factors as causal agents in disorder is far from established. The discoveries of neurochemical or other biological differences between people with disorders and normal (nondisturbed) people, for example, do not indicate whether the biological difference is the cause or merely a by-product of the presence of the disorder. Similarly, the success of medications in treating disorders is *not* itself evidence that the disorder arose from biological causes. We can successfully treat a fever with aspirin, for example, but that does not mean that the lack of aspirin was the underlying cause of the fever.

Behaviorism: The learning models

Rapidly growing since the 1960s, behaviorism concerns the manner in which human behavior is acquired or learned. Behavior occurs as a consequence of its having been learned in the past. Behaviorally oriented psychologists underscore the role of reinforcement, pleasant events, and a person's learning history, as well as the role of the current social and interpersonal environment, as forces contributing to adaptive as well as maladaptive (disordered) behavior.

The behavioral model emphasizes the observable behavior of the child and the environmental factors that maintain the action. Behaviorists believe that when other influencing factors are constant, the differences that exist among children are the result of learning. Behavior patterns, both normal and abnormal, are influenced greatly by the existing environment, and changes in the environmental influences will change the behavior pattern (Masters, Burish, Hollon, & Rimm, 1987; O'Leary & Wilson, 1987). Three forms of learning that can contribute to our understanding of psychological disorders are classical conditioning, operant conditioning, and observational learning.

Classical conditioning

A basic form of learning, classical conditioning involves a once neutral stimuli that comes to evoke involuntary responses. Classical conditioning (Pavlov, 1928) involves both conditioned (learned) and unconditioned stimuli and responses. If you found yourself stuck in a dangerous location, such as on the center lines dividing traffic on a major highway, then your being afraid would be perfectly normal and adaptive. However, people can learn to be afraid of things and situations when it is not normal or adaptive to be fearful. Classical conditioning helps us understand the development of these fears.

To begin, a realistically dangerous situation produces fear without prior learning or conditioning. Because this fear occurs without learning or conditioning, the dangerous situation is called an *un*conditioned stimulus (UCS) and the reaction, fear, is the *un*conditioned response (UCR). They occur naturally. A neutral stimulus does not itself produce a response. However, a neutral stimulus that is repeatedly paired with a dangerous situation becomes a conditioned stimulus (CS) and can itself lead to the UCR, fear. When the neutral situation itself becomes capable of producing fear, the fear it produces is called a conditioned response (CR). It is the conditioned (learned) responses that are of particular interest in psychopathology. For example, a specific piece of music played repeatedly in a dangerous situation becomes itself capable of producing fear. Think of the two-note theme from the movie *Jaws*. The music is a CS because it has acquired the fear-producing properties via conditioning, and the fear it produces is a CR.

Through conditioning processes, each of us has developed preferences and other reactions, and possibly even fears. Many researchers have used classical conditioning to explain the development of the psychological disorders called phobias, which are specific fears of a specific object or situation (e.g. fear of dogs). Fortunately, the principles of classical conditioning can and have been applied as a treatment to reduce and eliminate maladaptive fears.

Operant conditioning

Operant conditioning is concerned with the consequences of behavior— the probability that a response will be increased or decreased when it is followed by reinforcement or punishment (Thorndike, 1898). When responses lead to satisfying consequences, the responses are strengthened and more likely to occur in the future. When responses lead to unsatisfying consequences, they are not strengthened and are less likely to occur again in the future; this, then, was Thorndike's law of effect.

Skinner (1953) further developed the theory of behavioral consequences and used the principle of reinforcement to describe how behavioral consequences can strengthen the probability of behavior's recurring. There are numerous contingencies that have been described and researched, and Skinner's operant conditioning has had significant effects on psychological research and theory (see *American Psychologist*, 1992).

Punishment occurs when a response leads to a negative outcome. A dog who jumps on a visitor might be swatted on the rump, and a misbehaving student could be corrected in front of peers in class. Each of these illustrates the principle of punishment: Following an unwanted behavior with a negative outcome will reduce the likelihood of the unwanted behavior in the future. Although punishment can have desirable effects, it can also be detrimental. When harsh or excessive, punishment can cause serious inhibitions. A child who is punished too often may become overly withdrawn, unwilling to do anything, aggressive, and potentially depressed.

When positive consequences follow a behavior, the behavior is positively reinforced (rewarded) and the behavior is more likely to occur again in the future. Maladaptive behaviors, as well as desired patterns of behavior, can be acquired through their consequences. When a child screams or has a tantrum about a cookie, she may get her way because the parent simply wants to quiet her. But, the child is also learning that tantrums (or the screaming behavior) produce rewards. More tantrums will follow.

But what about more complex behavior? After all, human existence is not simply one behavior or another. Complex behaviors need not be directly reinforced for the behavior to be learned. The process of rewarding successive approximations, called shaping, does not require the learner to produce an entire new response pattern to receive the reinforcement. The shaping process is gradual, providing reinforcement for several interim steps. As the learner masters a new step, reinforcement shifts so that it is provided only after this new last step. Thus, an individual does not learn all at once to be verbally loud and vulgar—the undesirable behavior can be the result of a shaping process that has taken years to complete.

The shaping of behavior has important implications for child development (Gewirtz & Peláez-Nogueras, 1992) and for understanding and treating (Mash, 1998) childhood disorders. For instance, complex, disturbed behavior patterns need not themselves be reinforced. The maladaptive pattern can be shaped over time as small portions of the disturbed pattern are reinforced. A pattern of aggression, for example, might be shaped by rewards for successive approximations of violence.

> Matt was sloppily dressed and wore a sneer on his face. He sat quietly, slumped in a chair and gazing out a window, as the Principal dialed his mother's work phone number. It was his third visit to the office for disciplinary action, and he knew that he was about to be suspended from school for having been involved in a fight in the hallway. His year in school was not going well—grades were poor, he didn't do well in sports, and he wasn't exactly popular—but he really didn't care. Although there were many and varied reasons for Matt's situation, and many factors that contributed to his aggressive behavior pattern, a few of the early learning experiences described by his mother, Anita, stood out. It

seems that Matt, as early as age three, was being encouraged and taught by his father (Jerry) to "fight for his rights." Anita noted that when Matt was seven and was roughed up by a neighborhood boy who was a year older, Jerry was really upset and taught Matt how to fistfight. Anita also recalled that Jerry wouldn't discipline Matt or try to limit his fighting; instead he would pat him on the back for being tough. Matt wasn't a very thoughtful boy and he couldn't express his emotions well—instead, it seemed that he had learned from his father that fighting was the solution to problems.

Another type of reinforcement is negative reinforcement, in which the likelihood of a behavior increases by the removal of a negative (unpleasant) stimulus or situation. For example, if you politely ask a room-mate to turn off the television so you can study, and your room-mate does so immediately, the likelihood of your making a similar polite request in the future is increased. The polite request was reinforced by the removal of the unwanted (aversive) television distraction.

Additional stimulus-response relationships include escape and avoidance. An escape response stops a negative condition, whereas an avoidance response prevents a negative condition. Consider the following example:

> Sue had procrastinated on some tasks and had been up late the night before. Now she is sleeping with an alarm clock set to go off at 5:30AM. When the loud and aversive alarm rings Sue reaches out of bed and hits the snooze button. The snooze button "stops" the aversive alarm (an escape response) for 10 minutes. Sue returns to bed but in a few minutes realizes that the alarm will sound again at 5:40. When it does she slaps the snooze button again (escape response) for another ten minutes of rest. The alarm will sound again at 5:50, only this time Sue looks at the clock at 5:49 and presses the snooze button to "prevent" the alarm from sounding—an avoidance response.

In this case, the avoidance response works; however, people can learn avoidance responses that are not functional. As will be discussed in the chapter on anxiety disorders (Chapter 6), anxious people make responses that they believe will prevent an aversive situation but which, in fact, do not. The avoidance response offers a remarkable explanation for some of the anxiety disorders. For example, a young girl attends a school dance and is teased by a group of students. The teasing soon becomes harshly delivered ridicule, and it badly hurts her feelings. To stop the pain, she leaves the dance (an escape response). Because of this experience, in the future she will be more likely to run away from peers and potential ridicule, and will perhaps leave the presence of peers sooner. Eventually, staying away from peer interaction becomes associated with anxiety reduction—an avoidance response that prevents the experience of unwanted emotions. The avoidance response may continue despite the fact that students are no longer likely to tease and ridicule her. Patterns of behavior such as these are the result of avoidance learning. They occur, for example, in children and later adults with social phobia, in which individuals avoid feared social or performance situations, even though these behaviors may interfere with social and work relationships. Avoidance responses are persistent and, unfortunately, individuals who have acquired avoidance habits often continue to use them when they are no longer needed.

Observational learning

Modeling, or observational learning, is another manner of learning. Why was I embarrassed when my then 5-year-old son dunked his croissant in his milk at a somewhat formal brunch? The answer: I know where he learned to dunk breakfast pastry! Dunking is not genetic, nor did I ever reward him for dunking. He has simply watched me dunk various pastries into my morning coffee and has, through observation, learned to do the same. Modeling is the process of learning behavior by observing others (Bandura, 1969). A tennis trainee who watches the coach demonstrate (or model) the desired motions of a serve and then practices what she has seen is learning through observation.

Many behavior patterns can be traced to observation experiences. For instance, how little or how much alcohol a person consumes can be influenced by the drinking behavior that the individual observes from others. True, alcohol consumption can have many diverse causes, but modeling effects exist nonetheless. Alcoholics who observed several confederates consume wine at high or low rates adjusted their own wine consumption according to the models' consumption (DeRicco & Niemann, 1980). Aggressive acts such as karate kicks or chops can increase as a result of popular television programs or movies that model and highlight such attacks.

Observational learning is a part of social learning theory (Bandura, 1986), which proposes that behavior is the product of both external stimulus events and internal cognitive processes. An individual's social context is important because it provides many opportunities for behaviors to be observed and imitated. When researchers report that certain disorders run in families, it is often difficult to separate the effects of genetics from the effects of the shared social learning environment. Social learning explanations would discount head injury and downplay genetics, underscoring instead the role of what has been modeled for and observed by the child. If a child has witnessed his parents use aggressive solutions to problems, and has spent time with his uncle who is loud, vulgar, and aggressive and who has been arrested several times, then the child has been exposed to and may have learned a troublesome pattern of behavior.

Evaluating the behavioral approach

To its credit, the behavioral approach has produced voluminous research, including explanations for the development of certain types of abnormality, and specific methods for treating childhood disorders. Because the model focuses on the child's environment, it is especially sensitive to cultural and social factors. Similarly, by being concerned with the learning history and environment of individuals, there is an implicit concern with ethnic and gender influences.

Learning explanations of psychological disorders, however, have been criticized as oversimplified. For instance, behavioral studies of aggression and violence often rely on a count of aggressive acts. Critics argue that aggression results from complex causes including biological, familial, and cultural factors, and to explain them solely in terms of prior learning is too delimiting.

A second criticism of behaviorism is that its attempt to explain maladaptive behavior without considering the unobservable aspects of human existence downplays the role of cognition in abnormality. This criticism, however, has been addressed by the modern, integrative model (discussed later) called cognitive-behaviorism.

Cognitive model

How human beings perceive, recognize, attend, reason, and judge has come to play important roles in attempts to understand the development of disorders. Cognitive models emphasize that cognitive functioning contributes to emotional or behavioral distress. Misperceptions of social situations, a tendency to think negatively without sufficient data, and a habit of inaccurately blaming oneself for mishaps are examples of dysfunctional cognitive processing (see also Ellis & Harper, 1975).

Jonathan is a 10-year-old who lives with his mother, has few friends, and stays in his home most of the time, every day. Jonathan has developed a characteristic way of evaluating the world—a cognitive structure—based on the potential of threat. Jonathan can't do anything without thinking of and worrying about threat and danger, even in what appear to us to be the most innocuous and appealing activities. As a result, he perceives as threats the very situations and events that are not stressful for most people. When Jonathan is introduced to someone, he sees the experience not as a chance to make a friend, but rather as a risk that puts him in jeopardy. He frequently says to himself, "What will he think of me or do to me? Will he try to hurt me?" When at an amusement park, amusement does not come to Jonathan's mind as much as the risks of accidents on the rides, the possibility of getting separated or lost, and the risk of eating foods that will upset his stomach. Jonathan hardly notices the numerous opportunities for widespread fun.

Distortions and deficiencies

The cognitive processing of children can be differentiated in an important manner—distinguishing between cognitive distortions and cognitive deficiencies (Kendall, 1991, 1993). Cognitive deficiencies refer to the absence of thinking—such as when a child's responses and emotional states do not benefit from careful thinking or planning. In contrast, cognitive distortions refer to thought processes that are dysfunctional, such as active misperceptions and misconstruals of the environment.

The different types of cognitive processing mistakes have been linked to different types of childhood disorders (see Kendall & MacDonald, 1993). Distortions in information processing have been implicated in adult depression (Alloy, Abramson, Murray, Whitehouse, & Hogan, 1997; Beck, 1976; Ingram, 1984; Ingram, Miranda, & Segal, 1998), anxiety (e.g. Beck & Emery, 1985), and several other psychological abnormalities (see Dobson & Kendall, 1993; Ingram, 1986), as well as in childhood depression and anxiety (see also Leung & Wong, 1998). Deficiencies in active information processing are linked to other childhood disorders, such as the interpersonal problem-solving deficits and information-seeking deficits evident in impulsive children, and the related problems seen in related types of child psychopathology.

An example of a cognitive model is the one proposed by Beck to help explain depression. This model has received substantial research and clinical attention. According to Beck (1967, 1976, 1987), individuals, early in life, begin to formulate rules about how the world works, and that, for depressed persons, these rules are based on erroneous ideas and beliefs. An individual continues to distort life experiences through characteristic errors in perceiving and thinking about events, event outcomes, personal attributes, and interpersonal relations. These features define the cognitive model of depression. Accordingly, in depression, thought content centers on the experience of major loss, the anticipation of negative outcomes, and the sense of being inadequate.

Evaluating cognitive models

Criticisms have been leveled at the cognitive models. For example, "thought" is only part of the complex system in which people exist. What about the biological, emotional, and interpersonal factors that influence people's lives? Still others have commented that it is not yet clear whether cognitive factors are causally linked to disorder (e.g. Coyne, 1982): They have suggested that the cognitive dysfunctions that are found may be consequences or correlates of disorder rather than causes. These criticisms have led cognitive researchers to examine the role of dysfunctional thinking as a vulnerability factor (e.g. Ingram, 1998): People with maladaptive cognitive processes are at risk for psychological disorder (see Alloy & Clements, 1998; Ingram, 1998 and other articles in the same issue of the journal).

Critics of the cognitive model point out that many psychologically disturbed people live under objectively horrible life circumstances that are not easily reduced to "irrational" or distorted thinking. Another concern voiced about cognitive factors has to do with the difficulty of verification. People report their thoughts, but reporting one's beliefs is fraught with difficulties (Smith & Allred, 1986). A person who holds irrational beliefs, for instance, may not be aware that they are irrational. As the cognitive models of psychological disorder continue to make advances, these criticisms deserve further attention.

Cognitive-behavioral model

The cognitive-behavioral model emphasizes the learning process and the influences of the environment, while underscoring the importance of cognitive-mediating and information-processing factors in the development and treatment of psychological disorders (Kendall, 1993). Accordingly, this model proposes treatments aimed at modifying the client's perceptions, evaluations, and processing of events, while employing behavioral performance–based procedures, modeling, and rewards (e.g. Meichenbaum, 1985).

The cognitive-behavioral model is therefore an integrated model (Alford & Norcross, 1991). Cognitive-behaviorism is the result of movement from two perspectives (Kendall & Hollon, 1979; see also Craighead, Meyers, & Craighead, 1985): Behavioral theorists have shown increased interest in the cognitive aspects of psychopathology, and psychodynamic and cognitive theorists have shown greater concern for the performance-based learning aspects of psychological disorders. Not all members of each camp have come together, but there has been sufficient and noticeable movement from both sides toward a middle ground, and the cognitive-behavioral model has served as a functional vehicle to encourage such integration (Mahoney, 1977, 1993; Meichenbaum, 1977, 1993).

The increased acceptance of cognitive-behavioral approaches is evident in the impressive number of mental health professionals who identified themselves as holding a cognitive-behavioral orientation. Specifically, beginning as early as 1980 (Smith, 1982), there have been many survey respondents who said they were cognitive-behavioral. More recently, these self-identifications have grown. In 1998, the primary theoretical orientation of APA-approved programs in clinical psychology was endorsed as cognitive-behavioral by 68% of the programs: At other times, cognitive-behavioral is second only to those who named eclecticism (the practice of drawing from various therapeutic viewpoints) as a preferred self-identification. The increasingly popular cognitive-behavioral model has made great strides toward integrating the seemingly conflicting cognitive and behavioral theories that had previously been influential but less dominant in the study of psychopathology.

Psychodynamic model

The psychodynamic model has historical significance. Toward the end of the 19th century, Freud broke new theoretical ground by offering the first truly psychological account of abnormal behavior (Freud, 1913, 1914, 1917/1943). His psychodynamic model emphasized that an understanding of psychopathology lay in the analysis of mental structures in conflict, levels of consciousness, defense mechanisms, and stages of psychosexual development.

Freud's theory is called psychodynamic because it is based on the belief that personality and psychological disorders are the outcome of a dynamic interactions among mental (psycho) structures. According to Freud, thoughts, attitudes, and behaviors result from conflict among three mental structures—the ego, id, and superego (called intrapsychic conflict).

The part of you that wants satisfaction immediately was called the id. The id is an unorganized reservoir of wishes and passions of our basic sexual and aggressive drives; it strives for immediate gratification that bypasses the demands of reality, order, and logic. The superego is the storehouse of the moral and ethical standards taught by parents and culture (what we generally think of as "conscience"). When these standards are violated, the superego as conscience generates guilt.

Freud attributed finding a realistic means to resolve conflicts to the ego. The main function of the ego is to mediate the wishes of the id, the demands of reality, and the strictures of the superego. By regulating internal conflict and stress, the ego promotes adjustment. But, according to Freud, when the ego is not mediating effectively, conflict erupts and psychological abnormality emerges.

The conflicts Freud described may occur at various levels of awareness. Conscious material is that which we are aware of at any given time, and it changes constantly. Preconscious thoughts are those that are easily made conscious by the effort to remember or by the spark of a related idea. You may now be conscious that you are reading a book and, with a prompt, you could become conscious of the placement of your right foot. Some thoughts or memories are less accessible than others, but preconscious thought can potentially become conscious.

A major portion of mental activity such as the id is unconscious—that is, mental activity outside a person's normal awareness. Thoughts and ideas that are unconscious, according to Freud, press for expression, but may be withheld from consciousness because they are unacceptable to the ego or the superego. Sometimes, the ego is unable to gratify impulses or even unwilling to allow them access to consciousness. When these id impulses press for gratification or consciousness, the ego experiences intense anxiety.

When the ego experiences anxiety or the guilt induced by the superego, it protects itself with defense mechanisms. Defense mechanisms are said to be unconscious processes that try to protect the ego from anxiety provoked by unwanted or unacceptable impulses. These processes are defensive because they defend the self. As Brewin (1997, p. 107) noted in his discussion of the distortion of meaning, "the impact of unsettling thoughts and memories may be much reduced by mental operations that suppress or transform them." By avoiding our unwanted feelings we avoid looking unacceptable and having our security undermined, and we make ourselves look better and put ourselves in a more flattering light. Yet these mechanisms may not be true to reality or true to another observer.

For instance, repression is the unconscious but purposeful exclusion of painful thoughts or unacceptable desires or impulses from consciousness. A person might, for example, fail to recall—or repress—being mistreated as a child. Repression is often regarded as the primary defense mechanism. Denial is another defense mechanism: In denial, the person simply does not accept or admit the presence of the threatening condition. Projection is a defense mechanism in which the person with the problem attributes one's own unacceptable impulses or thoughts to others. When someone makes a socially acceptable explanation for a socially unacceptable behavior, this can be the defense mechanism called rationalization. Other defense mechanism have been described by scholars of this theory.

According to Erdelyi (1985), defensive processes are the foundation on which the structure of psychodynamic theory rests. But experimental research on defense mechanisms has produced ambiguous results. For example, Erdelyi's (1985) review of the evidence regarding repression concluded that there can be selective rejection of information from awareness, that organisms tend to avoid aversive stimuli and defend themselves against pain, and that some psychological processes can occur outside of a person's awareness. However, although each of these separate features has some support, there still is no clear-cut demonstration of the entire phenomenon taking place all at once. Thus, although psychological studies have helped us understand complex mental processes, unconscious defensive processes remain a challenge for research. The interested reader is referred to a contemporary "cognitive science" account of the unconscious (Power & Brewin, 1991).

According to Freud, if a person's defense mechanisms are unable to reduce or prevent unwanted anxious arousal, a neurosis may result. The term *neurosis* is of historical note (it is no longer used to label disorder) but it is still used on occasion to describe the conflicts seen in some persons. Neurotic individuals are said to exhibit intense infantile wishes and impulses. These impulses are so strong that they drive the individual to excessive and rigid use of defense mechanisms to contain them. Excessive repression, for example, keeps facts from awareness and can intensify personal conflict and interpersonal distress.

Although it was not central to Freud's theory, it is important to keep in mind that moderate use of numerous defense mechanisms is not abnormal. They can help us contain our own unwanted feelings, and they can keep us from behaving in less socially acceptable ways.

However, defense mechanisms are maladaptive, and abnormal, when a few defenses are relied on excessively or used extensively.

For Freud, the idea of sexuality includes all sensual striving and satisfactions (Brennan, 1955). As a person develops from infancy to young adulthood, the focus of sexual or sensual pleasure changes from the mouth to the anal area to the genitals. Freud in his theory of personality development, proposed five phases for psychosexual development.

In the oral stage, during which the major source of pleasure is the mouth, the infant seeks gratification through sucking, biting, and feeding. The oral stage covers the first year of life. The anal stage extends to about 3½ years of age, through the period of toilet training. During this phase the child derives pleasure from the retention and expulsion of feces. Boys and girls differ in their experience of the next phase, the phallic stage. From about 3 to 5 or 6 years of age, the child's interest centers on the genitals and on masturbatory activities. Borrowing from the theme of the Greek tragedy, *Oedipus Rex*, Freud proposed that the phallic-aged boy develops a sexual attachment to his mother and views his father as his rival—the Oedipal dilemma. He wishes to see his father gone, and fears that his father wishes the same toward him. These wishes and fears conflict with the young boy's genuine love for his father. An adjusted individual resolves his dilemma by renouncing his desire for his mother and identifying with his father.

The Electra dilemma is the phallic-aged girl's experience of the analogous situation with her parents. According to Freud, the girl's shift away from mother and toward father is facilitated by her belief that it was her mother who deprived her of a penis and her subsequent development of what Freud called penis envy. The theory holds that if the child—either boy or girl—is unsuccessful in resolving these dilemmas, the conflict will linger unconsciously and form the basis of maladjustment in adulthood.

The child then enters a latency stage, from 6 or 7 to 11 years of age, during which the sexual drives seem to be inactive. The next phase, the genital stage, begins with puberty and is characterized by a reawakening and maturation of the sexual drives.

With each successive phase, functioning is increasingly mature. Experiencing inordinate gratification or frustration at any given phase can cause psychological difficulties at a later stage. Fixation refers to an excessive attachment to someone or something that is appropriate to an earlier level of development. A regression is a reversion to an earlier, and therefore more immature, form of behavior, usually as the result of some external stress or in response to internal conflict. Regression can occur in both normal and disturbed persons.

Modern neo-Freudian reconsiderations

Few would dispute that Freud's views have been stimulating and provocative, yet his theory is more historical than contemporary. Some writers, although maintaining features of the initial theory, have made changes to modernize it. For example, whereas Freud saw sexual impulses as the basis for neurotic anxiety, the neo-Freudians shifted away when ascribing centrality to the role of sexuality.

One modern spin-off from psychodynamic theory is object relations theory (Kernberg, 1976; Kohut, 1977; Mitchell, 1988). This perspective, which is derived from the idea that people are often the object of others drives, de-emphasizes *im*personal forces and counterforces and focuses instead on the influences of early *inter*personal relationships. Contemporary object relations theorists are concerned with the role that human relationships play in the development of psychological abnormality. They believe that the early mother–child relationship is crucial to the child's development, self-concept, conceptions of others, and the quality of human relationships. Severe disturbances in early relationships can result in poor, if not chaotic, interpersonal relationships. Thus, the child's early interactions and impressions greatly influence later object relations.

Evaluating psychodynamics

Despite the impact of psychodynamic models, some have not withstood the test of time and many have not stood the tests of scientific study. After suggesting that there are only a few enduring contributions of the model, I note several of the weaknesses.

Some of Freud's observations were powerful and accurate. He recognized that a child's early experiences influences adult behavior and that internal conflict is an important source of psychological difficulty. The specific ideas about the dynamics of the conflict may not be correct, but there is widespread acceptance that human dysfunction can arise from the stress and conflict with which a person cannot cope effectively.

Perhaps one of his most enduring contributions, Freud described the unconscious and proposed that unconscious motives play a role in human behavior (see Freud, 1912/1984, 1915/1984). There is considerable agreement that human beings engage in behavior that appears to reflect processes they are not aware of, but exploring unconscious processes presents special problems for researchers.

Contemporary researchers are studying complex cognitive processes and their association to psychological disorders (see Dalgleish & Watts, 1990). Today, some researchers refer to unconscious processes whereas others refer to nonconscious processes (see Power & Brewin, 1991, for a discussion of this topic). Nonconscious processes have to do with the ways our learned experiences are organized and function without awareness (Kihlstrom, 1987). Well-learned and practical behaviors become automatic, and we may organize and implement our expectations, beliefs, and even memories without fully understanding or being aware of them.

Several items from Freud's original model have not been verified. First, regarding the universality of sexual and aggressive instincts as the basis for all human behavior—although these biological motives are powerful, other learned motives are powerful as well. Second, there is no evidence that human development unfolds according to Freud's psychosexual stages. Third, there is no compelling evidence that the hypothesized psychic structures (id, ego, superego) are needed as explanations of human disturbance.

Freud's theory was based on a sample of 20- to 45-year-old upper-middle-class women living in Vienna at a time when sexual expression was discouraged. Because his ideas were based on a sample that lacked the representativeness required for a comprehensive theory of human behavior, many have questioned whether the theories can be applied universally or generalized beyond the initial sample. Also, there is sexism in Freud's views, and this has been a source of criticism (Lips, 1988). He depicts women as inferior and suggested, for example, that women experienced envy or jealousy because they have no penis. Further, Freud theorized that a girl's belief that she had been castrated would produce feelings of inferiority in subsequent psychological development. Critics are quick to point out that Freud was not in a position to know what developing girls think as he did not study children—only the retrospective reports of frustrated adult female patients. When the theory is revised in a modern feminist fashion (Chodorow, 1978), some of the strengths of the theory can be sifted from its inherent sexism.

Systems models

Most models of psychological functioning address the individual. But, what about applying models of ongoing collection of or systems of people? Different perspectives have advanced different ideas about how a primary social system might contribute to childhood and to later psychological disorders. Often, a systems theory holds that the locus of pathology is not within the individual, who is designated the "patient," but within the family members' interrelationships.

Behaviorists emphasize the environment as a controlling and contributing factor in human behavior and identify the family system—especially the parents—as one of the most important environments (Braswell & Bloomquist, 1991; Forehand & McMahon, 1981; Patterson & Bank, 1989). Behaviorally, parents can be influential in several ways: (1) through their own behavior, where they serve as models; (2) through their selectively rewarding activities within the family; and (3) through their creation of a social climate—parents may be hostile and rejecting or warm and accepting. Parents are central players within the family system and carry a great deal of influence.

With less emphasis on the parents behavior but more emphasis on interpersonal relations, the object relations model also sees pathology as within the context of family relationships. One example of a psychodynamic family model addresses the eating disorder anorexia (see Chapter 8). Briefly, anorexia involves a preoccupation with "feeling fat" and accompanying efforts to lose weight—sometimes to the point of starvation. Anorexia typically occurs in female adolescents. Operating from what was once called the Philadelphia Child Guidance Clinic, Minuchin and his colleagues (Minuchin, Roseman, & Baker, 1978) described the characteristics of the family system with an anorexic child: These families were generally overprotective, rigid, and enmeshed and tended to lack skills for conflict resolution.

Enmeshment in a family system refers to a situation in which no member can have a separate identity. There is an insistence that everyone in the family must be together, with a resulting absence of privacy. Rigidity is evident in an unwillingness to tolerate change, and overprotection is evident in an expression of concern at the least sign of discomfort. When a family denies that conflict exists, or changes the topic of conversation to avoid it, conflict is not resolved. Minuchin's family systems view of anorexia places the abnormality in the family—the female adolescent cannot achieve separation from the family, is denied privacy, feels overcontrolled, and strives for independence by controlling eating. The anorexia isn't her disorder!

Systems models of psychopathology are beginning to receive research evaluation, and family systems notions are being included in integrated models of psychopathology. What remains of central importance is that, unlike other models of psychopathology, systems approaches do not place the locus of the disorder within the individual, but within the system. An individual does not have a disorder; instead, he or she has a problem with patterns of interaction within the social system. Because the family is the primary social network for children, it is the interaction pattern within the family that is seen as dysfunctional and it is often this same interaction pattern that is the target for change in family therapy.

Diathesis-stress model

In the example of schizophrenia cited earlier, recall that genetic forces were influential but the genetic factors did not account for all of the cases of schizophrenia. If the disorder were entirely genetic, then both members of an identical twin pair would receive an identical diagnosis. Therefore, nongenetic factors, such as environmental influences and stress, must also play a causal role.

The diathesis-stress model proposes an active interaction between genetic and other biological predispositions and stressful environmental influences. Diatheses are predisposing vulnerability factors, which include biological determinants and characteristic manners of responding. Stress is the current environmental factors that can, but do not always, contribute to the development of abnormal behavior. Common stressors for youngsters may include school, peer conflicts, loss of loved ones, physical accidents, exposure to family or community violence, or simply taking on too much responsibility or too many activities. According to this model, diatheses and stress are complementary; neither is sufficient by itself to cause abnormal behavior.

To further elucidate the diathesis-stress model, return to the example of schizophrenia where predisposing factors are involved, but they do not account for all of the data. The development of abnormality depends in part on the contribution of stresses and related environmental influences. As noted diathesis-stress theorist Meehl described in 1962, only those persons with a genetic makeup conducive to schizophrenia will develop the disorder, but they will become schizophrenic only if exposed to a detrimental learning environment and stressful life experience. This statement was designed for schizophrenia specifically, but has application to disorders in general: Complex interactions between the individual and the environment contribute to the behavior of the person (see also Rutter, Silberg, O'Connor, & Simonoff, 1999).

Changing times

Historically, models of psychopathology, including models of the childhood disorders, sought to explain all of human pathology and adjustment—they were universal models. One need not go beyond Freud's model to see the attempt to be all-encompassing. Such thinking is no longer advanced. Rather, grand and universal theories (models) are seen as so broad that they can never be adequately tested as a whole. Modern models of the development of childhood disorders do not expect universal applicability. Rather, there is an increase in the advancing of focused models—models that strive to explain single disorders. As will be evident throughout this book, certain models have been more or less successful in explaining some but not other disorders. Models specific to individual disorders are discussed in those chapters devoted to the specific disorders.

Another noteworthy trend is that models are becoming integrated. Although a full and comprehensive integration that receives uniform acceptances has not yet appeared, there are identifiable trends to support the view that modern integrative efforts, not unlike early integrations of psychodynamic and learning theories (Dollard & Miller, 1950), are reasonable and desirable. Both the diathesis-stress model and the cognitive-behavioral model, two models with fairly widespread acceptance, illustrate this integration.

Broad models of disorder have been offered as explanatory systems that hold true for boys and girls and for majority as well as minority ethnic groups. Future developments, however, may witness greater gender and ethnic specificity.

Summary

Models are guiding frameworks to organize information. The biological, behavioral, cognitive, psychodynamic, and systems models have been influential in understanding childhood disorders. Currently, integrative models such as the diathesis-stress and cognitive-behavioral models are receiving increased attention.

Biological models are concerned with the role of disease, individual biochemistry, and human genetics in psychological disorders. Biological models examine the genetics of behavior and how neurotransmitter substances influence behavior.

Behaviorists emphasize the observable behavior of the person and the environmental factors that maintain the action. The behavioral models are concerned with maladaptive learning and use the outcomes of laboratory research as the cornerstone for this understanding. Classical conditioning describes how a behavior called a conditioned response is acquired through the pairing of unconditioned and conditioned stimuli. Operant conditioning refers to the strengthening of responses that occurs when they are followed by rewarding experiences. Modeling refers to observational learning—when an individual's behavior is influenced by having observed and imitated the behavior of someone else.

The cognitive model emphasizes that an individual's cognitive functioning contributes to any emotional or behavioral distress. Cognitive functioning influence psychological maladjustment. Cognitive deficiencies are the lack of forethought when it would be useful, and cognitive distortions are dysfunctional thought processes. Although cognitive models are sometimes difficult to assess, data suggest that cognitive functioning is associated with various disorders.

The cognitive-behavioral model is integrative—emphasizing both the process of learning behavior and the cognitive information-processing factors that influence such learning.

Freud's theory suggested that psychological disorders result from intrapsychic conflict. This model places important weight on the unconscious causes of behavior. Contemporary revisions of this theory include the object relations approach, a theory that refers to persons as objects of drives and that places greatest emphasis on the interpersonal relationships and their role in individual psychopathology. One of Freud's lasting contributions was his identification of the unconscious. However, the nonrepresentativeness of his original subjects and the nonempirical features of the bulk of the theory are sources of concern.

Systems models suggest that an individual's symptoms are the result of a disturbed social system. For behaviorists, learning paradigms operate within the system. For psychodynamic theorists, it is the interpersonal dynamics that contribute to maladjustment.

The diathesis-stress model is a model of combined influences. Diatheses and stress interact. Diatheses are predisposing factors, whereas stress is current environmental factors: The model emphasizes the interaction of the predispositions and environmental stresses in psychological disorder.

The diathesis-stress model and the cognitive-behavioral model illustrate the current efforts to integrate models of psychopathology. Indeed, these models offer conceptualizations that have promise not only for understanding childhood disorders but also for guiding its treatment. Researchers and practitioners have given these integrated approaches widespread endorsement.

Issues facing the disorders of childhood 3

Children are not "little adults." Obviously, they are often physically smaller, but they are also emotionally less mature, socially and cognitively still in the process of development, and, in terms of sheer experience, they are not yet fully seasoned. Not surprisingly, it is extremely difficult for children to recognize their own psychological problems.

Children also differ from adults in the problems that bring them into treatment, in their response to certain therapies, and in the course of their disorders. Thus, the psychological difficulties of childhood require special study to be understood and treated.

Researchers have estimated that 15–22% of the children and adolescents in the United States have problems severe enough to need treatment (Costello, Burns, Angold, & Leaf, 1993), but fewer than 20% of youngsters with current problems actually receive services (Tuma, 1989). And, as was found in a 20-year follow-up of children in London (Champion, Goodall, & Rutter, 1995), many of these troubled children go on to become adults with psychological disorders. In several disorders, the median age of onset is between 13 and 25; other disorders can be identified before age 7.

Addressing these childhood difficulties is very important to both the individual and to society. If left untreated, children do not outgrow serious problems but instead can develop into adults with psychological disorders. For example, adults who are diagnosed as having an anxiety disorder have a very high frequency of having had anxiety disorders when they were children (e.g. Last, Hersen, Kazdin, Francis, & Grubb, 1987). Also, a grave psychological disorder in a child, even if transient, is likely to have serious consequences—often more serious than in an adult—because the disorder may interrupt the child's learning and development. A psychologically impaired child may fail to master key tasks that are faced at different ages such as developing self-esteem, establishing relationships with peers, resolving interpersonal conflict, and acquiring academic skills. These inadequacies may in turn lead to increased frustration and rejection. Moreover, once the developmental window for the establishment of self-esteem and other skills has passed, it may be difficult for some children to be given other opportunities to master the particular developmental challenges.

Almost all mental health professionals, across all of the models and theories that have been offered to explain human behavior, agree to one uniform tenet: The early formative years are important to later adjustment and difficulties during these years are the precursors of later maladjustment. The boy is father to the man. For example, once children learn to be unsociably aggressive, a substantial proportion tend to remain aggressive. Left untreated, aggression is a stable aspect of human behavior. In fact, the level of antisocial behavior in childhood has been found to predict the level of antisocial behavior in adulthood (e.g. Robins, 1966; Robins & Price, 1991).

In the chapters that follow, we describe the symptoms of disorders, provide information about their prevalence, discuss research findings, and describe the nature and status of treatments for the disorders. However, before we address the nature and treatment of the specific disorders, four general issues facing childhood disorders in general will be discussed: developmental psychopathology, parenting and family factors, assessing and classifying childhood disorders, and treating disorders of childhood.

Developmental psychopathology

One thing is for certain—the human organism completes many changes over the life span. Many of these changes occur during childhood. These changes include cognitive, emotional, social, sexual, and biological elements, to name just a few. One branch of psychology, developmental psychology, studies these and other changes as a part of the course of normal human development. Knowledge from the study of normal development plays an important role in the determination of what constitutes a deviation in adjustment.

Emerging from the study of normal child development and its interface with child maladjustment (Cicchetti, 1993), developmental psychopathology views psychological maladjustment in relation to the major changes that occur across the life cycle. No one theory of psychopathology is followed but emphasis is greatest on the rapid development that occurs between birth and maturity (Achenbach, 1990).

The importance of the interaction between the child and the social context is recognized and emphasized within developmental psychopathology. There are different behavioral styles as well as different beliefs about acceptable behavior, and if the "fit" between the person and the context is not good (e.g. an energetic child in a setting that is intolerant of even normal amounts of activity), maladjustment in the child may be what is seen by adults (Lerner, Hess, & Nitz, 1990). The person–context interaction of developmental psychopathology is embodied in the child's adjustment to the challenges of normal development (Sroufe & Rutter, 1984). For instance, consider the following developmental challenges. During ages 3 to 5, children face the developmental challenges of acquiring self-control, self-reliance, and peer contacts; ages 6 to 12 involve challenges of social understanding, whereas the challenges of adolescence address flexible thinking, emancipation, and identity. Success or failure in facing issues at one point in development are seen as laying the groundwork for success or failure when facing the issues that will need to be addressed later in life.

The disorders of childhood are best seen against the backdrop of normal development. An important feature of developmental psychopathology is that it judges child disorders using the backdrop of what is normal for a given age (Campbell, 1986). A specific behavior pattern is or is not considered maladaptive depending upon when in the child's development the behavior pattern is seen. A specific example will bring life to this point. Is it a disorder when a 4-year-old reports a specific fear—an extreme fear—such as fear of the dark? The parents are abashed and self-conscious about the child, and the child seems very distressed by even the mention of being in the dark. Normative data indicates that approximately 90% of children between the ages 2 and 14 reported at least one specific fear and that fear of the dark is a common fear for a child this age. It would hardly be fair to call such a fear abnormal when it appears instead to be a routine part of the challenges of normal development. In fact, it can be argued that it is through the overcoming of this fear or others like it that the child develops mastery and confidence for future encounters with novelty, the unknown, physical danger, or threat to self-esteem. The same fear in a 22-year-old might be abnormal. Defining fears as abnormal depends on the age at which the fear is expressed and on the disruption that results in daily functioning caused by such fears.

Parenting and family factors

The notion that the developing child's social context is important in psychological adjustment has been often stated and well ingrained, as noted in our earlier discussion of the systems and behavioral models of psychopathology. Not surprisingly, the child's family is considered a key social context in which the early years of development take place.

Early—and now known to be incorrect—explanations of certain severe disorders blamed the mother: A child with the disorder autism was thought to be the result of a cold and unloving mother. Although such an extreme explanation is now known not to be an accurate depiction of the causal pathway to autism (see Chapter 10), it nevertheless illustrates the prior tendency for mental health professionals, as well as nonprofessionals, to resort to early child rearing for explanations of psychological adjustment. Although this example was a fruitless path, other investigations have been more productive.

Some areas of research have been successful in identifying parenting styles that contribute to behavioral and emotional disorders of children. Later, in several chapters in this book, we review studies of the role of parenting behavior in the expression of conduct problems in the children, and the benefits of parent training to reduce child problems. Other research programs have identified biological causal factors, such as in Down's syndrome, a form of mental retardation. Because the conclusions that can be reached vary across the different childhood disorders, detailed discussions and comments about the role of parenting practices are presented within the specific chapters on the specific disorders. For now, let's consider one general parenting topic—divorce—and what we know about its effects on children.

Divorce: Solution or detriment for children?

Divorce is a worldwide phenomenon: Although the frequency and acceptance of divorce varies across cultures and generations, the dissolution of marriage occurs at alarming rates. Consider, for example, the data on divorce in the US. According to the data presented in 1997, half of the marriage contracts do not last. Approximately 40% of children grow up in a divorced family. How do children adjust to the changes associated with divorce? Children are not homogeneous on this issue, and their response depends in part on their age and gender.

According to experts, most preschool children experience a 2- to 3-year period of readjustment following divorce; they may show aggression, depression, noncompliance, acting-out, and problems in peer relationships (Hetherington, Stanley-Hagen, & Anderson, 1989; Wallerstein, Corbin, & Lewis, 1988; Weiss, 1979). After the initial distress, however, young children's adjustment appears to improve. Based on interviews with preschool and older children 10 years after the parents' divorce, researchers have reported that the younger children exhibited fewer problems than children who were older (Wallerstein & Blakeslee, 1989).

For preschoolers, the gender of the child influences their postdivorce adjustment. For boys, problems are more intense and enduring than for girls. Why might this be the case? Perhaps boys tend to find the breakup more distressing, perhaps they are less adept at coping with divorce, or perhaps they tend to show their distress more overtly than do girls. Another possibility is that girls fare better after divorce because mothers have custody in most single-parent homes and there is some evidence that children who are in the custody of a parent of the same gender show healthier emotional adjustment after divorce (Camara & Resnick, 1988; Furstenberg, 1988; Santrock & Warshak, 1986; Zill, 1988).

Based on other data, it is reasonable to speculate that the child's style of processing information—how a child makes sense of the social environment—contributes to postdivorce adjustment: Children who catastrophized about their social environment showed more symptoms, whereas children who perceived high personal control and were optimistic about the future showed fewer symptoms (Mazur, Wolchik, & Sandler, 1992; see also Kerig, 1998). One's attitudes about the event can influence one's adjustment to the event.

How do adolescents fare after divorce? Among early adolescents, the initial postdivorce response is often characterized by acting-out and difficulties in school and by early withdrawal and disconnection from the family (Hetherington, 1987; Wallerstein et al., 1988). This disengagement can have beneficial effects if the activities outside the family involve positive interactions with supportive care givers. However, early disengagement by boys from single-parent homes may expose them to higher rates of problem behavior and increase their susceptibility to antisocial peer pressure (Dornbusch et al., 1985; Steinberg, 1987).

Although not the central focus of this book, it is still worth noting that the responses of adolescents who are 13–18 years old at the time of their parents' divorce vary greatly. One longitudinal study found that middle adolescents, like younger children, expressed anger, depressive symptoms, and some acting-out behavior immediately after divorce (Wallerstein & Blakeslee, 1989; Wallerstein & Kelly, 1974). Additionally, it was reported that these same adolescents felt a sense of loss, betrayal, and concern about future financial resources and relationship stability. Middle adolescents also tended to distance themselves from their families. Generally, adjustment improved with time, but one-third of older children continued to express feelings of sadness and anger regarding the divorce 5 to 10 years after it had happened. For some, apparently, the effects are not short lived.

Why do children whose parents divorce show behavioral and emotional difficulties? Could it be that the divorce is a trauma, that the sense of family stability is forever disturbed, or that the parenting practices of the divorcing adults are severely disrupted. It could also be that the children are, before the divorce, doing less well than others. Methodologically, it is important to take into account the quality of the children's predivorce adjustment before examining any potential variations in their postdivorce adaptation. Important work along these lines was conducted and reported by Cherlin and his colleagues (1991). These investigators reported on the outcomes of two longitudinal studies, one conducted in the UK and the other conducted in the US. The results indicated that, for boys, the effect of separation or divorce on behavior and achievement was sharply reduced when one took into account the behavior problems, achievement levels, and family difficulties that were present earlier— before the divorce. The reduction in the apparent effect of divorce occurred for girls as well, but to a slightly lesser extent. Thus, conditions before the separation or divorce play a role in the prediction of childrens' adjustment postdivorce.

Perhaps the most difficult situation for the child is when the parents place the child in the middle of their conflicts. The following clinical case provides an illustration.

> Lisa was seen in therapy for severe separation anxiety—she was almost unable to be away from her mother. Indeed, on most nights, she slept in the same bed as her mother. When taken to school, she experienced inordinate distress. Her social life was affected as well. She would not go to sleepovers at friends' homes, and she often would exhibit amorphous physical complaints, as well as more severe symptoms, especially when her parents tried to force her to interact with peers or to sleep in her own bed. Lisa was 13 years old, and Lisa's parents had divorced when she was 11.
>
> Perhaps a main factor exacerbating Lisa's distress, and a factor that affects many children of divorce, was the degree to which the parents placed her in the middle of their conflict. Lisa's mom would disclose to Lisa that her father had been terribly mean ... and Lisa's father would complain to her about how her mother was taking all his money and not using it for the children as she was

instructed to do by the courts. Mom would confide in her daughter, disclosing personal matters that put her father in a bad light. When Lisa didn't want to spend time with her father, her father would express anger and blame the mother. The child was in the middle of the parents' conflict.

Belittling of the other parent's character, trying to sabotage Lisa's relationship with the other parent, and even trying to seduce Lisa in conspiracies with one parent against another were features of her parent's divorce that contributed to, exacerbated, and maintained her psychological distress. As is evident, the amount and quality of post-divorce contact with both parents can be an important factor in children's adjustment.

Assessing and classifying childhood disorders

Psychologists and other mental health professionals have designed and evaluated numerous methods for the measurement of human behavior. Like behavior in general, psychological disorders can be assessed by using methods such as self-report inventories, observations, structured interviews, and performance on laboratory tasks. With children, similar assessment procedures are used as with adults, but there are some important differences because young people may be inarticulate or uncooperative, or lack awareness about their emotions or actions. Accordingly, the psychological assessment of children includes ratings of the child's behavior by parents and teachers, structured interviews of the child and the child's parents, as well as self-report questionnaires and the use of structured behavioral observations.

Psychological assessments are useful to the extent that they are reliable and valid. Reliability and validity are the way psychologists test the merits of tests! For instance, reliability refers to the consistency of a test or measure: A reliable instrument is one that would be scored similarly by different examiners (interscorer reliability) and would produce scores that do not change dramatically over time (temporal stability or retest reliability). Reliability is necessary but not sufficient—validity is also required before a psychological assessment can be said to have utility.

A valid test or measure is one that actually assesses what it claims to measure. For example, if a test is said to measure aggression and scores on it correlate highly with scores on other valid tests of aggression it can be said to have concurrent validity. Moreover, if scores on the measure are found to predict the likelihood of aggressive actions, then it can be said to have predictive criterion-related validity.

Assessments involve the gathering of data, and it is preferred that reliable and valid psychological measurement instruments be used. These assessment data are then used by psychologists and other mental health professionals to help make informed decisions. The assessment process is complex, often including data gathered using multiple methods and data from multiple sources.

Assessing childhood disorders

The Children's Depression Inventory (CDI; Kovacs, 1981) is one example of a self-report measure used with children. It is noteworthy because of its widespread use with clinically referred and nonreferred children and because the scale includes a wide range of symptoms other than depressed mood (Compas, 1997). Parents may provide ratings using the Child Behavior Checklist (CBCL; Achenbach, 1991; Achenbach & Edelbrock, 1983), whereas the Diagnostic Interview for Children and Adolescents (DICA; Herjanic & Reich, 1982) and the Anxiety Disorders Interview Schedule–Child Version (ADIS–C; Albano & Silverman, 1996; Silverman & Albano, 1998) characterize the method of assessment using a structured diagnostic interview. The Response Class Matrix (Mash, Terdal, & Anderson, 1973) illustrates structured behavioral observations. More on each of these approaches as we proceed into this chapter.

Children are asked to report about themselves on the CDI—a 27-item scale that assesses depressive symptomatology in children (Kovacs, 1981). To respond to the items on the CDI, the child selects from among alternatives the one option that reflects the degree of the child's depressive symptoms. Consider these sample items from Kovacs (1991).

Pick out the sentences that describe your feelings and ideas in the past 2 weeks.

1. _____ I am sad once in a while
   _____ I am sad many times
   _____ I am sad all of the time
2. _____ I hate myself
   _____ I do not like myself
   _____ I like myself
3. _____ Nothing will ever work out for me
   _____ I am not sure if things will work out for me
   _____ Things will work out for me OK

Importantly, a specific interval of time is assessed: Children are asked to report how they felt over the last 2 weeks. Adequate reliability and validity data have been reported (Compas, 1997; Kazdin, 1981; Kendall, Cantwell, & Kazdin, 1989; Saylor, Finch, Spirito, & Bennett, 1984). Although a cutoff of 17 (Smucker, Craighead, Craighead, & Green, 1986) suggests maladjustment, more than the child's self-report on one questionnaire is typically needed to make an accurate determination of the presence of a disorder. Nevertheless, there is general agreement that for internalizing disorders, such as depression, there is great value in the child's perspective on the degree and intensity of his or her own emotional distress and this information can be gathered on a self-report instrument.

The Child Behavior Checklist (CBCL; Achenbach, 1991) is a rigorously developed and standardized rating scale, available for both parents and teachers (Teacher Rating Form; TRF). These scales are widely used for assessing the most common dimensions of psychological disorder in childhood (for example, social problems, aggressive behavior, anxiety, or depression). The CBCL presents parents with 118 descriptors—features of behavior problems. An additional 20 descriptors measure social competence. The scores of each child are based on the parent ratings of these descriptors and are then judged against a distribution of scores obtained by a normative sample of children with backgrounds representing the range of social and economic status. The normative data provide the backdrop for the profile of scores received by the target child. A sample CBCL report is presented in Figure 3.1. As can be seen, the parents of this child rated him as low on the first five dimensions and high (i.e. T score over 70) on the Delinquent behavior and Aggressive behavior scales, with the scores reflecting that the child is more delinquent and aggressive than 98% of male children of the same age.

> The CBCL profile shown in Figure 3.1 belongs to Gar, a 12-year-old boy who meets criteria for conduct disorder. The boy has been reported to engage in petty thefts, repetitive lying, fighting, bullying, disobedience, and arguing. His mother reports that he has "cut school," and that she also thinks that he has vandalized and started a fire in a nearby park.
>
> Although these behaviors are noteworthy in their own right, an advantage of the CBCL is the presentation of the data against a backdrop of the normal range of behavior (reflected in T scores). Thus, one can see that Gar's problems

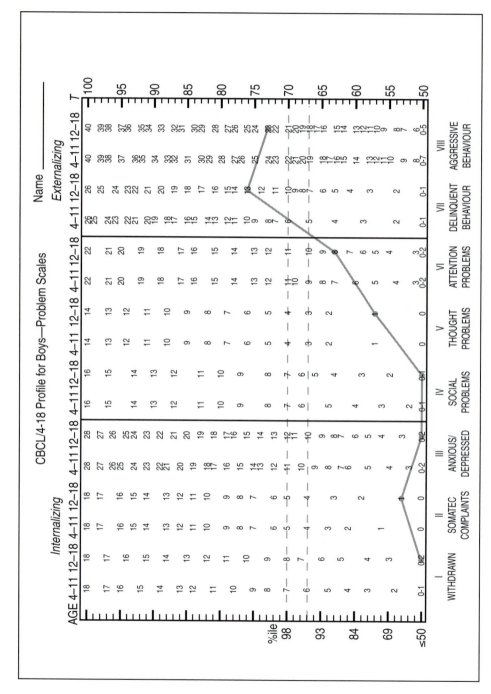

Figure 3.1. A sample CBCL profile. Copyright 1991 © by T.M. Achenbach. Reproduced by permission.

are well above that which would fall within the normal range of troubling behavior.

The Response Class Matrix is a method for observing and assessing parent–child interactions (Mash et al., 1973) and represents the effort to assess child behavior as part of a family system (Mash & Terdal, 1997). Trained observers record an observation every 10 seconds. They record both parent and child behaviors by placing a single check mark in one of the cells of a matrix. The rows of the matrix can be for different child behaviors (such as play and negative behavior) and the columns can be for different parent reactions (such as praise and commands). Thus, the matrix for one observation session might show that each negative child behavior was tied to a parental command and that desired child behaviors received no praise from the parent. By providing data about the pattern of interactions, the Response Class Matrix is helpful in identifying specific patterns that the therapist can target for change.

Information from direct observational methods, such as the Response Class Matrix, has the advantage of being representative of actual behavior in the real world. However, normative information about these interactions and behavior are lacking. That is, we do not yet know exactly what constitutes the healthy patterns of "good" parents and "well-adjusted" children. As a result, although observations are helpful to identify target behaviors for treatment, and useful to identify family influences (Mash & Terdal, 1997), they may not be as valuable as structured interviews or checklists for classifying abnormal child behavior or making a diagnosis.

The face-to-face interview can help establish rapport with children and families and permits asking questions that are geared to reaching designated diagnostic decisions. Structured diagnostic interviews are the preferred method of interviewing because the questions are arranged in advance, and the criteria needed to reach a diagnosis are delineated in the interview format. Most of the structured diagnostic interviews for use with youngsters follow an established diagnostic system (such as the DSM, or ICD-10) and include the full range of childhood disorders.

One structured diagnostics interview, the Anxiety Disorders Interview Schedule–Child (ADIS–C; Albano & Silverman, 1996; Silverman & Nelles, 1988) has received widespread application for use with children—especially children who may be suspected of suffering from an anxiety disorder. This structured interview, like the others that are available, provides the interviewer with specific questions, in an organized sequence and format, that can lead directly to decisions about the presence or absence of a disorder. The ADIS–C has adequate reliability over time (Silverman & Rabian, 1995) and inter-rater agreement (Rapee, Barrett, Dadds, & Evans, 1994). The instrument, when used before and after a psychological treatment, has also been found to be sensitive to treatment-produced gains (e.g. Kendall et al., 1997).

In addition to the ADIS–C, there has been considerable effort over the past several years to improve other structured interviewing procedures for use with children and adolescents (Edelbrock & Costello, 1988). For example, the Diagnostic Interview for Children and Adolescents (DICA; Herjanic & Reich, 1982) assesses 185 symptoms and can be conducted in 40–45 minutes with parents or children six years of age and older. As is true for structured interviews in general, the DICA has specific questions and scoring procedures that use a branching system to lead to diagnoses. Favorable reliability and validity data are available to support the use of structured diagnostic interviews (Edelbrock & Costello, 1988).

Although the child and the child's parents are typically interviewed separately, there is not yet a uniform method for the integration of these two sources of information. For some disorders, the parent report is given more emphasis, whereas for other disorders the child's perspective is given a major role. Researchers, as well as the developers of the structured interviews, are working to provide specific methods for the integration of child and parent interview data for use in reaching optimally accurate diagnoses (e.g. ADIS).

A diagnostic system for childhood disorders

Perhaps the most widely used classification system for disorders of childhood is the *Diagnostic and Statistical Manual,* 4th edition (DSM-IV) published by the American Psychiatric Association (APA, 1994). This system is largely in agreement with another often used system developed in conjunction with the World Health Organization—the International Classification of Diseases (ICD-10; WHO, 1992). Both systems use a categorical approach with specified criteria: There are categories of disorders each with their own criteria and a child who displays a sufficient number of the criterion behaviors (symptoms) is said to have the disorder. Although these systems are widely used, interesting and important points suggest that childhood disorders do not fall neatly into categories (Sonuga-Barke, 1999). For example, there is a high degree of co-occurrence of disorders (comorbidity) and symptoms of one disorder often overlap with symptoms of other disorders.

Conceptual considerations aside, much progress has been made with regard to the diagnosis of child disorders. For example, consider the fact that in the original DSM (APA, 1952), children were diagnosed using the adult categories because there were no categories specifically for childhood disorders. Over the years, the classification scheme has become increasingly data-based and responsive to input from researchers. The present version, DSM-IV, has a separate section for disorders usually first diagnosed in infancy, childhood, or adolescence. Also, children can receive other diagnoses (such as depression or generalized anxiety disorder) from the adult disorders sections of the DSM. For example, an early adolescent who displays symptoms of depression would be diagnosed and classified within the system as having a mood disorder, just as an adult. Box 3.1 provides an overview of the DSM classification of the disorders specific to youngsters.

As suggested earlier, not all psychologists endorse a categorical approach to defining childhood disorders. A related but contrasting approach for childhood disorders comes with an imposing title—multivariate statistical taxometric system—but the basic idea behind the

---

BOX 3.1   Classification of disorders of young people

Some of these disorders are among the adult disorders, others are specific to youth.

The diagnostic system permits children to receive some of the same diagnoses as adults, but it also includes disorders that are first identified in infancy, childhood, or adolescence. Here is a brief overview of these various disorders with some examples.

- Disruptive behavior disorders.   These disorders are associated with acting-out, such as destructive and dangerous behavior (conduct disorder) and extreme inattentiveness and restlessness (attention-deficit hyperactivity disorder).

- Emotional disorders.   These disorders involve disturbances associated with anxiety and depression. Within anxiety, there are several types of disorders such as generalized anxiety disorder, social phobia, and separation anxiety disorder. Depression, in varying degrees, can also be diagnosed for youngsters.

- Eating disorders.   Disorders associated with feeding, such as anorexia nervosa and bulimia nervosa.

- Mental retardation.   Substantial limitations in present functioning characterized by significantly subaverage intellectual functioning and limitations in adaptive living skills.

- Learning disorders.   Achievement substantially below that expected given age, intelligence, and education.

- Pervasive developmental disorders.   Impairment in communication and social interaction, together with restricted and stereotyped patterns of behavior. An example is autism.

- Tic disorders.   Sudden repetitive motor movements or utterances. For example, Tourette's disorder, which involves both motor and verbal tics that occur many times a day.

- Elimination disorders.   Encopresis, the repeated passage of feces into inappropriate places, and enuresis, the repeated voiding of urine into bed or clothes.

system is actually straightforward. The basic idea is to classify disorders along various continua by using statistical procedures to determine what symptoms occur together with what other symptoms. In this manner, human judgments are much less influential in determining the symptoms of disorders. Using correlations between pairs of symptoms or pairs of behavior ratings, the researcher then examines these relationships to look for patterns of co-occurring characteristics (Achenbach, 1982). This statistical approach to classification describes children in terms of their standing along several different continua of behavior—rather than as "in" or "out" of a category. Recall Figure 3.1 depicting the CBCL profile—it provided a picture of the degree to which the rated child was "extreme" on various dimensions of child behavior.

This method of assessment has led researchers to describe childhood disorders as falling into two broad categories: (1) internalizing disorders and (2) externalizing disorders (Achenbach & Edelbrock, 1978). Internalizing disorders are psychological difficulties that are considered inner-directed; core symptoms are associated with overcontrolled behaviors (Reynolds, 1992). Internalizing disorders include such psychological disorders as anxiety, depression, social-withdrawal and isolation, and the eating disorders. Externalizing disorders are maladaptive behavior patterns in children, across several situations, that create problems for others. In these undercontrolled disorders, which are also called behavioral disorders, the child's behavioral problems result in conflicts between the child and the social context. Conduct disorder, discussed in Chapter 4, is an example.

Studies of adolescents, including studies of African-American youngsters (Resnicow, Ross-Gaddy, & Vaughan, 1995), suggest a gender distinction; more females report internalizing disorders, whereas more males are identified with externalizing difficulties. By a ratio of 2:1 or 3:1, boys show more problems linked to externalizing than girls (Quay, 1986). For instance, boys, by a ratio of between 2:1 and 9:1 (Barkley, 1997b), are more likely to be diagnosed with attention-deficit hyperactivity disorder (ADHD). Somewhat surprisingly, however, when boys and girls aged 9–13 are studied, the incidence of one internalizing disorder—the anxiety disorders—is equally represented across gender.

Some critics of the distinction between internalizing and external-izing disorders hasten to point out that many externally disordered children also have very tormented inner lives—if not because of their own internal personal turmoil, then perhaps because of the punishment, ridicule, or unwanted attention that their externalizing behavior generates. In response, advocates of the distinction have suggested that children with externalizing disorders display their problems outwardly, but may still experience some inner distress and that these variations can be seen in the profile describing the child's level of distress on each of the dimensions. When there are elevations in the externalizing dimensions, and less elevation on the internalizing dimensions, for example, the child suffers less internally relative to the problems that are discharged onto the environment. As discussed in later chapters, the taxometric approach and its distinction between internalizing and externalizing disorders has led to valuable and informative cognitive and behavioral distinctions (Kendall & MacDonald, 1993) that have important implications for psychological therapy.

Treating disorders of childhood

As noted earlier, children typically come to the attention of the mental health system when parents, teachers, or officials of some type decide that the youngster needs professional assistance—the children themselves do not self-refer. Indeed, I have never received a telephone call or any other form of contact from a troubled child who was seeking or asking for psychological help for him- or herself. The fact that children are sent for or brought to treatment, whereas adults may seek it, is an important distinction with implications for treatment.

A variety of theories and types of therapy have been applied to children and adolescents (Kazdin, 1994; Kendall, 1991; Kratochwill & Morris, 1993). For example, young persons may be treated individually using behavioral procedures, a cognitive-behavioral approach (Kendall, 1991, 2000), or psychodynamic (Target & Fonagy, 1994) strategies, or within the family using any of the various theoretical approaches. In other instances, the parents may be given parent training to alleviate child problems. Which of the various treatments should be used? How does one decide which treatment to implement?

One way to select an intervention is to refer to the empirical literature on the efficacy of the different treatments for specific child problems (see Hibbs & Jensen, 1996). Numerous research studies—referred to as treatment outcome studies—have been conducted and reported, and we will discuss several of them in some detail within our consideration of each of the disorders. For now, the general and overall reviews of the full complement of research studies about the effectiveness of therapy with children can be used to draw suggestions about which treatments to use. These reviews often indicate that several of the interventions based on a behavioral or cognitive-behavioral perspective tend to be the more effective (Weiss & Weisz, 1995; Weisz, Weiss, Hans, Granger, & Morton,

1995), although there does not appear to be any one treatment that is consistently more effective than others. The absence of a universally effective treatment, however, is to be expected. It is unlikely that one method of treatment would be effective for all childhood behavior disorders (Shirk & Russell, 1996). Other reviews of the literature, such as those that apply specific criteria for the determination of efficacious treatments (e.g. Kaslow & Thompson, 1998; Kazdin & Kendall, 1998; Kazdin & Weisz, 1998; Kendall, 1998; Lonigan, Elbert, & Johnson, 1998; Ollendick & King, 1998) find several treatments to meet the criteria/standards and thereby earn the designation of "efficacious" or "probably efficacious." Interestingly, an examination of these treatments yields some consistencies: The efficacious treatments are time-limited and focused on a specific problem with a relatively homogeneous sample of children. The treatments include behavioral components, attention to cognitive processing and emotional experience, and have an action-oriented infrastructure. With regard to the action orientation, the efficacious treatments generally include role-plays, practice exercises, exposure to distressing situations, or behavioral experiments as ways for the child to test ideas and learn and practice new skills. Like the earlier mentioned reviews, treatments with a behavioral or cognitive-behavioral orientation can be said to meet the criteria for being classified as probably efficacious or efficacious. Later in this book, when treatments for specific disorders are described, you will recognize the features listed here as they will likely be a part of the treatments that have been found in methodologically sound empirical evaluations to be effective.

Are child therapy and adult therapy alike? Yes, to a degree, child and adult psychological treatments have like-minded theoretical orientations, schedules and structures, and professional ethics. But there are three important differences between adult and child therapy: (1) the role of parents, (2) the use of play in therapy, and (3) the relevance and efficacy of psychoactive medications.

Parents play a central role in children's lives, and the degree to which parents and other family members are involved in the problem or the treatment requires consideration. Instead of working one-to-one with the child, therapists who work with children often choose to spend at least some time teaching the parents to work with the child. Such parent training is often used with younger children. In other instances, the family may be seen together in family therapy (Fauber & Kendall, 1992; Fauber & Long, 1991).

Recall that children did not seek treatment on their own, and recognize that, in the beginning, they may not want to be there. Play is used by a variety of therapists as a means to involve children in the tasks of treatment. One specific form of "play therapy" follows psychodynamic theory and uses play as a means for the child to express thoughts and emotions. This method remains somewhat popular despite a lack of data to support its use. In contrast, the treatments that have received empirical support use play not as a means of child expression, but as a way to engage the child in the action-oriented experiences that are designed to be therapeutic.

Biomedical treatments, specifically medications, have also been used for childhood and adolescent disorders. Many people think that children's disorders can be treated with the same medications that are used for adults. However, with the exception of Ritalin, which is used to treat childhood attention-deficit hyperactivity disorder (ADHD; see Chapter 5) and has begun to be applied with adults as well, there are far fewer controlled studies on the effectiveness of psychotropic medications for children than there are for adults (Biederman, 1992), and the studies that have been done sometimes paint a less optimistic picture of the effects of the medications for children than for adults. For instance, several medications that are effective in the treatment of adult depression are not effective with depressed children (Gadow, 1992; Sommers-Flanagan & Sommers-Flanagan, 1996), and medications for adult anxiety disorders have not yet been evaluated adequately for their use with anxiety-disordered children. Also, the use of neuroleptics with children may result in high levels of neurological symptom side-effects that are different from those of adults (Richardson, Haugland, & Craig, 1991). When the research evidence provides a basis for their use, medications can play an important role. In the absence of empirical evaluation and support, use of certain psychoactive medications with children can be questioned.

Summary

Normal development offers an important perspective for under-standing psychological disorders in children. In developmental psychopathology, maladjustment is seen in relation to the major changes that occur across the lifespan. Assessing and diagnosing child disorders use assessments often similar to those used with adults (e.g. self-reports, structured diagnostic interviews). Some assessments are specific to use with children such as the Child Behavior Checklist (CBCL) and the Response Class Matrix. Psychological disorders of childhood can be classified into categories or described along several continua in an effort to guide treatment. Child problems can be treated individually, in school- or clinic-based programs, in families, or using medications.

Conduct disorders 4

Depression and anxiety are the leading reasons that adults seek psychological help, but this is not the case when it comes to children. The majority of difficulties in childhood that are brought to the attention of mental health professionals have to do with externalizing, undercontrolled behavior problems. Our focus in this chapter will be on one of these behavior problems—conduct disorder (CD). In the next chapter we will address attention-deficit hyperactivity disorder (ADHD).

> Large for his age, physically strong, and aggressive, Josh was not bullied by the other children, even though he associated with kids several years his senior. Josh was 12 years old when he was brought home at 1:30AM by the police. He had run away from home the day before, slept in a parked car that he had broken into, and was identified as the perpetrator of a theft at a neighborhood convenience store. He had also been sought by school officials because, on more than one occasion, he had been in fights and had skipped school for several consecutive days. Josh's mother claims that she can't control him, and his teachers report that he is defiant and uncooperative in class and cruel to some of the other children. Josh did not report feeling emotional distress—"I ain't got no problems"—but the reports indicated that those around him had suffered from his lack of socially appropriate behavior. Indeed, Josh's mother reported several bouts of emotional distress exacerbated by Josh's misbehavior.

Phenomenology and classification

Many if not all children have broken social or familial rules or been disobedient to adults in authority. But, certainly one cannot categorize all children as conduct disordered. What level of defiance is needed for a child to be deemed conduct disordered (see also Hinshaw & Zupan, 1997)?

According to DSM-IV, the essential features of conduct disorder are a repetitive and persistent pattern of behavior that involves violation of the basic rights of others and of the major age-appropriate social norms. The problem is not situation-specific: Rather, the conduct problems are evident at school, in the home, within the community, and with peers. A common feature of conduct disorder is physical aggression, taking the form of cruelty, damage to the property of others, or starting fires. For example, Jamie, described in Chapter 1, was considered by some to be a suspect in setting fire to his home. Stealing, lying, and cheating are also common among children diagnosed with conduct disorder. To warrant a diagnosis of conduct disorder, the behavior pattern must include three or more of the criteria (listed in Box 4.1) during the past 12 months, with at least one present in the last 6 months. Conduct disorder has been described as an "acting-out" behavior problem (McMahon & Estes, 1997) and, as seen in the table, represents a variety of serious antisocial acts.

BOX 4.1   DSM criteria for a diagnosis of conduct disorder

Conduct disorder involves a repetitive and persistent pattern of behavior in which the rights of others or societal rules are violated. At least three of the following must be present within the past 12 months, with at least one present in the last 6 months.

- aggression to people and animals:
  - often bullies, threatens, or intimidates others:
  - often initiates physical fights
  - has used a weapon that can cause serious physical harm
  - has been physically cruel to people
  - has been physically cruel to animals
  - has stolen while confronting a victim
  - has forced someone into sexual activity

- destruction of property:
  - deliberately set fires with intent to cause serious damage
  - deliberately destroyed others' property

- deceitfulness or theft:
  - has broken into someone else's house, building, or car
  - often lies to obtain goods or favors or avoid obligations
  - has stolen items of nontrivial value without confrontation

- serious violations of rules:
  - often stays out at nights despite parental prohibition (beginning before age 13)
  - has run away from home overnight at least twice while living with parents/guardians
  - often truants from school (beginning before age 13).

DSM distinguishes between childhood onset (prior to age 10) and adolescent onset (after age 10) and specifies three levels of severity: mild, moderate, or severe.

There is a less serious expression of acting-out behavior disorder that is referred to as oppositional defiant disorder (ODD). In several ways, oppositional defiant disorder resembles conduct disorder. However, whereas conduct disorders are essentially concerned with serious violations of the basic rights of others, oppositional defiant disorder involves a pattern of negativistic, hostile, and defiant behavior that has lasted a minimum of 6 months. A diagnosis of oppositional defiant disorder requires evidence of a pattern of behavior (lasting 6 months) during which there is evidence of the presence of four of the following behaviors:

- often loses temper
- often argues with adults
- often defies rules, or refuses to comply with adult requests
- often intentionally annoys people
- often blames others for mistakes or misbehavior
- is often touchy or easily annoyed by others
- is often angry and resentful
- is often spiteful and vindictive.

As is evident, the construct of oppositionality is a central feature of this disorder.

When conduct disorder is present, the behaviors associated with oppositional defiant disorder are also likely to be present. Therefore, a diagnosis of conduct disorder preempts a diagnosis of oppositional defiant disorder.

Although the one category of conduct disorder does reflect a pattern of behavior, the actual children in this diagnostic group are quite heterogeneous. One child might be a firestarter, whereas many others have never started a single fire. There are cases with and without significant aggression: Not all youngsters receiving a diagnosis of conduct disorder engage in physical fighting. There are still others with and without illegal activities, with and without the presence of family psychopathology, and with and without comorbid diagnoses such as ADHD or learning disabilities. In general, conduct disordered youngsters are often impulsive, have a high need for stimulation, are low in empathy and moral development, and have troubled interpersonal relationships (Martin & Hoffman, 1990). Not surprisingly, substance abuse is also a common concern.

How can we better understand such noncompliant acting out? Loeber, Van Kammen, and Maughan (1993) studied about 500 boys aged 3 to 16 over a 3-year period and identified three developmental pathways or trajectories that lead to disruptive behavior problems.

According to Loeber et al., the overt behaviors pathway consists of those antisocial actions that are confrontive such as fighting, arguing, and temper tantrums. The covert behavior pathway consists of concealed actions such as stealing, truancy, and lying. A third pathway—early authority conflict (e.g. stubborn, defiant)—was also identified. The lowest rates of offending were seen in boys in the overt and authority conflict pathways, whereas those with highest delinquency and most violent offenses showed escalation over the years on scores on all three pathways. Researchers may come to further identify different etiological pictures and, eventually, distinctions such as these may produce subgroups of children who are differentially responsive to interventions.

Who are the conduct-disordered youngsters?

Conduct problems are prevalent in the general population and especially so in the samples seen in child clinics. According to McMahon and Estes (1997), conduct problems are among the most frequently occurring child disorders, with prevalence ranging from 2% to 9% for CD and from 6% to 10% for ODD. When teenagers are asked to self-report their experiences with the specific behaviors that comprise conduct disorder, the results are alarming: More than 50% admit to theft and 45% admit to having caused property destruction. Based on a review of several studies of the prevalence of conduct disorder conducted with clinic-referred children, Wells and Forehand (1985), while at the University of Georgia, noted that 33–75% of the referrals were for conduct-disordered behaviors.

Boys and girls differ in the prevalence of conduct disorder. The precise gender ratio in the prevalence of the disorder is difficult to determine because of the varied diagnostic criteria and the varying types of assessments that have been used. Nevertheless, estimates that vary from 3:1 to 7:1 (males–females) are common (Earls, 1994), with biological and psychosocial theories offered to explain the observed difference (Eme & Kavanaugh, 1995). Gender differences are apparent in the age of onset of conduct disorder (Kazdin, 1990)—whereas most boys had an onset before age 10, the onset of conduct disorder in girls was concentrated in the early teens (ages 13–16). Some gender differences are noticeable in symptoms as well: For instance, theft is more common among males, and sexual misbehavior is more common among females. Early age of onset is also seen as a poor prognostic indicator (Werry, 1997).

Are these gender differences important in determining the cause or designing the optimal treatment? What can be said about the meaning of these gender differences? Clearly, one cannot determine the causes of the observed differences without further investigation. However, one speculative explanation is that the socialization process, in both families and schools, shapes boys and girls in different directions. For example, in most Western cultures, aggressiveness is tolerated more in boys than in girls, and boys are expected to discharge their tensions in more physical ways. There is also some evidence that, whereas girls may be less likely to engage in serious and persistent conduct problems, they may be at risk for a broad range of other behavior problems including internalizing disorders (Loeber & Keenan, 1994; Zoccolillo, 1993). Others have speculated that there are biological differences, as well as biological predispositions, toward different types of behavior problems.

Although culture and socialization play a role in the development and expression of conduct disorders, conduct disorders are found around the globe (see Rutter, Tizard, Yule, Graham, & Whitmore, 1976). In a sample of youngsters in New Zealand, 9% of boys and 4.6% of girls were found to have chronic antisocial behavior patterns (McGee, Silva, & Williams, 1984). Conduct problems are more prevalent among those of low socioeconomic status, and from urban (8%) rather than rural (4%) settings (cited in Barclay & Hoffman, 1990), although an urban–rural difference was not found in one study (Offord, Boyle, & Racine, 1991).

Causes

Are conduct disorders the product of genetics? Of social and peer influences? Of biology? Of parental child-rearing practices? What accounts for the onset of conduct disorder? Although no one factor can provide a full explanation of the cause of conduct problems, there are several types of influence that have been identified and supported by research. We will discuss cognitive factors, biological forces, and the role of the family.

Cognitive processing in conduct disorders

The factors most often associated with risk of conduct disorders include features of the individual child, the child's parents, and the interaction patterns between child and parent. Investigators have found that academic and intellectual difficulties, for example, predict conduct disorder (West, 1982), although many children with limited academic abilities do not display antisocial actions. Other aspects of the child that are possible risk factors include cognitive and biological characteristics. Let's look more closely at the child's manner of making sense of the environment—cognitive processing—as a contributor to problems of conduct.

Aggressive youngsters often show cognitive deficiencies (e.g. Seguin, Pihl, Harden, Tremblay, & Boulerice, 1995). They lack problem-solving skills (Spivack & Shure, 1982), scoring low on measures of the ability to generate multiple solutions to problems. Also, conduct-disordered children seem more likely than nondisordered children to think of solutions that others would rate as aggressive, and less likely to think of socially appropriate solutions to interpersonal problems (Fischler & Kendall, 1988).

Aggressive children also display cognitive distortions when thinking about social interactions. Dodge (1985) documented this tendency in a series of studies. He presented children with videotaped vignettes that showed one child doing something that caused a negative outcome for another child. In some of the tapes the intention of the actor who caused the negative outcome was ambiguous. The children who participated in the research were then asked to choose an explanation for the actor's behavior. The studies showed that relatively aggressive children were more likely than nonaggressive children to believe that the actor in the ambiguous tapes had hostile intentions—as if the actor had caused the negative outcome on purpose! In contrast, non-aggressive youngsters were likely to see the ambiguous actions as having been accidental. To illustrate this cognitive distortion, suppose that you have a new Discman player. While en route to a school activity you loan it briefly to a friend and, when it is returned, the headphones no longer work properly. The cause of the damage is uncertain. Why did this happen? A greater percentage of aggressive than nonaggressive children are likely to say that the damage was done on purpose, perhaps offering an explanation akin to "He did it to get me mad" or "He did it because he was jealous." Nonaggressive youngsters are more inclined to attribute the headphone damage to causes other than the hostile intentions of the other child and seem more willing to accept that "stuff happens."

The research findings have led to the conclusion that, in short, aggressive children have a hostile attributional bias: When a situation is ambiguous, they tend to attribute negative motivations to others. This distortion may then prompt the aggressive child to retaliate, and a vicious cycle can result.

Genetic factors

To determine the contribution of genetic factors it would be necessary to have longitudinal data on numerous sets of monozygotic and dizygotic twins, raised together and raised apart. At present, there are no such twin studies reporting on conduct disorders as currently conceptualized (Earls, 1994). A recent study of adoptees (Cadoret, Yates, Troughton, Woodworth, & Stewart, 1995), however, sheds some light on the issue. These researchers studied the male and female offspring, separated at birth, of parents with known antisocial behavior. If the parents are known to be antisocial, is it more likely that their offspring will display conduct disorder? The results indicated that a biological background for antisocial behavior was predictive of adolescent aggression and conduct disorder. Importantly, however, the study also examined the adoptive home environments: It was found that adverse home environments independently predicted later conduct problems. As the authors concluded, an adverse adoptive home environment and biological background of antisocial behavior interact in producing increased aggression and conduct disorder—an instance of the meaningfulness of the diathesis-stress model.

The many labels used to describe externalizing behavior problems—conduct disorder, aggression, antisocial behavior—have clouded our ability to better understand the causes. Among twin studies that specifically examine aggression, no consistent pattern of genetic influence on aggressiveness has been reported (e.g. Plomin, Nitz, & Rowe, 1990). In contrast, genetic contributions to antisocial behavior clearly exist, and have been found in lesser amounts for adolescent delinquency as well (DiLalla & Gottesman, 1989; Wicks-Nelson & Israel, 1991). Based on the diverse studies to date, there may be a genetic component to conduct disorder as well.

The role of the family

The family is the primary context for the socialization of children and many research findings have supported the idea that the family is a major factor in the cause of conduct disorders (e.g. Jouriles, Bourg, & Farris, 1991). Four alternative patterns are common in the families of youngsters with conduct disorders: parental deviance, parental rejection and coerciveness, lack of discipline or supervision of children, and marital conflict and divorce (see Hetherington, Law, & O'Connor, 1993).

The parents of children with conduct disorders are themselves often deviant, displaying maladjustment, anger, and sometimes criminal behavior. Overt marital conflict can contribute to oppositional behavior in children (Mann & MacKenzie, 1996) and many children with conduct disorder have a parent with antisocial personality disorder (Rutter & Quinton, 1984). More extreme patterns, such as criminal behavior and alcoholism, particularly in the father, put the child at an especially high risk for conduct disorder (Robins, 1966; West, 1982). Separation from an antisocial father does not seem to protect the child from this risk, perhaps suggesting a genetic causal pathway, or perhaps because with the father absent, discipline may weaken.

Parenting practices are said to contribute to behavior problems. Parents of conduct-disordered children tend to respond coercively and often negatively to their children. Although precise measurement of parental practices is difficult, there seems to be a strong association between negative parent–child relations and antisocial conduct in youngsters (see Loeber, 1990). An extreme form of parental negativism is physical abuse. In a US study of 584 Caucasian and African-American youth (grades 1 to 4), those who had been physically abused had significantly more conduct problems than those not abused (Dodge, Pettit, Bates, & Valente, 1995). These data are correlational, and although such a correlation does not permit a causal statement, it can be suggested that the experience of abuse fashions these children's view of the world as a dangerous place in which aggression is a conceivable way to solve problems. In a study of Danish sons of alcoholic fathers, a past history of severe physical abuse by the father was a significant predictor of antisocial traits in the son (Pollock et al., 1992).

The occurrence and observation of the use of weapons in interparent violence could be a powerful contributor to child conduct disorder (see Widom, 1997). Jouriles and colleagues (Jouriles et al., 1998) studied knives, guns and interparent violence and its relationships with child behavior problems. The sample consisted of youngsters from families characterized by interparent violence: Some children had observed the use of weapons when used, others did not witness weapons but they were reported to have been used, and the third group consisted of families where the mother did not report the use of weapons. Interestingly, children from families when weapons violence had occurred and children who had observed violence involving weapons had higher levels of behavior problems that the group where violence did not involve weapons. Marital violence contributes to the likelihood that children will have behavior problems, and the situation seems to worsen when the interparent violence involves weapons.

Let's take a closer look at the specific patterns of parent–child interactions that are said to be related to antisocial activity. Such a close-up is made possible by the work of Patterson (1982) and his associates (Patterson, Chamberlain, & Reid, 1982). His research included observations of parents and their conduct-disordered children, and the results indicated that these parents had difficulties appropriately disciplining their offspring. According to Patterson's analysis, the parents of children with conduct disorder tended to reward positive and negative behaviors inconsistently. In particular, the parents often reinforced—such as by attention or laughter—coercive child behaviors, such as demanding, defying, yelling, and arguing. Thus, consequent to the reinforcement provided by parental attention, the child learns to use coercive behaviors. Over time, the child learns to be even more coercive, possibly escalating to hitting and verbally attacking. Meanwhile, positive behaviors by the child were often ignored or responded to inappropriately by the parents. In effect, the youngster was rewarded for displaying antisocial actions and failed to learn alternate adaptive behavior. Thus, according to Patterson, families with children with conduct disorder are characterized by coercive interactions. Poor parenting skills, he argued, produce and promote antisocial behavior.

Research has provided some support for this conceptualization of the role of parents in child conduct problems. The coercive interaction parenting style was studied in 708 families, some of which had monozygotic (93) and dizygotic (99) twins (Reiss et al., 1995). These authors reported that almost 60% of the variance in adolescent antisocial behavior could be accounted for by conflictual and negative parenting behavior directed toward the adolescent.

Finally, high rates of divorce have been found to be associated with conduct disorders (Rutter & Quinton, 1984) but, as discussed earlier, the divorce itself may not be the sole contributing factor to the problem. Instead, there is some evidence that divorce is frequent among parents and families with certain characteristics, and that those characteristics—not divorce itself—contribute to the onset of conduct disorder. Independent of the cause of conduct disorder, what happens to these children when they reach adulthood?

The course of conduct disorder

A large number of youngsters engage in single behaviors that may resemble some of the actions listed as criteria for conduct disorders. But, it should be highlighted, one incident or one brief conflicted experience does not make a disorder! Of those children who continue, and who show wider ranges of conduct problems, there is increased likelihood of antisocial behavior in adulthood. However, the pattern is not simplistic. Those adults identified as severely antisocial have long histories of disruptive behavior in their childhood, but most conduct disordered children do not grow up to be severely antisocial adults (Maughan & Rutter, 1998).

There is some evidence of transgenerational consistency in antisocial and aggressive behavior patterns. Indeed, perhaps the most troublesome feature of conduct disorder—not the occasional act of a nondisturbed child—is its stability over time (Lahey et al., 1995). Early evidence of conduct disorder in a child is related to later aggression, antisocial behavior, and other adult difficulties (see Robins, 1978). As argued by Eron and Huesmann (1990), aggressive behavior, if untreated, has been shown to be stable over a 30-year period of time. However, as noted by Maughan and Rutter (1998), when details of the studies are examined there are both continuities and discontinuities across time. For example, male gender, hyperactivity, aggression, poor verbal skills, low achievement at school, peer problems, and family disruption are risks for child-onset conduct disorder (e.g. Dishion, French, & Patterson, 1995). Some differences emerge for adolescent onset: Gender differences are less marked, aggression and learning problems are not central, and adolescent-onset offending is sometimes associated with peer popularity, close peer orientations, and peer delinquency (e.g. Stattin & Magnusson, 1998). Age of onset is a strong predictor of continuities in disruptive behavior problems (Moffitt, 1993a).

Although there are many factors that influence the relationship of child conduct problems and adult antisocial behavior (e.g. age of onset, gender, presence of other disorders, intervening treatment), the presence of conduct disorder in childhood carries predictive information for a wide variety of later adjustment problems (including antisocial activities and alcohol and substance abuse). Identification of the mechanisms that account for these trajectories is a major challenge facing the field (Maughan & Rutter, 1998).

Treatments

From several vantage points the conclusions appear consistent: Family conflict and poor parenting skills characterize the family relations of children with conduct disorders, and the children themselves display cognitive as well as behavioral difficulties. These characteristics suggest several possible approaches to treating these children, and recent reviews have suggested that treatments for young children with emerging conduct disorders can be beneficial. Many of the more effective methods involve system-wide programs in schools or communities (e.g. Hawkins, Arthur, & Olson, 1997), behaviorally oriented parent training (see Southam-Gerow & Kendall, 1997), cognitive-behavioral therapy for the children themselves (e.g. Kazdin,

1996; Lochman, 1992; Lochman, Burch, Curry, & Lampron, 1984), or for the child–parent interaction (e.g. Eyberg, 1988).

Wouldn't it be great if interventions, implemented at a school-wide level, could catch the problem early and prevent the emergence of conduct disorder? In one example of a school-based program, Weissberg and associates (Caplan et al., 1992; see also Braswell et al., 1997) taught broad-based problem-solving skills and included specific applications of problem solving to problems facing inner city youth (12- to 13-year-olds). After the program, the youngsters were rated as improved in handling personal problems, impulse control, and popularity. Excessive alcohol use was also reduced. Long-term follow-ups and rigorous research designs are needed, including measurement of delinquent and criminal acts, but prevention is a first and worthwhile step in dealing with aggressive and antisocial behavior problems.

Parent training is another oft-used and oft-studied approach to the treatment of conduct problems (Foote, Eyberg, & Schuhmann, 1998). Such an approach is suggested and justified by the association between conduct disorders and ineffective, punitive, and inconsistent parenting practices. In action-oriented family therapy, parents are directly taught skills for managing their children (see Alexander, Holtzworth-Munroe, & Jameson, 1994; Vuchinich, Wood, & Angelelli, 1996; Webster-Stratton, 1996). These treatments aim to undermine the coercive family interactions associated with antisocial behavior. The family and the therapist set goals in terms of changes in target behaviors. Through written manuals, practice with the therapist, and homework assignments, parents learn to identify problem behavior, to observe and record the frequency of the behavior, to reward proper behavior effectively, and to stop rewarding unwanted behavior (see also Henggeler & Borduin, 1990).

Sundry studies have indicated that action-oriented family therapy can lead to improvements in children's functioning, reductions in antisocial behavior, and continuing improvements for at least brief follow-up periods. For example, in one of the early studies in this line of work, Patterson (1974) documented that after treatment the frequency of a target unwanted behavior dropped to a level within the range found in nondeviant families. In another later study (Patterson, Chamberlain, & Reid, 1982), the changes in parental discipline were accompanied by reductions in children's antisocial behavior, whereas there was no change in antisocial behavior in families whose discipline practices were found not to change. Though not always measured, home-based parent training programs have sometimes been associated with improvements in child behavior in the classroom and even with reductions in siblings' deviant behavior (see also Forehand & McMahon, 1981). A more recent example is the multisystemic family therapy evaluated by Henggeler, Melton, Brondino, Scherer, and Hanley (1997). This work provided coordinated interventions for juvenile offenders and their families and the effects were reported to be superior to routine care.

Despite some promising results, much more research is needed to identify the specific types of antisocial conduct and specific groups of children and families that benefit from parent-training programs (Dumas, 1989). Studies of the effectiveness of these programs are often marred because some families drop out before completing the therapy. Treatment success is greater when the problem children are identified early and is probably also better for families that are less stressed and relatively better off socioeconomically. The published data are supportive, yet the outcomes do not reveal an eradication of conduct problems but a reduction in them. These intervention programs tend to be relatively brief, and it may be the case that antisocial conduct problems represent a long-term problem requiring long-term treatments.

Another approach to treatment focuses on the child's cognitive processing: The therapy targets the deficient and distorted thinking tied to conduct disorders. Cognitive-behavioral treatments, for instance, aim to teach children to stop, think, and engage in reflective problem solving before impulsively engaging in an action. These programs often teach problem-solving skills and provide role-play or real experiences to help the child rectify social misperceptions such as the hostile attribution bias. In one program that aims to train children to cope with their anger, the therapist teaches the children the process of problem solving and models how to manage arousal without getting upset (Lochman, White, & Wayland, 1991; see also Nelson & Finch, 1996). The therapist assigns out-of-session homework tasks, provides the children opportunities to practice their new skills in provocative situations, and gives rewards for improvements.

The empirical studies of cognitive-behavioral treatments have examined various measures for evidence of success, such as ratings by parents and teachers, number of behavior problems, progress in school, participation in social activities, and amount of cooperative play. These studies, and follow-up reports of the effects of booster sessions (for example, see Lochman, 1992), begin to testify to the value of teaching children cognitive and behavioral skills for solving interpersonal dilemmas. For example, cognitive-behavioral treatments have shown some success in decreasing aggressive behavior and increasing prosocial behavior (see data in Figure 4.1).

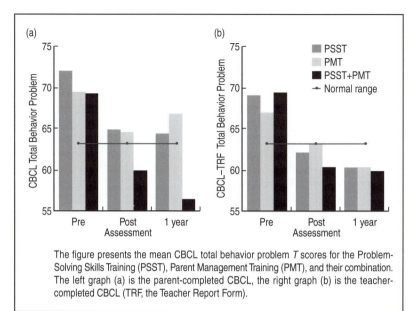

Figure 4.1
Outcomes from cognitive-behavioral skills training and parent management training in the treatment of antisocial behavior in children.
Adapted from Kazdin, Siegel, & Bass (1992, p. 744).

The figure presents the mean CBCL total behavior problem *T* scores for the Problem-Solving Skills Training (PSST), Parent Management Training (PMT), and their combination. The left graph (a) is the parent-completed CBCL, the right graph (b) is the teacher-completed CBCL (TRF, the Teacher Report Form).

In one study, 20 sessions of a program that taught impulse control and problem-solving skills produced significant improvements in social behavior (Kendall et al., 1990), but some youngsters continued to display conduct-disordered behavior even when their prosocial interactions increased. The outcomes offer some encouragement but additional treatment development and outcome research is needed to enhance and fine-tune the interventions for children of different ages, to foster widespread changes in behavior, and to ensure the longer-term maintenance of any gains from the treatment.

Where do we turn in our search for more potent intervention programs? Promising leads for future treatment of children with conduct disorders come from programs that improve either parents' behavior-management skills or the child's cognitive processing. In addition, we have learned that preventive efforts are best directed toward younger children who have not yet become immersed in delinquent or antisocial behavior patterns. One prime example is the work of Tremblay and colleagues in Montreal, Canada (Tremblay et al., 1990). This research team provided a 2-year intervention program to oppositional and aggressive kindergarten boys from low-income families. The intervention included parent training and child social skills development. At 3-year follow-up, the program, compared to control conditions, resulted in some crucial changes: The treated participants showed less fighting and delinquent behavior, as well as less-frequent grade retention. Early intervention is pivotal because once the problematic behavior patterns become more entrenched, they are also more resistant to treatment.

Summary

Conduct disorder involves behavior that violates the basic rights of others and of the age-appropriate social norms. Aggression, property damage, stealing, and cheating occur among conduct-disordered youngsters. Conduct disorder is more common among boys and evident worldwide. Research indicates that conduct-disordered youth evidence a hostile attributional bias by which they tend to attribute negative motivations to others. Family distress and ineffective parenting, for example, are implicated in the cause of conduct disorder. Although treatments such as action-oriented family therapy, school-based prevention, and cognitive-behavioral therapy have produced beneficial outcomes, the effects are greater for younger participants. Problems with conduct disorder can persist into adult life.

Attention-deficit hyperactivity disorder 5

Even at age 6, Zach was, according to each of his parents, "unpredictable" and "antsy." His mother, a real estate agent, reported that "he's always on the go, but I'm not always sure where he is going. He's into so many things." Zach's father, an attorney for a large firm, described Zach as "rash and impetuous" and "having his engine running constantly." Both parents were distressed when Zach's school performance suffered because of his impulsivity and poor attention: He was determined to be a bright child, but his teacher suggested that Zach might have ADHD and that the ADHD was interfering.

Phenomenology and classification

Hyperactivity is perhaps the most common or popular term for the psychological problem of childhood that is technically known as attention-deficit hyperactivity disorder (ADHD). Other terms professionals have used include hyperkinetic reaction, minimal brain dysfunction, and attention deficit disorder. Today it is formally designated attention-deficit hyperactivity disorder (ADHD), a disorder of limitations in behavioral inhibition that has three essential features: developmentally inappropriate levels of inattention, impulsivity, and hyperactivity, with onset before age seven (Barkley, 1997b, 1977c; Bauermeister et al., 1995; Iaboni, Douglas, & Baker, 1995). Cross-cultural consistency has been supported by research, with comparable features of ADHD being identified in 9- to 17-year-old Puerto-Rican children.

Few if any childhood disorders have received the degree of widespread attention from professionals, teachers, and parents as has ADHD. During the last decade, for example, ADHD has been one of the most widely observed, described, studied, debated, and treated childhood disorders. DSM-IV provides criteria for different types of ADHD: ADHD—predominately inattentive type; ADHD—

predominantly hyperactive type; and ADHD—combined type. Descriptively, these conditions are different, but the possibility that these are separate disorders requires additional research.

No doubt you have experienced a time when your interests or your attention shifts from one activity to another. Or the topic of your conversation, or the theme of your thinking changes from one idea to another. Is this a sign of disorder? What constitutes an attentional or hyperactive problem? Is it a diagnosable problem and, if so, can it be treated? Should the 3–5% of children who receive this diagnosis be medicated? Discussions of these and other questions have made "hyperactivity" a topic of substantial scholarship and considerable controversy.

Assessing and diagnosing ADHD

One of the advances over the years of scrutiny is that researchers and practitioners have come to recognize that the problem is not simply excessive levels of motor activity (hyperactivity). Difficulties in the three essential features of inattention, impulsivity, and hyperactivity need to be seen across situations—at school, at home, and in social contexts—before one can declare the presence of ADHD.

Inattention is observed in behaviors such as seeming not to listen and failing to complete tasks. More specifically, a short attention span is seen in rapid shifts from one activity to another before the first activity is completed (Alessandri, 1992). The child goes from one toy to another without focused play with either toy; in the classroom, the child is easily distracted and fails to pay attention to directions. Is the problem tied to an inability to pay attention, or to difficulty in sustaining attention? Attentional difficulties are required, but the exact nature of the attentional problems seen in ADHD children is still a theme of debate, requiring further research.

Impulsivity is acting without thinking. Although many children can be impulsive (especially at younger ages), ADHD children routinely interrupt others, blurt out responses to questions, and fail to wait their turn. ADHD youngsters are impaired in their ability to inhibit inappropriate responding (Jennings, Van der Molen, Pelham, Brock, & Hoza, 1997; Schachar, Tannock, Marriott, & Logan, 1995). They have problems organizing schoolwork and a general need for greater supervision. The problem can be seen in different contexts. Consider the following example which comes from an actual experience with children engaged in athletics. When joining a game of soccer, the impulsive child runs onto the field and chases the ball, eager to kick it. Unfortunately, the child did not yet know the team he was on or which goal to shoot toward. In another context, such as the classroom, the impulsive child tries to answer questions before the question is completely stated by the teacher.

Hyperactivity is often reported by parents and teachers who cannot keep up with these children. The children are described as fidgety, restless, and unable to sit still. Using direct observations and mechanical recordings, researchers have substantiated an excess of activity among diagnosed hyperactive children (e.g. Milich, Loney, & Landau, 1982). These children are "on the go," unable to play quietly, and inept at shifting from free to structured activities such as from recess to a classroom activity.

Peer relationships are, increasingly, viewed as central difficulties for the ADHD child, with rule violations and aggression often linked to ADHD children's behavior being viewed negatively by their peers. Moreover, the social rejection experienced by children with ADHD appears to develop after only brief periods of interaction with others (Bickett & Milich, 1990). Erhardt and Hinshaw (1994) asked youthful students what factors contributed most to the peer status of children with ADHD. They reported that physical attractiveness, athletic skill, intelligence, and academic achievement, for example, were not the main concerns. Aggression and noncompliance were two specific social behaviors that contributed to initial peer impressions of previously unfamiliar ADHD children.

In a different line of research, one that focuses on family relationships, ADHD children showed less compliance and more opposition to their parents than non-ADHD children. Interactions between ADHD children and their parents were marked by greater than normal levels of parental commands, reprimands, and punishment (Barkley et al., 1991).

ADHD, quite commonly, does not exist by itself. Rather, there is a high degree of comorbidity among ADHD children. According to one source, up to 44% of children with ADHD have at least one other disorder (Szatmari, Offord, & Boyle, 1989). For example, researchers have estimated that 20–25% of ADHD children also have learning disabilities (Barkley, 1990). In both the US and the UK (McArdle, O'Brien, & Kolvin, 1995) ADHD children have also been found to have problems with aggression (such as conduct disorder). The possibility of different types of ADHD is gaining attention, and one important distinction may be between ADHD youth with and without comorbid conduct disorder (Hinshaw, 1987).

Making a diagnosis about the presence of ADHD is not simplistic. Identifying ADHD in children should involve several separate assessments:

- *Ratings of the child's behavior by parents and teachers.* The CBCL (Child Behavior Checklist), mentioned earlier, can be used to place the level of the child's problem in comparison with other children (recall Figure 3.1). Other parent rating forms are also available, such as the Conners Rating Scales (Conners, 1990; Conners, Sitarenios, Parker, & Epstein, 1998a, 1998b) and the ADHD Rating Scale—Home version (DuPaul, Anastopoulos, Barkley, & Murphy, 1994, cited in Barkley, 1997b).
- *Interviews with the child, parents, and teachers.* The details of the child's behavior or social context that may be lost with rating scales can be gathered through interviews. Interviews with parents and teachers can be especially helpful in assessing whether the child's behavior is consistent across different situations and what conditions exacerbate or reduce the problematic behaviors. For instance, the presence of certain classroom peers or a certain classroom seating arrangement may be associated with a worsening of an ADHD child's symptoms in the classroom.
- *Direct observation of behavior and task performance.* Observing the child provides valuable information in assessing ADHD. For example, trained observers can reliably distinguish hyperactive from nonhyperactive children by observing and recording behavior— such as out of seat activity and disruptiveness (e.g. Milich, Loney, & Roberts, 1986). As an example of a performance task, consider a match-to-sample problem where a standard picture is shown above six others, only one of which matches the standard (e.g. Matching Familiar Figures Test; Kagan, 1966). The child's task is to find the one of the six that match the standard at the top. ADHD children react to this situation of high response uncertainty by behaving impulsively, showing short latencies to respond and a high rate of errors. It is as if they rush to guess, without looking carefully at the alternatives. In one study, performance on this match-to-sample task (one of more than twenty-five tests given) was found to be useful in identifying hyperactive children (Homatidis & Konstantareas, 1981).

Most assessments of ADHD employ a combination of data-gathering techniques and strive to determine if the child meets the criteria needed for a diagnosis. Structured diagnostic interviews, for example, are typically used to gauge the child against the diagnostic criteria (see Box 5.1).

Reprinted with permission from the Diagnostic and Statistical Manual of Mental Disorders, Fourth Edition. Copyright 1994 American Psychiatric Association.

BOX 5.1 Assessing and diagnosing ADHD

Several methods are typically used to assess ADHD, and the DSM criteria are often used to reach a diagnosis.

Assessments:
- Teachers and parents provide ratings of the child's behavior in the classroom and at home, respectively.
- Psychologists conduct interviews with the child, the parents, and other relevant individuals as needed.
- Psychologists conduct structured diagnostic interviews with the child and the parents.
- Psychologists make observations of the child in certain situations.
- Psychologists have children perform certain tasks.

Diagnostic criteria:
- INATTENTION, as seen in at least six of the following.
  - Often fails to give close attention to details or makes careless mistakes in school, work, or other activities
  - Often has difficulty sustaining attention in talks or play activities
  - Often does not seem to listen to what is being said to him or her
  - Often does not follow through on instructions and fails to finish schoolwork or chores
  - Often has difficulties organizing tasks and activities
  - Often avoids or strongly dislikes tasks that require sustained mental effort
  - Often loses things necessary for tasks
  - Is often easily distracted by extraneous stimuli
  - Is often forgetful in daily activities
- HYPERACTIVITY/IMPULSIVITY, as seen in at least six of the following.
  - Hyperactivity:
    - Often fidgets with hands or feet or squirms in seat
    - Often leaves seat in situations when remaining seated is expected
    - Often runs about or climbs excessively in situations when it is inappropriate
    - Often has difficulty playing or engaging in leisure activities
  - Impulsivity:
    - Often blurts out answers to questions before the questions have been completed
    - Often has difficulty awaiting his or her turn
    - Often interrupts or intrudes on others.

Who are the children with ADHD?

Although gender differences are routinely recounted, ADHD has been identified in both boys and girls. A male–female ratio of between 4:1 and 8:1 is typical (Barkley, 1996). Gender differences have also been reported in the expression of ADHD. Among clinic-referred children, girls with ADHD have fewer behavior and conduct problems (less aggression) and more social withdrawal and anxiety and depression than boys with ADHD.

No one culture breeds ADHD. ADHD has been identified in a variety of ethnic groups and across cultures, with some cross-cultural differences emerging. For instance, there is a lower prevalence of ADHD in the UK (Taylor, 1994) and a high rate of hyperactivity in China (Luk & Leung, 1989). Because of inconsistent diagnostic practices, however, interpretations of these rates must be made with caution (Mann et al., 1992).

Although ADHD children come from urban and rural as well as rich and poor families, socioeconomic status differences have also been reported: There is a somewhat greater frequency of children with ADHD from the lower social classes. Several possible explanations have been suggested. Lower socioeconomic class mothers are likely to have poor nutrition and care during their pregnancies, as well as a high incidence of complications, perhaps affecting the developing brain of the as-yet unborn child. Second, the troubled environment of low socioeconomic status families might account for higher rates of family instability, divorce, and parental psychological disorders (Biederman et al., 1995). Last, the high incidence of ADHD among low socioeconomic children may be due to a predisposition on the part of teachers and others to expect ADHD behavior among them.

Causes

There is no one, single cause of ADHD. Rather, there is general consensus that many factors contribute to the onset of ADHD. Genetically determined predispositions, brain damage and dysfunction, diet and toxic substances, and environmental forces have all been implicated. What does the research tell us?

Some evidence has suggested that genetic factors play a role in the disorder. For starters, it is widely accepted that genetic transmission influences individual differences in general activity level. But do genetics contribute to the disorder? Some data have suggested that the answer is yes—an individual may genetically acquire a predisposition to develop ADHD in response to environmental events. For monozygotic twins, the concordance rate was 81%, but only 29% for dizygotic twins (Gilger, Pennington, & DeFries, 1992), and ADHD occurs more often in first-degree biological relatives of those with the disorder than would be expected in the general population. Approximately 25% of the natural parents of ADHD children, compared with 4% of adoptive parents, had histories (gathered retrospectively) of ADHD (Deutsch, 1987). Interestingly, there is also a higher incidence of other disorders (such as mood disorder) among the natural parents and extended relatives of children with ADHD (Biederman et al., 1987).

Siblings of a person with ADHD are at greater risk for ADHD, especially when parents have a history of ADHD, and monozygotic twins are more likely to be concordant than dizygotic twins (McMahon, 1980). The data also suggest that the more serious the symptom picture, the greater the genetic contribution to the disorder. The evidence supports a genetic contribution, but a specific mechanism for the genetic transmission of ADHD, although there is mounting evidence, has yet to be completely identified. Several studies have identified an association between the dopamine transporter gene and ADHD (e.g. Cook et al., 1995; Gill, Daly, Heron, Hawi, & Fitzgerald, 1997). At least one study (Waldman et al., 1998) reported stronger relationships for the hyperactive-impulsive symptoms than for the inattentive symptoms of ADHD. The fact that the results of several studies replicate the relationship of the gene to the psychological disorder is an exciting step toward understanding. However, given that ADHD is often comorbid with other childhood disorders, more research is needed to determine if the genetic link is specific to ADHD.

What about impairment to the brain of the child? Researchers have studied the possible role of brain damage, brain dysfunction, and neurological immaturity in ADHD. Several decades ago the label "minimal brain damage" was used for the behaviors currently seen as ADHD. Consistent with the label, researchers were eager to try to document a link between brain damage and ADHD. The results, however, did not often fall in line. In studies of identified ADHD patients, only 5–10% were found to have histories suggestive of brain damage, and most children with well-documented brain damage did not develop ADHD (Rutter, 1977). The use of computerized axial tomography (CAT) scans also failed to reveal anatomical brain differences (Shaywitz, Shaywitz, Byrne, Cohen, & Rothman, 1983) and brain metabolism differences (Zametkin et al., 1993) between ADHD children and non-ADHD controls. These results led to the conclusion that brain damage is clearly not the sole cause of ADHD and may not even be a correlate of ADHD.

However, studies have suggested that brain functioning of children with ADHD may be impaired: ADHD children show performance deficits on tasks sensitive to brain function (e.g. August, 1987; Douglas, 1983), and they perform less well on measures requiring vigilance and impulse control (e.g. Homatidis & Konstantareas, 1981). Specific parts of the brain, such as the frontal and frontal-limbic areas, have been implicated in ADHD. The "so-called" neurological immaturity of

ADHD children refers to their being chronically delayed relative to same-aged peers. The attention span, social behavior, and even EEG patterns of ADHD children suggest immature brain activity. Although research results are consistent with the hypothesis that brain function is involved in ADHD, poor task performance and delayed functioning could be due to other influences.

Have you read or heard the notion that a person's diet may cause ADHD? This hypothesis holds that hyperactivity is related to the child's food choices, such as consumption of large quantities of sugar. In fact, the idea that excessive sugar can cause ADHD is properly considered a myth. Also, eating foods with artificial dyes and preservatives is likewise a nonsupported notion about the etiology of ADHD. In the early to mid-1970s, however, after claims that a change in diet could reduce hyperactivity were published (Feingold, 1975), parents eagerly implemented changed diet programs. Concurrently, scientists undertook rigorous tests of the diet hypothesis. Overall, the accumulated evidence was a bit equivocal but generally failed to support the hypothesis that diet, or diet modifications, could have a significant impact on ADHD (Conners, 1980). After reviewing several studies, Swanson and Kinsbourne (1980) made a very informative observation—they noted that the more rigorous the investigation, the less support it provided for the diet hypothesis.

Others have hypothesized social and environmental causes for ADHD, particularly the child's failure to learn adequate cognitive and behavioral skills. Perhaps, like socially appropriate behavior or behavior in general, ADHD behaviors are shaped by the social environment (O'Leary, 1980). A lack of a structured learning environment, observing inappropriate behavior by others, receiving rewards for fast guessing, not being taught cognitive strategies for modulating attention, and disruption and disorganization in the home can contribute to a child's failure to acquire sufficient self-control. For example, Wahler and Dumas (1989) viewed a variety of childhood problems as the result of dysfunctional parent–child interactions (see also Barkley, Guevremant, Anastopoulos, & Fletcher, 1992). Overall, however, few studies have examined the social environmental factors suggested as causal in ADHD. Data have suggested that parents of ADHD children provide more direct commands and supervision than others, but these actions seem the result rather than the cause of the ADHD behavior. Also, following effective use of stimulant medication, mothers show a diminished pattern of control (Barkley, Karlsson, Pollard, & Murphy, 1985). As Braswell and Bloomquist (1991) astutely noted and registered, environmental factors seem to play a more important role in the course and ultimate outcome of ADHD than in its initial cause.

Controversial if not bizarre explanations for ADHD have also been offered. Are the soft X-rays emitted from fluorescent lighting to blame? Although one study (reported by Mayron, Ott, Nations, & Mayron, 1974) claimed that children exposed to full-spectrum lighting systems showed greater reduction in hyperactivity than did children who were exposed to standard cool-white fluorescent lamps, the study had several flaws. The observational period was quite brief, and the authors did not specifically control for the level of illumination produced by the two lighting systems. Another study (O'Leary, Rosenbaum, & Hughes, 1978) alternated broad-spectrum and standard cool-white fluorescent systems at the end of each week of an 8-week period. This research team took care to ensure equivalent illumination and brightness across the weeks of the study and their findings were clear: Lighting conditions had no significant effect on hyperactive behavior.

What then is the accepted etiological explanation for ADHD? In general, the accepted explanation of ADHD invokes a multiple pathways model, not unlike the diathesis-stress model that was described in Chapter 2. The growing consensus is that persons with ADHD have a biological predisposition and that the disorder can be exacerbated by environmental forces. The predisposition is necessary but not sufficient, and there is no single environmental factor, alone or in combination, that is unique or specific to ADHD. Both causes— biological disposition and environmental forces—are implicated in the disorder.

The course of ADHD

But, you might be saying to yourself, "Don't all children show difficulties in attention and impulsivity?" And "Aren't lots of kids really active?" "Isn't it a part of normal development for children to run about and play spontaneously?" In part, your thoughts are accurate and the implications for ADHD are real. Importantly, diagnoses of ADHD should be made in terms of the developmental appropriateness of the behavior. Only those children whose attention and/or activity problems are judged to be excessive relative to what is appropriate for the child's level of development should contribute to a diagnosis of ADHD. Certainly, children's ability to exercise selective attention improves with age (Hagen & Hale, 1973); a 4-year-old is not expected to have the attentional focusing skills of a 12-year-old. The impulsivity of a child just beginning school (6 years old) may be evident in fast and inaccurate responding to assigned math problems, whereas an impulsive adolescent is more likely to display impulsiveness in an increase in accidents (Barkley, Guevremant, Anastopoulos, DuPaul, & Shelton, 1993). Indeed, evidence supports the association between dangerous driving and disorders such as ADHD (Jerome & Segal, 1997). For a well-reasoned diagnosis, the developmental inappropriateness of the behavior that is thought to be symptomatic is an essential element in an accurate determination of the presence of ADHD.

As recently as the late 1980s, some people continued to believe that hyperactive children didn't need treatment—that they would "outgrow" their problems. Some parents therefore refrained from seeking help and waited, and hoped, for a natural change to occur at puberty. In fact, some ADHD children did show a decrease in excessive motor activity at puberty, but the other ADHD problems do not seem to go away (Cantwell, 1987; Weiss & Hechtman, 1986). In approximately one-half of the children with ADHD, and some suggest in as many as three-quarters, the problems of attentional focus and related academic and social difficulties persist into adolescence (Fischer, Barkley, Edelbrock, & Smallish, 1990; Gittelman, Mannuzza, Shenker, & Bonagura, 1985) and potentially into adulthood. A recent follow-up report indicated that young adults with ADHD appeared to have overcome some of the educational and legal difficulties that they experienced during high school, but they continued to report psychological problems and continued to seek mental health services (Hansen, Weiss, & Last, 1999).

It was possible to investigate the characteristics of children with ADHD that may predict later problems by following up ADHD youngsters 4 years later when they were adolescents (see Greene, Biederman, Faraone, Sienna, & Garcia-Jetton, 1997). Marked impairment in social functioning of ADHD children was found to predict later conduct disorder and some substance abuse in these same youngsters. In a study conducted in New Zealand, however, attentional difficulties were unrelated to juvenile offending or substance use (Fergusson, Lynskey, & Horwood, 1997). Currently, there is much debate about the meaningfulness of predictions associated with childhood ADHD and the validity of the claim that with advancing age comes declining ADHD (Barkley, 1997a; Hill & Schoener, 1997; Toone & van der Linden, 1997).

A longitudinal look at adolescents and adults

A diagnosis of ADHD is typically made at about age 6, when a child begins formal schooling. Do ADHD children become ADHD adolescents, and then grow to be ADHD adults? To determine the adolescent and adult outcomes of children with ADHD, longitudinal research is required. But even this desirable research strategy has potential problems.

Barkley and his associates at the University of Massachusetts Medical Center (see Barkley, Fischer, Edelbrock, & Smallish, 1991) studied 100 ADHD and 60 non-ADHD children eight years after their initial diagnosis. Ratings of behavior problems and family conflicts as well as direct observations of mother–child interactions were taken in childhood and again at adolescence. The hyperactive children were rated by their mothers as having more numerous and intense family conflicts than the non-ADHD controls, although the adolescents themselves did not differ in their own ratings of family conflict. Observations of mother–adolescent interactions revealed more controlling and negative behaviors and less positive and facilitating behaviors among the hyperactive dyads than the controls. Interestingly, the presence of conduct-disordered behavior was associated with the persistence of the conflictive family situation—a finding that suggested that at least part of the persistence of ADHD can be explained by the comorbid existence of other behavior problems.

There is clear value in prospective longitudinal research. Nevertheless, certain problems emerge whenever researchers try to measure the same psychological dimension at two different points in time. For example, observations of mother–child interactions are different at age 6 and age 14. At age 6 mother–child interactions are observed within a free play situation; at 14, however, mother–child interactions are observed while the participants engage in neutral and conflictive verbal discussions. Different behavioral observation coding systems are needed for these two different interaction situations. The Barkley study used age-appropriate interaction situations, and the findings nevertheless evidenced meaningful consistencies. Children who were noncompliant as youngsters (in the free play situation) continued to be difficult with their parents at adolescence (in the discussion situation).

A different approach could have been chosen. Barkley and colleagues could have opted to use the same assessment situation at both points in time (e.g. parent–child interactions in free play), but such a choice, while creating equivalence of measurement at different ages, would have reduced the meaningfulness and relevance of the second assessment. Reviewers could have criticized the work for having used a developmentally inappropriate context for assessing mother–adolescent interaction. As it turned out, the use of the developmentally appropriate situation provided the opportunity to observe and record behavior that permitted reasonable tests of the hypotheses. It also permitted reasonable confidence in the conclusion that the mother–child interaction conflicts continue to be significantly greater in hyperactive than non hyperactive children at 8-year follow-up.

The likelihood that ADHD will persist into adolescence depends in part on several factors. First, how were the children with ADHD first identified? When ADHD is first seen in clinic-referred children, 50–80% may continue to have the disorder into adolescence (Barkley, 1996). This estimate is lower when the ADHD children are first identified via a school screening procedure. Also, the persistence of ADHD problems into adolescence is associated with other features of ADHD children at the time of the initial identification: the presence of conduct problems, the presence of oppositionality, and poor family relations. When these factors are present, ADHD is more likely to persist into adolescence.

The likelihood that ADHD persists into adulthood cannot be answered with complete confidence at this time. Few studies (e.g. Mannuzza & Klein, 1992) provide substantive data on the topic, and there are features of the studies that may restrict the estimation of adult prevalence. That is, children with conduct problems—those most likely to have persistent ADHD—were excluded from the Mannuzza and Klein initial sample of ADHD youth who were later assessed in adulthood. Thus, the 30–50% estimate of adult ADHD is likely to be lower than other estimates based on the full range of children with ADHD at the initial identification. Although the exact adult prevalence awaits further research, the distractibility, inattentiveness, and difficulties with goal-directed persistence remain a serious concern for those adults with chronic ADHD (Biederman et al., 1993; Mannuzza et al., 1991; Spencer, Biederman, Wilens, & Faraone, 1994; Weiss, Hechtman, Milroy, & Perlman, 1985). Babinski and colleagues (Babinski, Hartsough, & Lambert, 1999) followed children 9 years after parent and teacher ratings identified them as ADHD and found that hyperactivity/impulsivity (in several ways) was predictive of both self-reported and official records of adult criminal activity. Despite our less than full understanding of the course of ADHD, several approaches to treatment have been developed and evaluated.

Medications and psychosocial programs for ADHD

Currently, the foremost treatments for ADHD are medications and psychosocial programs employing behavioral and cognitive-behavioral strategies (see Abikoff & Hechtman, 1996; Anastopoulos, Barkley, & Sheldon, 1996; Hinshaw, 1996; Pelham & Hoza, 1996). Both pharmacological and psychological treatments for ADHD have received considerable application and study. In many instances, the approaches are combined, and the efforts of parents, professionals, and schools are included and integrated.

Medications for ADHD typically involve stimulants. These stimulants, in proper dosage, have what has been described as a "focusing" effect. Because the effects wear off within hours, the medication is commonly given two or three times a day. A review of over 150 studies (Spencer et al., 1996) concluded that use of psychostimulant (typically methylphenidate [Ritalin], but also pemoline [Cylert] and dextroamphetamine [Dexedrine]) by children with ADHD can increase their ability to sustain attention, decrease impulsiveness, and improve performance on fine motor tasks. Although the outcomes are not always consistent for ADHD children with co-occuring internalizing symptoms (e.g. DuPaul, Barkley, & McMurray, 1994), the positive response rate has been estimated to be approximately 70%. Also, numerous investigations have indicated that children's performances on a wide variety of cognitive tasks improve while on stimulants (Klorman, Brumaghim, Fitzpatrick, Borgstedt, & Strauss, 1994; Rapport & Kelly, 1991) and a recent study (Spencer et al., 1995) reported that ADHD adults benefited from methylphenidate.

Although we are not certain of the mechanisms involved, stimulants probably have a positive effect on attentional symptoms, which leads to a decrease in physical hyperactivity. However, the attentional focusing doesn't always translate into increased academic performance. Although there has been reservation about the use of medications for ADHD children who have tics (involuntary rapid stereotyped motor movements), recent data suggest that medications did not alter tic frequency (Gadow, Sverd, Sprafkin, Nolan, & Ezor, 1995).

History has been witness to changing information about ADHD. For example, it was once believed that because stimulant medications have a quieting effect on ADHD children the effects were "paradoxical." Indeed, for some years parents and professionals alike thought a paradoxical effect occurred when an ADHD child was quieted by a stimulant. Moreover, the quieting effect was thought to be evidence of the presence of attentional hyperactive problems. We know now that this belief is false. Stimulant medications have a quieting and focused effect on all children, both ADHD and non-ADHD (Rapoport et al., 1978; Weingartner et al., 1980). Relatedly, it would be an error in reasoning to assume, because a child is more focused on even a trial dose of stimulant, that he or she has ADHD. Such thinking—using a positive response to the medications to confirm a diagnosis—is not supported by the data.

Despite some positive effects linked to stimulant medications, there are shortcomings that are worth noting. Researchers have estimated that 70% of children with ADHD show a positive response to stimulants (Cantwell & Hanna, 1989), but stimulants also have potential, unwanted side-effects—including anxiety, insomnia, irritability, weight loss, increased blood pressure and heart rate, and occasional motor tics (Barkley, McMurray, Edelbrock, & Robbins, 1990). Also, not all children can be given these medications, nor do all who take them improve (Whalen & Henker, 1991). In the majority who improve, the effects are short-lived, persisting only as long as the drugs are taken.

In the very recent past, and perhaps continuing today, the number of children given the diagnosis of ADHD has been rising rapidly. Correspondingly, increasing numbers of children were being placed on medications (e.g. Ritalin). In the US alone, some 750,000 children take Ritalin (Rapport & Kelly, 1991). Based on biannual surveys conducted in Baltimore since 1971 (Safer & Krager, 1988), the prevalence of medication treatment for ADHD has doubled every 4 years, with approximately 6% receiving such treatment in 1987. The trend is said to have continued, resulting in widespread use of medications for inattention and hyperactivity.

How can we explain the increase in ADHD diagnoses and in the use of medications? Some researchers suggest that 30–50% of those taking Ritalin may not even have ADHD (Bocella, 1995). In the US, misidentification of ADHD is said to be on the rise, perhaps in part because government regulations now provide special education services for children with ADHD. Thus, there is an incentive for some parents to seek and receive an ADHD diagnosis for their child.

There is an emerging emergency problem: Because of the heightened sense of well-being produced by the drug, there are increased reports of children selling their ADHD medicine, with some youngsters breaking the pills and snorting the drug. Additional monitoring, and preventive intervention, may be needed to quell this trend.

Psychosocial approaches to treating ADHD emphasize teaching children the skills necessary to pay attention, engage in self-control, and reduce or better modulate excessive motor activity. Following the statement of O'Leary in 1980 that hyperactive children need skills, not just pills, these methods have continued to aim to modify the environment and provide structured opportunities for children to learn the self-control skills that they can take into new situations.

Psychological treatments characteristically teach behavioral management and may feature parent training, structured classroom programs, and training in cognitive skills (see Bloomquist, 1996; Carter, 1993; Goldstein & Goldstein, 1998; Hinshaw & Erhardt, 1991; Pelham & Sams, 1992).

Independent of the type of treatment provided to the child, programs that provide parent training are considered worthwhile. Comprehensive parent-training programs typically provide parents with some basic education about ADHD and teach them behavior management skills to use with their child (e.g. Anastopoulos, 1996; Braswell, 1991). As Barkley (1990) argued, many of the interpersonal difficulties associated with hyperactivity come from the child's noncompliance and lack of self-control. Accordingly, parents are taught skills to reduce noncompliance (see Forehand & McMahon, 1981) and to help the child develop self-control (for example, see Braswell & Bloomquist, 1991; Kendall & Braswell, 1993). Parents learn to reward appropriate behavior, shape desired responses, reduce and eliminate inappropriate behaviors, and use additional rewards to maintain behavior gains. In addition, use of a brief "time-out" from desired activities can be an effective punishment for misbehavior. Parents are also taught how to ignore unwanted actions, provide nonabrasive commands, and pay attention to positive behavior. Based on the positive outcomes of a comparison between parent training and a wait-list condition, researchers have stated that parent training increased parents' self-esteem, reduced their stress, and produced overall improvements in their children's ADHD symptoms (Anastopoulos, Shelton, DuPaul, & Gouvremont, 1993). Not all skills that are evident during parent training, however, are maintained after the program is completed.

Because a child's ADHD has an unwanted impact that is evident in school, classroom management programs are designed to develop the child's ability to benefit from classroom instruction, decrease activity levels, and increase focused attention. For example, in one 10-week program, teachers first determined academic and behavioral goals and reinforcers for each child (O'Leary, Pelham, Rosenbaum, & Price, 1976). The teachers completed a daily checklist rating the child's behavior in the classroom, and the child could receive reinforcers according to the results of the checklist at the end of the day and at the end of each week. Compared with untreated children, the children who completed this program were rated as being less hyperactive and as showing improved behavior. Like parent training, classroom skill training is effective while the program is operating, but diminishes in effectiveness after the program is discontinued. Pelham has further developed the classroom approach and employs a version of it in summer camps for children with ADHD.

Programs strive to produce change that persists across settings, but this does not always occur. Overcoming this backsliding—by shaping and encouraging the child to internalize and take to other situations the skills trained in behavioral management programs—has been one of the goals of cognitive-behavioral treatments. Thus, cognitive-behavioral treatments combine behavioral management training with direct efforts to teach both self-control skills, such as self-evaluation and self-reward, and attention-focusing skills. The treatment strives to instill problem-solving skills that the child can apply in the classroom and with parents and peers, but the goal of generalization outside and after the program is quite challenging and has not always been met (Abikoff, 1985, 1991). For clinical cases of ADHD, generalization of behavior change has not been reported. Only a few research reports have shown generalization of one aspect of ADHD (impulsivity) but other reports have been disappointing.

In one comparative study (Abikoff & Gittelman, 1985; see also Brown, Wynne, & Medenis, 1985), the authors reported greater effectiveness for medications over parent and teacher contingency management in reducing ADHD behavior. Separate applications of behavioral therapy and medications produced relatively comparable effects on classroom behavior in one study (Carlson, Pelham, Milich, & Dixon, 1992), whereas, although both treatments were effective, medications were superior to behavior modification in another study (Pelham et al., 1993).

Recall that many children with ADHD have other problems, and that these other difficulties are often associated with an oppositional quality. Recognizing the central role of anger management for ADHD youth, Hinshaw, Henker, and Whalen (1984a,b) provided and compared a cognitive-behavioral anger control program and Ritalin. Relative to the ADHD childrens' behavior before treatment, children in all conditions displayed less fidgeting and verbal aggression. The children receiving the cognitive-behavioral treatment were rated as having higher degrees of self-control and displaying more appropriate coping behaviors than the children receiving just medication. Although medications did not alter the content of the child's response, they did produce changes in the intensity of the child's behavior. Unfortunately, no follow-ups were done to determine if these beneficial gains were lasting.

Although there are inconsistencies, the findings generally indicate that stimulants and behavioral programs can have desirable effects on

ADHD. Such a conclusion has sparked a growing belief that the combination of medication and behavior therapy may offer the most promising comprehensive treatment for these children. A series of research studies has questioned the potential utility of such treatment combinations. What are the outcomes of programs that employ both medications and behavioral or cognitive-behavioral training?

Although research on combined treatments has been described as having major methodological barriers (e.g. Brown, Borden, Wynne, Schleser, & Clingerman, 1986; Whalen & Henker, 1991), the field seems to have reached some tentative conclusions. In an examination of a combined medication and cognitive therapy, the combined treatment was compared to cognitive therapy alone and medication alone (Abikoff et al., 1988). In this study, the cognitive therapy focused on academic work. All three conditions demonstrated comparable levels of improvement, suggesting not only that each approach is useful, but also that the academically focused cognitive components did not add meaningfully to the effects achieved by medications. Again there are inconsistencies, but the generally accepted conclusion is that the medications are fast-acting and effective on some measures, but that the effects are gone when the medications are discontinued. Psychosocial treatments are not as fast-acting, and the effects may be somewhat less apparent. However, when the effects are observed, and to the extent that the skills taught in the therapy were actually learned and continued to be applied, they are thought to have the potential for persistence over time.

Summary

Attention-deficit hyperactivity disorder (ADHD) is characterized by inattention, impulsivity, and overactivity. Seen more in boys than girls, the symptoms of ADHD affect academic and social arenas and may persist into adolescence and sometimes adulthood. Multiple causal pathways are implicated in the onset of ADHD and there have been some positive results from treating ADHD with psychostimulant medications as well as with behavioral approaches.

Anxiety disorders 6

Emotional development is a challenge for all human beings. Over the course of less than a decade, children move from a state of limited emotional understanding to become complex emotional individuals. With age, the number and complexity of emotional experiences, as well as the demands for modulating emotional expression, all increase. It is not surprising that some children are overwhelmed by these challenges and experience emotional disorders. Anxiety disorders have a chronic course (Keller et al., 1992), can produce severe interference in the lives of adults (Rachman, 1998), and are among some of the most prevalent emotional problems of childhood (Barrios & Hartmann, 1997).

When children are asked to answer a question in the classroom, to compete in athletic activities, to be participants in social activities, or to perform in front of friends and relatives, they may become anxious. These reactions are normal. The anxiety disorders of childhood are characterized by more extreme and persistent emotional reactions. It is the severe manifestations of emotional behaviors that require intervention. Another type of emotional disorder, the depressive disorders, are discussed in the next chapter. We are here concerned with the anxiety disorders that are seen in childhood.

Normal emotional development

Before we embark on a discussion of emotional disorders of childhood, let's begin by asking ourselves a question: Have we ever felt great worry or extreme emotional upset? The answer is most probably yes. Everyone has, and alone it is not sufficient to warrant a judgment of abnormality or to contribute to a negative reflection on one's character. Children, too, experience fears and anxieties—normal emotional challenges—and these fears and anxieties signal psychological disorder only when they are intense, prolonged, and interfering.

Consistently, research findings over the past 50 years indicate that fears and anxieties in childhood are numerous and common (Jersild &

Holmes, 1935; Lapouse & Monk, 1958; McFarlane, Allen, & Honzik, 1954; Ollendick & King, 1991). Miller, Barrett, and Hampe (1974) assessed 249 children aged 7 to 12: 25–45% showed no fear, 50–60% showed normal fear, and 4–6% showed excessive fear. It should not be surprising that the vast majority of children (86% of the 568 studied) exposed in 1992 to Hurricane Andrew reported at least mild disaster-related symptoms (Vernberg, LaGreca, Silverman, & Prinstein, 1996). Regarding gender, some studies have found that girls report more fears than boys (Ollendick & King, 1991), although other studies of clinic cases have found no gender differences (Treadwell, Flannery, & Kendall, 1995) and several studies suggest that both genders report fears associated with the same stimuli (such as getting lost in a strange place, a burglar breaking into the house).

Development is important: There are different fears for different years. Children aged 8 months to 2 years fear separation from the caregiver, though this diminishes between ages 1 and 2. Between ages 2 and 4 the tight attachment weakens and new fears appear—such as fears of animals and the dark. Between ages 4 and 6 the child's imagination develops and creates visions of ghosts, half-human/half-animal monsters, and unexplained sounds in the night. After age 6 children are more likely to have fears of injury, death, or natural catastrophes. Both Caucasian and African-American youth reported similar fears (Neal & Knisley, 1995), centering around harm befalling self or others. As adolescence approaches, the child may fear not being an accepted member of the peer group.

At different points along the lifespan, the social environment presents different challenges that require the development of new skills, beliefs, or feelings. Fears and anxieties represent such challenges during childhood. Through learning to cope with anxious and fearful situations in childhood, children learn ways to cope with the fears and anxieties of later life. For instance, recognizing a fear, addressing the fear, coping with the fear, and eventually no longer experiencing the fear is a developmental sequence that will bolster the individual's ability to cope with fear and anxiety in the future.

Fears and anxieties are normal developmental challenges facing the maturing individual. During adolescence, autonomy and independence become major developmental challenges and the adolescent must establish a difficult balance between complying with rules and expressing independent competency. Again, it is normal to be involved in the conflicts of emerging independence, but the challenge posed by autonomy can trigger or exacerbate interpersonal problems. Child behaviors that may or may not be signs of psychological disorder must consider the culture (Lambert et al., 1992) and be judged against the frequency of the same behaviors among nontroubled children. The relative intensity, frequency, and duration of the behaviors must be evaluated, and their role in the course of normal development must be considered.

> Unlike her 12-year-old peers, Marsha doesn't go to school with classmates, choosing instead to walk to school alongside her mother. On many days Marsha refuses to go to school because she does not want to be separated from her mother. Following an interview and discussion, the clinician learned that Marsha preferred not to have friends over to her home because she again feared that she might be away from her mom. The clinician also learned that Marsha worried excessively every night, typically crawling into bed with her parents for security.

Phenomenology and classification

Children can be diagnosed as having any of several anxiety disorders, including but not limited to generalized anxiety disorder (GAD), obsessive-compulsive disorders (OCD), and separation anxiety disorder (SAD). In general, the symptoms associated with these anxiety disorders in children resemble those found in adults, including physiological, behavioral, and cognitive manifestations. Although the symptoms of anxiety disorders in children may be seen in expressions such as stomach aches, headaches, muscle tension, sweating, jittery behavior, or feelings of suffocation or choking, not all youngsters recognize these bodily reactions as related to anxiety. Cognitively, anxious children worry, often based on misperceptions of the demands in the environment and underestimates of their abilities to cope. A closer look at several of the anxiety disorders will provide more of the details and the distinguishing characteristics.

Generalized anxiety disorder (GAD). The hallmark of GAD is unrealistic and excessive anxiety and worry that do not present as linked to a specific situation or external stress. According to Strauss (1994), this feature was present in over 95% of children diagnosed GAD. Children with GAD report worries about future evaluations, social events, family activities, athletics, health issues, and simply what will happen the next day or even the next hour. Although children do not always use these phrases, GAD is also characterized by tension, nervousness, or being on the edge. This chronic persistent anxiety has been referred to as "anxious apprehension" (Barlow, 1988).

GAD involves excessive and unrealistic anxiety that is present more days than not, for a minimum of 6 months, it is experienced as difficult to control, and it is associated with some physical symptoms (e.g. restlessness, irritability, difficulty concentrating, muscle tension, sleep problems; Strauss, 1994).

Four per cent of the adult population is said to suffer from GAD (Rapee, 1991) and, although the number of studies with children are fewer than those with adults, these studies have produced varying estimates that average at about the same rate (see also Beidel, 1991). For example, Costello (1989) studied outpatient clinic participants and reported 4.6%, whereas Anderson, Williams, McGee, and Silva (1987) studied a large sample of the general population in New Zealand and reported 2.9%.

Obsessive-compulsive disorder (OCD).   OCD involves the presence of recurrent obsessions or compulsions that are time-consuming, cause distress, and lead to impairment in the person's functioning. More specifically, obsessions are recurrent intrusive thoughts or images that are perceived as senseless and inappropriate and cause marked anxiety. Compulsions are repetitive behaviors whose primary purpose is to reduce anxiety or distress.

Studies of childhood OCD have identified patterns in the content of the obsessions and compulsions. Common obsessional themes include contamination, dirt, violence, harm, or religious themes. Frequently reported compulsive rituals include cleaning, ordering, or arranging. In one of the largest prospective studies, Swedo, Rapoport, Leonard, Lenane, and Cheslow (1989) studied 70 consecutive cases of OCD in children. Washing rituals were most often reported (85%), with repeating tasks and checking rituals also occurring frequently (51% and 46%). Dirt and germs were the most often reported obsessions (40%). Rituals were most frequently reported by children with obsessions, whereas the instance of pure obsessions was found to be rare. Do children even experience an obsession without a compulsive ritual? Consider Jim, an 11-year old boy.

> Jim came to treatment following a phone call from his father. Dad reported that Jim recently disclosed that he was imagining and thinking about his teachers being naked. Jim stated that he couldn't pay attention at school, would occasionally break out into laughter in class, and was

distressed even at home in his room when the thoughts would re-enter his mind. Jim reported that the images of naked teachers were "on his mind a lot of the day" and that he couldn't "get them out of his head." Though not a complete explanation, it was discovered that an older sibling's "sex talk" coupled with Jim's having discovered and viewed a "nude video" preceded his obsessional thinking.

OCD in childhood is relatively rare, once thought to occur less than the 2% prevalence seen in adults. Presently, although different studies have reported wide ranges, there is growing acceptance that OCD in childhood is not as rare as once thought (Henin & Kendall, 1997). Also, it is worth noting that a follow-up of persons with OCD over 40 years after the initial identification of the problem conducted in Sweden (Skoog & Skoog, 1999) revealed that an early age on onset (in youngsters; under age 20) was associated with a worse outcome (less evidence of recovery).

Separation anxiety disorder (SAD). One anxiety disorder, separation anxiety disorder, is specific to children and remains a distinct category in DSM-IV. Separation anxiety disorder (SAD) is manifested by obvious distress from and excessive concern about being separated from those to whom the child is attached. Refusing to sleep away from home, staying excessively close to a parent while at home, and separation problems occurring when the child is about to begin school are relatively common. Marsha, described earlier, had been diagnosed with SAD.

What distinguishes SAD from normal behavior is the persistent and unrealistic concern—the child is overly worried about the harm that might befall major attachment figures. The diagnostic criteria appear in Box 6.1. When such symptoms are present and cause clinically significant distress or impairment in social, academic, or other important areas of functioning, a diagnosis of SAD is appropriate.

The contrast between normal and abnormal anxiety, depending on the child's age, is well illustrated by separation anxiety. Anxiety about separation involves a child being distressed in anticipation of or subsequent to being apart from an attachment figure (caregiver). New parents customarily note that around the ages of 6 to 8 months their child seems extremely "clingy." The child's demands for being in the same room as the adult, being able to see the adult, and being held by

Reprinted with
permission from the
Diagnostic and
Statistical Manual of
Mental Disorders,
Fourth Edition.
Copyright 1994
American Psychiatric
Association.

BOX 6.1   Separation anxiety disorder (SAD)

SAD is developmentally inappropriate and excessive anxiety concerning separation from home or from those to whom the child is attached. One of the anxiety disorders specific to young people, this diagnosis is only used for persons younger than 18 years of age. For a diagnosis, the problem must persist for 4 weeks or more and must evidence at least three of the following.

- recurrent excessive distress when separation from home or major attachment figures occurs or is anticipated
- persistent and excessive worry that an untoward event will lead to separation from a major attachment figure
- persistent reluctance or refusal to go to school or elsewhere because of fear of separation
- persistent and excessively fearful or reluctant to be alone or without major attachment figures at home or without significant adults in other settings
- persistent reluctance or refusal to go to sleep without being near a major attachment figure or to sleep away from home
- repeated nightmares involving the theme of separation
- repeated complaints of physical symptoms when separation from major attachment figures occurs or is anticipated
- persistent and excessive worry about losing, or possible harm befalling, major attachment figures.

---

the adult are heightened during this time, and the presence of strangers produces more noted discomfort. It is reasonable to conclude, therefore, that, at this period in development, attachment and separation are major issues for the challenge of growth and competence.

Infant–adult attachment (Bowlby, 1969) plays an important role in development, and its disruption can have unwanted effects. In early childhood, separation anxiety appears and recedes naturally as part of normal development. In contrast, when separation anxiety occurs in a 12-year-old, it signals anxiety that is beyond the normal developmental timetable, evidences attachment problems, and can reflect maladaptive adjustment (Jones, 1996). Data gathered in the UK suggest that SAD is a precursor of an adult anxiety disorder known as panic disorder-agoraphobia (Silove et al., 1995).

School phobia.   School phobia, a specific phobia seen in children, is a fear and avoidance that is relatively well circumscribed to the school environment. Whereas the separation anxious child will avoid a variety of situations that are related to separation, the school phobic child will be fearful and avoid school alone. Separation anxious children often stay in the presence of the attachment figure (or at home), whereas a child with a school phobia can be comfortable in any setting other than the school environment (Last, 1992).

Assessing anxiety disorders in children

Given our earlier discussion of the methods typically used for the assessment of psychological disorders in children it should not be at all surprising to read that the assessment of anxiety in youngsters is accomplished using self-report measures, structured diagnostic interviewing, and parent and teacher ratings.

There are several self-report scales that measure anxiety in children. The State-Trait Anxiety Inventory for Children (STAI–C; Spielberger, Gorsuch, & Lushene, 1970) uses 20 items each to measure the state of anxious arousal and the personality characteristic of trait anxiety. The Revised Children's Manifest Anxiety Scale (Reynolds & Paget, 1982; Reynolds & Richmond, 1985) assess three factors within anxiety: physiological anxiety, worry and oversensitivity, and concentration/ fear. A contemporary measure of anxiety in children is the Multidimensional Anxiety Scale for Children (MASC; March & Albano, 1998; March, Parker, Sullivan, Stallings, & Conners, 1997). The MASC consists of 39 items that assess physical symptoms, social anxiety, harm avoidance, and separation concerns. Because the psychometric qualities of the MASC are good, it is likely that this instrument will receive increased use.

Although self-reports are useful, reaching a diagnosis usually requires a clinician-administered structured interview. As noted in Chapter 3, the ADIS–C is a semi-structured clinical interview for the diagnosing of child disorders such as the anxiety disorders (Silverman & Albano, 1998). Two separate interviews are conducted—one with the child and one with the parent. As with the MASC, solid psychometric data support the use of this interview.

The CBCL contains items that assess emotional distress associated with anxiety. Within the Internalizing side of the CBCL, the anxiety-depression scale provides a parent-rated data base for evaluating children. An advantage of the CBCL is that it has normative data against which the child's ratings are judged. A parent's ratings can produce a score, and the score can be evaluated against the normative data that are provided. This process enables the user to determine the degree to which the child's scores are within or outside the normative range. A teacher rating version of the CBCL, the Teacher Rating Form (TRF), is also available.

Understanding the problem and making a determination of the presence of a disorder benefit from multimethod measurement, including self-reports, interviews, and parent and teacher ratings. Careful observation of the child's behavior in several settings would also be very valuable.

Who are the children with anxiety disorders?

As noted earlier, when community samples of children are studied, fears and worries are found to be quite common. In terms of meeting diagnostic criteria, less is known, with estimates of 5–8% (slightly higher in mid-adolescence; Kashani & Orvaschel, 1988) considered credible. However, it is difficult to reach definitive conclusions on the prevalence of anxiety in youth because of methodological and diagnostic variations across the studies.

In terms of meeting diagnostic criteria, boys and girls are relatively comparable in the prevalence of anxiety disorders in childhood, but the ratio changes in adolescence to 1:3. Some recent research has examined the fears and anxieties of minority group children. In two studies, African, American and Caucasian children showed similarity in the situations that were feared (Neal, Lilly, & Zakis, 1993) and clinical features of anxiety disorder (Last & Perrin, 1993), although rates of diagnoses were higher for African-American than for Caucasian children (Kashani & Orvaschel, 1988).

Causal forces

Emotional development is influenced by a variety of factors, including genetic predispositions, parental psychological disorder, early trauma, the child's cognitive and behavioral learning history, and peer and familial interrelationships. Biological, cognitive and behavioral, and family factors offer the greatest promise. These explanations, often offered as explanations of anxiety disorders in adults, apply to disorders in children as well.

Studies of the genetic contribution to the anxiety disorders have indicated significant, though modest heritability. One adult anxiety disorder—panic disorder—has been found to occur in nearly one-quarter of the close relatives of panic patients compared to 2% among controls (Crow, Noyes, Pauls, & Slymen, 1983). Research using twins (Torgersen, 1983) reported 31% of monozygotic twin pairs, but none of the dizygotic twin pairs, both had panic disorder. Simple phobias also seem to run in families (Fyer et al., 1990). In contrast, research suggests that there is little genetic contribution to generalized anxiety disorder (GAD) (Kendler et al., 1992). Apparently, not all of the anxiety disorders are alike in terms of the genetic contribution.

The basic idea behind the cognitive explanation is that anxiety results from dysfunctional ways of making sense of the world. Perhaps due to prior experience, or early mistaken interpretations of events, individuals who suffer distressing anxiety process their social world in anxiety-provoking ways. Holding irrational expectations for oneself, for example, can produce anxiety. To be unwilling to participate in a new game for fear that you won't be the best player ever is to hold too grand an expectation. Other cognitive functions are associated with anxiety as well. For example, anxious persons bring a tendency to perceive threat to a variety of situations. Being concerned about evaluation may be rational in a job interview situation, but the anxious person brings evaluative threat to situations that are potentially playful, relaxed, and comfortable. Interestingly, anxiety-disordered children recognize emotions but do not seem to understand how to think about emotions in order to change them (Southam-Gerow & Kendall, in press).

The behavioral explanation of anxiety disorders was discussed in Chapter 2 when we considered the classical conditioning of fear and when we examined the contingencies involved in avoidance learning. As was stated, avoidance responses are responses that are made to prevent an unwanted situation or outcome. The relief of avoiding something unpleasant serves as a positive reward. Consider the child who is being teased by classmates in the playground at school recess. To stop the teasing, the child does not go outdoors during recess. In the future, staying indoors is associated with reduced anxiety. To avoid future anxiety, the child continues to avoid peers and continues to avoid social interactions. Such avoidance responses prevent the unwanted emotions from being experienced. As was also stated, avoidance responses that are not functional—they do not in fact continue to be effective in preventing the unwanted situation—are characteristic of anxious persons. In other words, even though the response (staying inside) is made to prevent a negative condition, the negative condition was not going to occur whether or not the response was made. In our example, the peers had matured, were socially supportive, were favorably interested in the isolated child, and were no longer teasing each other. The avoidance response is maintained, nevertheless, by the persons' perception that it has been effective—in fact, the avoidance response was unnecessary.

Other behavioral forces contribute as well. Modeling, for example, plays an important role. A child can acquire dysfunctional behavior by observing a parent's reactions and behavior patterns, and hearing a parent's explanation for social events (Barrett, Rapee, Dadds, & Ryan, 1996b). The child can develop an anxious style without direct experience with anxiety-provoking situations by watching someone else. A child walking with a parent witnesses the parent crossing the street to avoid someone, not entering a store because there are people already inside, or declining an invitation to a social event and comes to see the presence of other people as threatening. The child can learn to avoid through the vicarious experience.

Considerations of the family system as a contributor to children's anxiety disorders is an area just beginning to receive research attention. Initial work suggests that children with an anxiety disorder are more likely to have a parent who is reluctant to grant autonomy and is somewhat controlling (Siqueland, Kendall, & Steinberg, 1996). Other work suggests that parents contribute to the child's tendency to avoid by encouraging them to solve problems in ways that are more avoidant than even the initial ideas of the child. That is, the anxious child may be somewhat avoidant, but becomes increasingly so after discussing problems to be solved with the parent (see Rapee, 1997). It appears that parent–child interactions contribute to the development of childrens' problems with anxiety.

Treatment

The late 1990s have witnessed an emerging literature that describes the procedures in therapy and documents the efficacy of treatments for childhood anxiety disorders (see Ollendick, King, & Yule, 1994). For example, there are treatments for specific phobias (Silverman & Rabian, 1994) and social phobias (Beidel & Randall, 1994; Heimberg et al., 1990), obsessive compulsive disorder (Henin & Kendall, 1997; Leonard, Swedo, Allen, & Rapoport, 1994; March, 1995; March & Mulle, 1998; Piacentini, Gitow, Jaffer, Graae, & Whitaker, 1994), and generalized anxiety disorder (Kendall, 1994; Kendall et al., 1997).

The psychosocial treatments designed for youngsters with GAD— typically identified as cognitive-behavioral—often combine skill in the management of unwanted arousal with exposure to the feared or distressing situation (e.g. Kendall, Kane, Howard, & Siqueland, 1990). That is, children are first taught about their unwanted emotional, cognitive, and behavioral reactions, and then they are taught strategies to manage the arousal. The educational component of the treatment helps children identify their anxiety-arousing thoughts, teaches relaxation responses, and provides strategies for use to moderate anxious arousal. These parts are integrated:

F   stands for <u>Feeling Frightened?</u>
E   for <u>Expecting bad things to happen?</u>
A   is for the <u>Attitudes and Actions</u> that you can take
R   stands for the <u>Results and Rewards.</u>

As an illustration, the Coping Cat program (Kendall, 1992) uses the acronym FEAR to put the pieces together and empower children with a plan for mastering anxious distress. Children take the FEAR plan with them into the anxiety-producing situations.

Exposure is critical (Barlow, 1988) in treating anxiety—once the children learn the skills, they practice them in the once-feared context. Investigators on two continents have found that various versions of this approach (Kendall, 1994; Kendall et al., 1997 in the US: Barrett, Dadds, & Rapee, 1996a in Australia) have been an effective means of treating youngsters diagnosed with anxiety disorders such as generalized anxiety disorder, social phobia, and separation anxiety disorder (see also Kendall et al., 1997; regarding obsessive-compulsive disorder see March, 1995). Because anxiety and depressive symptoms often co-occur, the treatment of anxiety can be modified for comorbid depression (Kendall, Kortlander, Chansky, & Brady, 1992).

A diagnosis of school phobia is appropriate in the presence of severe difficulty in attending school that results in prolonged absence from school, severe emotional upset, staying home from school with the parent's knowledge, and the absence of antisocial or conduct problems (Ollendick & Mayer, 1984). In the UK, Blagg and Yule (1984) conducted a comparison of (1) behavioral treatment, (2) hospitalization, and (3) psychotherapy with home tutoring for school phobic children. In the behavioral treatment, coping strategies were taught, behavior consequences were put into effect, and the child was placed in school directly. Members of the hospital group discussed issues of separation, were encouraged to be independent, and received exercises to build self-concept and self-esteem. Tranquilizers were sometimes prescribed. Members of the home-tutoring group were allowed to remain at home while receiving individual therapy at a community clinic and educational tutoring in the home. Using regular school attendance and improved psychological adjustment as the criteria for success, the behavioral group's success rate of 93.3% was significantly superior to the 37.5% for the hospital group and the 10% for the home treatment group. This study provides a clear indication that certain kinds of treatment can be effective.

Antidepressant medications (SSRIs such as clomipramine) have been used to treat obsessive-compulsive disorders in children (for example, see Leonard et al., 1989) and to a lesser extent school phobic children. There are a few uncontrolled reports of the use of adult anti-anxiety medications with children, but there is a marked absence of empirical research evaluating such use and, taken with the fact that medications for adult depression do not work the same with children as with adults, there is an apparent need for caution and for research. In the absence of the data, one cannot recommend the use of anti-anxiety drugs with children.

Studies of the cognitive-behavioral treatment of children who are diagnosed as suffering from an anxiety disorder have produced fairly comparable outcomes: Approximately 70% of children show marked improvements. Importantly, efforts are being made to improve the outcomes and recent studies are beginning to include and address parents in the child's treatment (Kendall, MacDonald, & Treadwell, 1995), and some initial data suggest that adding parent training to the child's cognitive-behavioral treatment produced improved outcomes (Barrett, Dadds, & Rapee, 1996a). The anxiety disorders of childhood have, until recently, taken a back seat to the study of the disruptive behavior problems. The added attention being given to anxiety problems will likely produce noted improvements in our knowledge of the causes and our application of treatments for children with anxiety disorders.

Summary

Fears are a normal part of development, but extreme fears can be a part of an anxiety disorder of childhood (e.g. separation anxiety disorder). Children can suffer from generalized anxiety disorder, separation anxiety, and other types of anxiety problems (e.g. school phobia, obsessive-compulsive disorder). Family influences, learning histories, cognitive processing distortions, and biological predispositions all contribute to the onset of anxiety disorders in childhood. Several studies indicate that cognitive-behavioral procedures have been found to alleviate clinical levels of unwanted anxiety.

Depression 7

José was 13 when he was first seen in therapy. His parents made an appointment with a clinical child psychologist at the recommendation of a psychiatrist who had been unable to get José to talk. His parents reported that he stayed in his room, did not play with other kids, and often awoke during the night and very early in the morning. School was said to be uninteresting, sports were out of the question, and even youthful music was unfavored. After several sessions during which the psychologist was very calm and patient, José began to talk. Weeks later, he expressed hatred toward his hypercritical parents, an absence of closeness with any of his siblings, and extreme disappointment with himself. His emotional state was one of depression.

Phenomenology and classification

Believe it or not, depression was once thought to be a disorder limited to adults only! Depressive disorders impair the functioning of numerous adults (see Hammen, 1997), but experts now recognize that children, too, can and do experience clinical depression. Early on, childhood depression might have been overlooked simply because no one asked the child about his or her feelings and moods. Children who were brought to clinics for behavior problems might have also suffered from depression, but clinicians did not take notice. Unfortunately, children who were quiet and withdrawn, and perhaps dysphoric or depressed, were often ignored. When researchers began to ask children directly about depressive symptoms, it became apparent that children can and do suffer depression (Harrington, 1994), and childhood depression is associated with a wide range of negative outcomes, including future episodes of depression, impaired social adjustment, academic difficulties, and in some cases an increased risk of suicide.

In the DSM-IV diagnostic system, adult criteria for a depressive episode can be applied to children (see Box 7.1)—although there are some differences in how the disorder is expressed. For instance, younger children might complain of physical symptoms more than adults and might be irritable. Older children might have more subjective symptoms than younger children, such as helplessness and pessimism. In general, however, most experts believe that depression generally presents a similar clinical picture regardless of the person's age. Major depressive disorder is the diagnosis when there is evidence of a major depressive episode—an episode that is not better accounted for by the presence of another disorder and there has never been a manic episode. Based on the number of episodes, major depressive disorder is divided into two categories: single episode and recurrent.

Although the symptom picture is similar for youngsters and adults, we know a lot less about childhood and adolescent depression than

---

BOX 7.1   Criteria for major depressive episode

A: Five (or more) of the following symptoms during the same 2-week period and representing a change from previous functioning; at least one of the symptoms is either (1) depressed mood or (2) loss of interest or pleasure.

- depressed mood most of the day, nearly every day, as indicated by either subjective report (e.g. feels sad or empty) or observation made by others (e.g. appears tearful).
  Note: In children or adolescents, can be irritable mood.
- markedly diminished interest or pleasure in all, or almost all, activities most of the day, nearly every day (either subjective or observed by others)
- significant weight loss when not dieting or weight gain (more than 5% change in a month), or increase or decrease in appetite nearly every day.
  Note: In children, consider failure to meet expected weight gains.
- insomnia or hypersomnia nearly every day
- psychomotor agitation or retardation nearly every day (observable by others)
- fatigue or loss of energy nearly every day
- feelings of worthlessness or excessive or inappropriate guilt (which may be delusional) nearly every day
- diminished ability to think or concentrate, or indecisiveness, nearly every day
- recurrent thoughts of death (not just fear of dying), recurrent suicidal ideation without a specific plan, or a suicidal attempt or a specific plan for committing suicide.

B: The symptoms do not meet criteria for a mixed episode (i.e. evidence of mania).

C: The symptoms cause clinically significant distress or impairment in social, occupational, or other important areas of functioning.

D: The symptoms are not due to the direct physiological effects of a substance (e.g. drug abuse, medication) or a general medical condition (e.g. hypothyroidism).

E: The symptoms are not better accounted for by a bereavement (i.e. after loss of a loved one), the symptoms persist for longer than 2 months or are characterized by marked functional impairment, morbid preoccupation with worthlessness, suicidal ideation, psychotic symptoms, or psychomotor retardation.

Reprinted with permission from the Diagnostic and Statistical Manual of Mental Disorders, Fourth Edition. Copyright 1994 American Psychiatric Association.

about adult depression. Nevertheless, there are several facts that are clear. One is that depressive syndromes are relatively rare in early childhood but become more common with increasing age. About 1% of preschool children, especially those older than 2 or 3, have been said to have clinically diagnosable depression (Kashani & Carlson, 1987). In middle childhood (ages 6 to 12), the estimate rises to 2%, based on large samples gathered in New Zealand and the US (Anderson et al., 1987; Costello et al., 1988). By the time the child reaches adolescence, the rates of depression jump enormously, up to about the same rates as adults— between 4% and 8% if both major depression and dysthymia are combined (Cooper & Goodyear, 1993; Roberts, Lewinsohn, & Seeley, 1991). Comorbidity adds to the number of youngsters who are depressed: Children who meet criteria for other disorders, such as an anxiety disorder or ADHD, may also meet criteria for a secondary diagnosis of depression.

Gender differences in depression exist, and they evidence a developmental pattern. A 1:1 (male–female) ratio in childhood changes to 1:2 in adolescence. One study reported rates of major depression to be 4.5% for girls and 2.9% for boys (Whitaker et al., 1990). With further development, the ratio reflects an increasing incidence among females (see also Gladstone, Kaslow, Seeley, & Lewinsohn, 1997).

The occurrence of depression among youngsters may be on the rise. Although we do not have high-quality surveys from previous generations for comparisons, some evidence that those born in more recent decades are more likely to meet criteria for major depression than are their older counterparts (Klerman & Weissman, 1989; Lewinsohn, Rohde, Seeley, & Fischer, 1993). Whether this change reflects a real increase or an epiphenomenon linked to increased searching for the disorder remains to be addressed by research.

One of the consistent findings with regard to youngsters with depression is the high rate of comorbidity. A recent review (Compas, 1997) reconfirmed an earlier observation that comorbidity is the rule (Brady & Kendall, 1992). From data reported by Lewinsohn, Rohde, Hops, and Clark (1991), 43% of adolescents identified as depressed received at least one additional diagnosis. Current comorbidity was highest for anxiety disorders (18%), substance use disorders (14%), and disruptive behavior disorders (8%) (as cited in Compas, 1997).

Assessing depression in children

Measuring depression in children has proven more complex than once thought. There are structured interviews, self-report questionnaires, peer nomination methods, and parent and teacher rating forms, yet the data produced by these various sources show limited cross-informant agreement. Depression as assessed by one method is not the same as assessments of children's depression gathered in other ways (for example, see Kazdin, Esveldt-Dawson, Unis, & Rancurello, 1983; Saylor, Finch, Baskin, Furey, & Kelly, 1984; Wolfe et al., 1987). The dilemma is evident in the following: Peer and staff ratings of depression are not meaningfully related to children's own reports about their level of depression. Self-reports of anxiety are often more highly correlated with depression than are self-reports and teacher ratings of depression (Wolfe et al., 1987), and a mother's depression may influence her report of her child's emotional well-being (e.g. Conrad & Hammen, 1989).

As noted earlier, the emotional disorders of anxiety and depression are highly related (Kendall & Watson, 1989). Further research is needed on the overlap between anxiety and depression and to better understand the differences between self-reports of these disorders and the symptom reports of others. Still, because the child's experience is important, the child's self-report remains an essential part of the assessment of emotional distress (Finch, Lipovsky, & Casat, 1989). Indeed, when we need to assess clinical depression in children, researchers recommend that children and their parents be interviewed separately because parents, who can report their observations of some symptoms, simply do not know what their children's private experiences might be.

Causal forces

Clinical levels of depression, in any of its forms, are not caused by a single environmental event or sole biological ingredient. Nevertheless, each of the various factors have been found to contribute to our understanding. Most of the research has been conducted with adults (see Hammen, 1997), and most of the investigations pertain to one of the major models discussed in Chapter 2.

Extensive evidence is available on the genetic contribution to depression. According to Hammen (1991), depression runs in families. Genetics research results, using family history, twin, and adoption studies, support the conclusion that there is a meaningful genetic component to clinical depression (e.g. Paykel, 1992). Environmental factors are still important, however, as evident in the fact that the risk for depression among youngsters is increased when the history of the parent's depression includes onset before the age of 20. Recent data suggest that a genetic component contributes to the co-occurrence between antisocial and depressive symptoms over a 3-year period (O'Connor, Neiderhiser, Reiss, Hetherington, & Plomin, 1998).

Cognitive models of depression focus on the attributional styles that persons use to explain negative outcomes, and are, in various ways, offshoots of Beck's (1967) model of depression. This view holds that depression is linked to negative views of the self, the world, and the future. A related model (e.g. Abramson, Metalsky, & Alloy, 1989) emphasizes hopelessness and a depressogenic attributional style. When negative outcomes occur, depression-prone children attribute the outcome to stable, internal, and global aspects of the self. Misattributions with regard to loss, separation, and abuse are especially potent. An emerging research with children has documented that attributions and misperceptions are related to depression (Kaslow, Brown, & Mees, 1994).

In one study, children (grades 3–6) identified as depressed were found to evaluate themselves more critically than their nondepressed peers (Kendall, Stark, & Adam, 1990). To determine if the ratings were based in reality, or were a cognitive distortion, teachers also provided ratings of all of the children. The teacher's blind ratings showed no significant difference between the evaluations of the depressed and nondepressed children. The depressed children were showing their bias in harsh self-judgments.

Other data also support an information-processing problem in childhood depression. Judy Garber and her colleagues (Garber, Braafladt, & Zeman, 1991) examined how depressed and nondepressed children addressed negative affective experiences. Nondepressed children were able to identify ways to cope with affective distress, whereas the depressed children were more inclined to choose strategies such as distraction. Depressed children were also less likely to process negative emotions in ways that recognize that negative mood can be modified.

Behavioral explanations of depression (e.g. Lewinsohn, 1974) emphasize problems in the person's response to the environment. Reduced experiences with reinforcement, limited pleasant events, and nonresponsiveness to cues were thought to contribute to the emotional sadness. Interpersonal models emphasize parent–child interactions, with special limited contact given special notice as a risk factor.

Probably the most accepted model for understanding depression is the diathesis-stress approach. In this instance, biological and genetic predispositions interact with family distress and personal cognitive distortions. Depression runs in families, so it is possible that the early childhood onset of depression represents a genetically transmitted tendency (Strober, 1992). However, stress is a contributor as well.

Family disruption is a common feature associated with childhood depression. For example, several sources of evidence link negative quality of relationships between parents and children with depression in these youngsters. In depressed adults' reports of their own childhoods they report a variety of problems such as rejection by parents, neglect or lack of interest, hostility, or overcontrolling behaviors by the parents (Hammen, 1991). One might be skeptical of the accuracy of these results if they were the only information available because depressed people might be biased to report only the negative memories of their childhoods. However, evidence suggests that retrospective reports are not necessarily unreliable or biased (Brewin et al., 1993)—evidence from studies of depressed children and from studies of children of depressed parents has also indicated hostility, arguments, and generally negative quality of interactions (see Hammen, 1991). Apparently, having a poor relationship with one's parents may set the stage for childhood problems. One might speculate that depression is especially likely to occur when the child feels bad about him- or herself because of feeling unloved, unwanted, or insecure (for example, as a result of a poor early mother–child bond; Cummings & Cicchetti, 1990).

The course of childhood depression

Until we have sufficient longitudinal studies that have followed depressed children into adulthood, we can only speculate about the relationship between depressed children and depressed adults. The likely answer is that there is a meaningful relationship, especially if the depression is left untreated. Some depressed youngsters do indeed have problems with depression in adulthood (Garber, Kriss, Koch, & Lindholm, 1988). Kovacs and her colleagues found that 72% of the depressed children they studied had a relapse within 5 years (Kovacs, Feinberg, Crouse-Novak, Paulauskas, & Finkelstein, 1984). UK researchers recontacted former child patients and found that 60% of those treated for depression in childhood an average of 18 years earlier had experienced at least one recurrence of major depression during adulthood (Harrington, Fudge, Rutter, Pickles, & Hill, 1990). Certainly not all children who are clinically depressed will continue to have depressive episodes, but episodes of depression in childhood do seem to be predictive of future depression (Lewinsohn, Clark, & Rohde, 1994) and there appears to be continuity in major depressive disorder from adolescence to young adulthood (Lewinsohn, Rohde, Klein, & Seeley, 1999).

Treatment

Interestingly, one of the major treatments for adult depression—antidepressant medications—has been found not to be effective with all children (see Sommers-Flanagan & Sommers-Flanagan, 1996). That is, the effects of some forms of antidepressant medications are no greater than the effects produced by a placebo. There is an exception: A study reported by Emslie et al. (1997) found that Prozac (an SSRI) was superior to a placebo for the treatment of depressed youth. The absence of extensive evidence requires that caution be exercised when considering antidepressant medications with children.

A variety of psychological treatment approaches are used in clinics, but evaluations of the outcomes have not often been conducted. One approach, cognitive-behavioral therapy, has been used successfully with adults, and has been applied and evaluated with children. So far, based on a few controlled studies, the gains are promising.

In one of these outcome evaluations, Stark, Reynolds, and Kaslow (1987) compared a self-control training program, a problem-solving therapy, and a wait-list control condition. The two treatments, each focusing in different ways on the teaching of self-management skills, self-monitoring, and social problem solving, were found to produce meaningful gains in both child self-report and interview measures of depression. Participating youngsters learned to plan and schedule potentially pleasant activities, to be less critical in their self-evaluation, and to view social dilemmas as problems to be solved. The positive gains from such treatment remained evident at an 8-week follow-up. (For examples of a school-based program for pre-adolescents, see Butler, Mietzitiz, Friedman, & Cole, 1980; Stark, 1990).

A study with depressed adolescents reported encouraging outcomes. Lewinsohn and his colleagues (Lewinsohn, Clarke, Hops, & Andrews, 1990) provided and evaluated a treatment that involved a cognitive-behavioral group that taught skills for increasing pleasant activities, controlling depressive thoughts, improving social interactions, and resolving conflict. In a research design that allowed for the examination of the effects of parental involvement, parents of some of the depressed adolescents were told of the program given to their teens and were encouraged to be supportive and reinforcing, especially when the adolescent used the coping skills to address family problems. A look at the overall effects, in terms of self-reported depression and the percentage of patients meeting diagnostic criteria, showed that improvements were achieved. Indeed, the significant reduction in symptoms and diagnoses held up at a 2-year follow-up evaluation.

Reinecke, Ryan, and DuBois (1998) reported that, based on a meta-analysis of six studies of depressed adolescents, cognitive-behavioral treatment was generally found to be useful in reducing dysphoria and depression, and the effects were found to have been maintained at follow-up. Although these outcomes are encouraging (see also Brent et al., 1997), not all of the treated adolescents responded equally favorably to the treatment. Based on a study of 50 depressed adolescents, Jayson and colleagues (Jayson, Wood, Kroll, Fraser, & Harrington, 1998) reported that 60% of adolescents experienced symptom remission, but that adolescents with more severe psychosocial stress and with greater symptom severity were less likely to exhibit remission of symptoms. Given the likelihood of persistent depression if left untreated in childhood and adolescence and the likelihood for cognitive-behavioral treatment-produced gains (Clarizio, 1994), it is reasonable to recommend that depressed youngsters seek and receive psychological intervention (see also Rehm & Sharp, 1996; Rudolph, Hammen, & Burge, 1997; Stark et al., 1996).

Summary

Children can and do experience depression. With age, more females are found to have the disorder: If children are left untreated, they are at significant risk for depression in adulthood. Family influences, learning histories, cognitive processing distortions, and biological pre-dispositions all contribute to the onset of depressive disorders in childhood. Though the number of studies is limited, the effects of medications have not been uniformly supported. Cognitive-behavioral procedures have been found to help reduce depression.

Eating disorders 8

Because eating disorders are characteristically first identified during the pre-adult years, they are considered psychological problems of youth. When the problems persist, however, they are troublesome for adults as well (see Wilson, 1999). Eating disorders often have emotional and behavioral qualities as well as physical consequences. Although many persons with eating disorders do not have other problems, of those who do, they may be comorbid with any of a wide variety of other disorders. The two major disturbances in eating behavior that we discuss are anorexia nervosa and bulimia nervosa. However, before we examine these disorders we will first consider feeding difficulties seen in infancy and early childhood.

Feeding disorder of infancy or early childhood

Feeding is the first task in which the parent and child work together for a common goal. Not surprisingly, many parents show interest in the details of their newborn's eating habits and disturbances in the area of feeding can contribute to parental distress (Budd & Chugh, 1998).

Estimates of the extent of feeding problems vary a great deal—with higher rates reported by studies using more inclusive criteria and lower rates reported by studies with rigorous criteria. Many children may show finicky eating, selective eating, overeating, or vomiting, but these variations are within normal limits and do not reflect disorder. When the stringent criteria are applied, only 1–2% of infants evidence persistent feeding problems.

The central feature of feeding disorder of infancy is the persistent failure to consume adequate food as evident in a failure to gain weight or significant weight loss over at least one month. For a diagnosis, the child must be under age 6, and must show a problem that is not the result of a general medical condition or gastrointestinal disorder.

As is true for the majority of childhood disorders, a wide variety of etiological models have been proposed (e.g. physical, child temperament, modeling, parent behavior, family factors) to explain variations in eating behavior. For example, maladaptive patterns of parental interaction with the newborn have been implicated in the onset of feeding problems. Nonresponsiveness to the child's needs (Bradley, Casey, & Wortham, 1984) and power struggles over feeding (Chatoor & Egan, 1983) illustrate parental behavior that can contribute to feeding problems. Although the amount of research is limited, the field is increasingly adopting a diathesis-stress model in which the interplay of physiological, social, and behavioral factors explain the nature of feeding disorders (Budd et al., 1992).

Once a feeding problem has been identified, the typical approach to remediate the problem is to work with the parent(s) to alter feeding-related behavior patterns. Parent guidance and education can be useful, as can repeated exposures to models who are responsive to child needs, avoid power struggles, and who are tolerant of individual variability in feeding styles. The infants can also be exposed to various foods, and can receive differential attention for eating increasingly diverse foods. It should be kept in mind that mild feeding difficulties are common in infancy and childhood and they do not require excess attention. However, there are serious eating disorders that emerge during childhood and these often do require professional attention.

Anorexia nervosa

"Nervous loss of appetite" is the exact meaning of the phrase *anorexia nervosa*.

> At 15, Alma had been healthy and well-developed, had menstruated at age 12, was five feet six inches tall, and weighed 172 pounds. At that time her mother urged her to change to a school with higher academic standing, a change she resisted. Her father hounded her to watch her weight, an idea that she took up with great eagerness—and she began a rigid diet. She lost weight rapidly, and surprisingly to her, her menses ceased. She enjoyed becoming thin, as it gave her a sense of pride, power, and accomplishment. She also began a frenetic exercise program, swimming hundreds of laps, running on the treadmill for hours, or doing calisthenics to the point of exhaustion. Whatever low point her weight reached, Alma feared that she might still become "too fat" if she regained as little as an ounce. After several months of the extreme exercise, most of the time her weight

was less than 70 pounds, and when she temporarily yielded to others' efforts to make her gain weight, she lost it again almost immediately. There was also a marked change in her character and behavior. Formerly sweet, obedient, and considerate, she became more and more demanding, obstinate, irritable, and arrogant. There was constant arguing, not only about what she should eat but about all other activities as well.

(Adapted and modified, from Bruch, 1978.)

Phenomenology and classification

Anorexia nervosa was originally applied because theoreticians believed that anorectic patients did not experience pangs of hunger. As it turns out, they do experience hunger pangs, often intensely, so the phrase may be a misnomer. Nevertheless, anorexia nervosa is an eating disorder characterized by an intense fear of becoming obese, a distorted self-perception of body image, refusal to maintain minimal normal body weight (significant weight loss), and, in females, the cessation of menstruation.

Individuals with anorexia are persistent in the desire for additional weight loss. They believe that they are fat when others would evaluate them as thin or even emaciated. They have a distorted self-perception of body size; they fail to recognize successful weight loss and their need to control their body by weight loss. Whereas it is safe to say that the average dieter does not share these characteristics, certain groups (such as ballet dancers and female athletes) that are quite conscientious about weight may be considered at risk. The exact DSM criteria are presented in Box 8.1.

The risk for onset of anorexia is high at ages 14–18 (Foreyt & McGavin, 1988)—the average age of onset is 17 years. The estimates of

---

BOX 8.1   DSM criteria for a diagnosis of anorexia nervosa

- Refusal to maintain body weight at or above a minimally normal weight for age and height (e.g. weight loss leading to maintenance of body weight less than 85% of that expected; or failure to make expected weight gain during periods of growth, leading to body weight less than 85% of that expected).
- Intense fear of gaining weight or becoming fat, even though underweight.
- Disturbance in the way in which one's body weight or shape is experienced, undue influence of body weight or shape on self-evaluation, or denial of the seriousness of the current low body weight.
- In postmenarcheal females, amenorrhea, i.e. the absence of at least three consecutive menstrual cycles. (A woman is considered to have amenorrhea if her periods occur only following hormone, e.g. estrogen, administration.)

Reprinted with permission from the Diagnostic and Statistical Manual of Mental Disorders, Fourth Edition. Copyright 1994 American Psychiatric Association.

prevalence vary greatly, depending on the manner used to identify persons with anorexia, but there is one consistency: The disorder is eight to eleven times more common in females than males (Steinhausen, 1994), but those men and women with eating disorders are quite similar (Olivardia & Pope, 1995). Some early data (Pope, Hudson, & Yurgelun-Todd, 1984) suggested that 1 in every 200 school-aged girls qualified as anorexic, whereas more conservative estimates have placed the prevalence at 1 in 200,000.

Anorexia nervosa has been identified worldwide. Incidence rates in the US vary (Jones, Fox, Babigian, & Hutton, 1980; Lucas, Beard, O'Fallon, & Kurland, 1991), but it is generally accepted that anorexia affects less than 1% of the adolescent population. Anorexia is quite rare in China (Lee & Chiu, 1989), but quite common in Japan (Suematsu, Kuboki, & Itoh, 1985). An incidence of 6.3 per 100,000 was reported in a Dutch study (Hoek, 1991). Whereas anorexia is rare among African-Americans in the US (Dolan, 1991), Africa, and the UK, there are documented cases (Nwaefuna, 1981).

Is the problem of anorexia on the increase? There are more reported cases of anorexia nervosa now than there were a few years ago, but does this mean the disorder is on the rise? Some researchers believe that the change reflects increases in the number of young women in the population and an increased awareness of the disorder, however, and not true changes in frequency (Williams & King, 1987).

Unlike many psychological problems, anorexia can lead to serious physical illness and even to death. Estimates vary, but a typical estimate holds that two-thirds of cases are treated successfully and one-third are chronically ill. Less than 5% of anorexics are said to die from the disorder (Steinhausen, 1994).

Causes and course

Persons with anorexia have been described as obsessional, neurotic, having a heightened need for personal control, and they have been found to have low estrogen levels (Leon & Phelan, 1985). They hold more negative attitudes about sexuality and rarely engage in sexual activity (Coovert & Kinder, 1989).

Eating disorders are most likely to appear in adolescence because of the convergence of physical changes and psychosocial challenges. The increase in body fat, which is most dramatic in adolescent girls, is frequently associated with concerns about increased weight and the need to do something about it. Researchers and theoreticians have amassed considerable data about anorexia nervosa, but no one explanation is accepted by all of the workers in this field.

Psychological factors. Psychodynamic theorizing (such as Bruch, 1973, 1978) has argued that because of disturbed mother–child interactions anorexic children failed to develop a body identity and a sense of owning their own bodies. They are said to be overpowered by the body's needs; not eating can provide a false sense of control. The sense of control derived from not eating also appears in explanations based on other theoretical points of view.

Are there personality traits that have been linked to anorexia? Although limited by retrospective reporting that is typical in clinical history taking, a pattern of compliance, perfectionism, and dependence, as well as the absence of school or educational problems, has been described as characteristic of anorexic youngsters (Steinhausen, 1994). Obsessive-compulsive tendencies and early eating and digestive problems may be present (Manchi & Cohen, 1990).

Minuchin and his colleagues (Minuchin et al., 1978) viewed the family as a system and argued that the symptoms of anorexia cannot be understood outside the system. As noted in Chapter 2, the family of an anorexic child, in this view, is marked by enmeshment. In an enmeshed family, each member lacks a distinct identity. A child in such a family can feel protected by the group, but also fails to develop a personal sense of autonomy or independence. The anorexic individual challenges the family system and wants to break out; failure to eat is the rebellion.

In the view of Minuchin et al. (1978), rigidity and a failure to resolve conflicts are theorized to be a mark of the families of anorexic children. According to Minuchin, the symptoms of the anorexic child regulate the family by keeping parental conflict from getting out of control. The symptoms thus protect the stability of the family. Although these ideas have not received rigorous research evaluations, data are consistent with the view that the families of anorexics have increased parental conflict (Kalucy, Crisp, & Harding, 1977).

Anorexia has also been described as an avoidance response, where excessive anxiety is associated with the avoidance of food. The food avoidance is then reinforced by the attention that it brings to the individual (Leitenberg, Agras, & Thomson, 1968). The anorexic, therefore, is seen as having learned that not eating is a successful way to get attention.

The social pressure to be thin is emphasized in other learning explanations of the disorder. It is easy to imagine how one might learn the expected body size: Evidence of the pressure for thinness is in the photos and articles in newspapers and magazines and in the ads and scripts of television programs and movies. Thinness is often a part of the developing self-concept of teenage girls.

Cultural forces are said to be operative in the eating disorders. In many cultures, the ideal for female beauty has increasingly become a lean woman, and the influence of this ideal is spreading to other cultures. Using a bust-to-waist ratio calculated on female figures in popular magazines, researchers have documented that the cultural ideal of beauty has become increasingly leaner (Williamson, Kahn, Remington, & Anda, 1990). However, the discrepancy between ideal and real has created a widespread desire for "magical" programs that make women healthier, slimmer, and more aesthetically appealing (Brownell, 1991). There are mass-marketed diet aids and stimulant drugs that curb hunger, and many infomercials airing on late-night television. The pressure is on women, and it seems to be internalized in adolescence (Wadden, Brown, Foster, & Linowitz, 1991).

Follow-up reports from former anorexics have suggested another explanation to Garner and Bemis-Vitousek (1985). They saw a persistent pattern of distorted thinking among anorexic individuals and built the beginnings of a cognitive model of the disorder. They noted that the behavior of anorexic individuals reflect their conviction that they "must" be thin—not just a desire or wish to be thin, but a controlling and demanding must. The striving to lose weight may be a route to alleviate the dysphoria, isolation, low sense of self-worth, and sense of inadequacy often felt by young adolescents. Anorexics also make inaccurate cognitive evaluations: for example, "I must lose more weight since I am not yet thin" and "I must continue to lose weight so I can continue to be in control of my body." While losing weight at alarming and dangerous rates, the anorexic processes the weight loss as success, as evidence of power and control. More is better, so the weight loss continues as the sense of power continues. This aberrant thinking leads to and maintains the eventually self-destructive behavior.

Biological factors. Hormones, genetics, and brain functioning are three areas where biological models have been applied to eating disorders. The hypothalamus has been considered the brain area likely to control eating. Possible biological factors in anorexia, therefore, included malfunctioning of the hypothalamus. For example, researchers found that animals will stop eating, and can literally starve to death, when they are given lesions in one portion of the hypothalamus, or when stimulation is applied to other areas of the hypothalamus. Currently, the hypothalamus is considered important in controlling a variety of motivated behaviors (eating, drinking, temperature, sex).

Studies have shown correlations between anorexic behavior and changes in norepinephrine and serotonin (Fava, Copeland, Schweiger,

& Herzog, 1989), but the direction of influence is not clear. The extended starvation might cause physiological malfunctioning, just as it is possible that the physiologic dysfunction produces the eating symptoms (Weiner, 1985).

Genetic factors may predispose some people to the onset of anorexia. A review of twin studies remarked that monozygotic twins had a concordance rate that was higher than that for dizygotic twins (Scott, 1986). In one illustrative study (Holland, Sicotte, & Treasure, 1988), 56% of monozygotic twin pairs were concordant for anorexia nervosa and only 5% were concordant among dizygotic twins.

The course and outcome of anorexia nervosa is quite varied: some individuals recover after a single episode, whereas others experience patterns of weight gain and successful weight maintenance followed by periods of relapse. Indeed, severe cases of anorexia have required hospitalization. As mentioned earlier—though it occurs in a small percentage—death can result from extreme cases.

Given the evidence to date, the diathesis-stress model has merit in understanding anorexia nervosa (Bemis-Vitousek & Orimoto, 1993). Indeed, as is true for many other disorders described in this book, it is the interaction between a biological predisposition and adverse environmental forces that affects the individual.

Bulimia nervosa

The rapid consumption of a large quantity of food in a discrete period of time, and the feeling of a lack of control over the eating, characterizes bulimia.

> Dieting was a common practice for Jenny, with small portions of food at meals and exercise in both the morning and evening being a regular part of every day. Often on weekends when she was home alone, however, Jenny would make eggs, bacon, and pancakes, with whipped cream and syrup, and eat massive quantities of these breakfast foods at one sitting. Soon after the feast, and the cautious and meticulous kitchen clean up, she would go to the bathroom and self-induce vomiting. During the week, the feast was an entire pizza, again followed by vomiting. For many months, she told no one of her habit. In therapy, however, as her therapist asked the proper questions and her comfort level was sufficient, she disclosed the binge–purge habit.

Phenomenology and classification

Bulimia is characterized by self-induced vomiting, use of diuretics, fasting, vigorous exercise to prevent weight gain, and a persistent overconcern with body weight and shape. A diagnosis of bulimia requires a minimum of two binges per week for at least a three-month period (see Box 8.2). Bulimia has been referred to as the binge–purge syndrome because massive quantities of food are eaten and then actions are taken to rid the body of potentially fat-producing calories. DSM includes patients with bulimia episodes in the diagnosis of anorexia nervosa, and not surprisingly there is substantial debate as to whether bulimia is a separate syndrome or merely a manifestation of anorexia nervosa (Foreyt & Mikhail, 1997).

Fairburn and Beglin (1990) concluded that the prevalence of bulimia among adolescents is about 1%. Although epidemiological data are often based on questionnaires, a number of studies (e.g. Timmerman, Wells, & Chen, 1990) have documented the existence of bulimia in a variety of countries. The majority of studies have focused on North American youngsters, but there are data on binge eating among various racial groups in Zimbabwe (Hopper & Garner, 1986). Given the worldwide occurrence of binge eating, a purely cultural explanation is not likely to be entirely satisfactory.

Bulimia, like anorexia, occurs much more often in females, although the age of onset of bulimia is typically in later adolescence (18.4 years; Fairburn & Cooper, 1984), as opposed to early adolescence for anorexia. Bulimia has often been linked to anorexia—in fact, roughly 50% of anorexic cases show some evidence of bulimia. Apparently, a sizeable

---

BOX 8.2   DSM criteria for a diagnosis of bulimia nervosa

- Recurrent episodes of binge eating. An episode of binge eating is characterized by both of the following:
  1. Eating, in a discrete period of time (e.g. within any 2-hour period) an amount of food that is definitely larger than most people would eat during a similar period of time and under similar circumstances
  2. A sense of lack of control over eating during the episode (e.g., a feeling that one cannot stop eating or control what or how much one is eating).
- Recurrent inappropriate compensatory behavior in order to prevent weight gain, such as self-induced vomiting; misuse of laxatives, diuretics, enemas, or other medications; fasting; or excessive exercise.
- The binge eating and inappropriate compensatory behavior both occur, on average, at least twice a week for 3 months.
- Self-evaluation is unduly influenced by body shape and weight.
- The disturbance does not occur exclusively during episodes of anorexia nervosa.
- DSM specifies purging (regularly engaged in self-induced vomiting or the misuse of laxatives, diuretics, or enemas) and nonpurging types.

Reprinted with permission from the Diagnostic and Statistical Manual of Mental Disorders, Fourth Edition. Copyright 1994 American Psychiatric Association.

number of persons with anorexia use binge eating and purging as part of their effort to be remarkably thin. This practice has unwanted effects, with potentially serious health ramifications such as the acids from vomiting damaging the enamel on your teeth and chemical imbalances in the body—and it isn't even all that effective in getting rid of the calories!

Causes and course

The etiological models that have been advanced for anorexia are often applied to bulimia. For example, Humphrey, Apple, and Kirschenbaum (1986) studied the interpersonal behavior of families with a normal adolescent female and others with an anorexic-bulimic female. The families interacted around the topic of the daughter's separation from the family, and trained observers recorded the frequencies of specific target behaviors. The frequencies of "helping" and "trusting" behavior on the positive side and "ignoring" and "walling off" on the negative side differentiated the families. Families with an anorexic-bulimic daughter displayed more of these negative and fewer of these positive interactions. Although these observed differences may possibly be the result of having a family member with an eating disorder, problematic family interactions are one proposed causal factor.

Regarding the role of cognitive factors in bulimia, an interesting series of studies was reported by Polivy and Herman (1985). Normal eating is generally under the control of appetite; when people feel full, they stop eating. According to Polivy and Herman, however, people who watch their weight (restrict their eating) use cognitive strategies to control their eating. That is, they eat when they believe they "should" eat, and ignore biological signals of hunger and fullness. Unfortunately, this pattern is said to set them up for binge eating. Polivy and Herman identified groups of normal eaters and restrained eaters (those usually dieting) and had them participate in what they believed were studies of taste preferences. The participants consumed high-calorie milkshakes and then were led to a room with unrestricted access to snacks—they could eat whenever they wanted—while they awaited the next part of the study. Normal eaters did not eat much; they were already full. But the restrained eaters ate a lot—as if once they decided that their diets were broken by the milkshake, they figured they might as well eat what they wanted. Because they do not detect the physical cues of satiation, they don't know their bodily cues for when to stop. Polivy and Herman (1985, 1987) speculated that the line between this eating pattern in typical dieters and clinical bulimia may be only a matter of degree.

Bulimia usually begins in late adolescence, and binge eating is sometimes associated with an episode of dieting. Until a recent report by Keel and colleagues (Keel, Mitchell, Miller, Davis, & Crow, 1999), very little was known about the long-term outcome of bulimia. Keel et al. (1999) tracked down 173 women who had been identified as having bulimia nervosa during the years between 1981 and 1987 (average of 11.5 years after the initial presentation). At the point of follow-up, 11% of the sample again met criteria for bulimia. Only 0.6% met criteria for anorexia; yet 18.5% met criteria for an unspecified eating disorder. Of note, 70% of the sample no longer met any criteria. Also of interest, a history of substance-use problems and a longer duration of the disorder at the time of initial presentation was found to be associated with a worse outcome at follow-up. Although these data contribute to our understanding, some of the women in this study had received psychotherapy and medications at some time during their history and such a situation complicates an understanding of the course of bulimia. Despite our limited knowledge, bulimia is often categorized as either chronic or intermittent.

Again, a diathesis-stress model serves as a reasonable integration of what is known about the cause of bulimia. Biological predispositions and environmental forces interact. It is not sufficient to have the predisposition or the environmental conditions—each contribution is needed.

Treatment

Treatments for anorexia nervosa include psychodynamic, behavioral, cognitive, and family systems approaches. Hospitalization, diet modification, medications, and force feeding have also been tried.

Psychodynamic treatments of anorexia have reported gains (Bruch, 1973), but research evaluations using acceptable methods are lacking. Minuchin and colleagues (1978) reported a successful family systems treatment, claiming that 86% of the 53 patients recovered from the anorexia. These results could be considered encouraging, but the evaluation was methodologically lacking.

Well-controlled outcome evaluations have primarily looked at behavioral or cognitive-behavioral treatments for anorexia (Vitousek & Orimoto, 1993). These programs aim to modify eating patterns, offer specific rewards for eating larger amounts of food, help the client identify faulty beliefs or expectations, and introduce doubt about the beliefs to diminish them.

One study compared cognitive-behavioral, interpersonal psychotherapy, and behavioral therapy for bulimia nervosa (Fairburn, Jones, Peveler, Hope, & O'Connor, 1993). The outcomes (see Figure 8.1) indicated that cognitive-behavioral therapy and interpersonal psycho-therapy produced comparable beneficial effects. The behavioral treatment was less effective than the other two. Over 5½ years later, Fairburn and colleagues followed up 90% of the treated cases and reported that over 50% of those receiving cognitive-behavioral or interpersonal therapy no longer qualified as having an eating disorder. The figure shows the proportions of the 75 participants who had not only ceased to have binge-eating episodes but who also ceased to vomit and take laxatives. The behavior therapy condition produced half the positive results of the other treatments. As can be seen, the different treatments had differential effects on the target problem. Results such as these indicate that bulimia can be treated with some success. Studies such as this—treatment-outcome research—provide invaluable information about the efficacy and effectiveness of various treatment efforts.

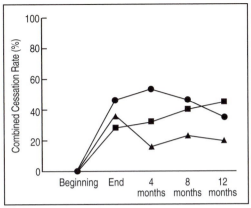

Figure 8.1.
Outcomes for different therapies for bulimia nervosa. Cognitive-behavioural (circles), interpersonal (squares), and behavioral (triangles) therapies were compared, with the evidence suggesting that not all treatments for bulimia nervosa are comparably effective. Fairburn et al. (1993, p. 423). Copyright 1993. American Medical Association.

Cognitive-behavioral and pharmacological treatments have also been used to treat bulimia (Craighead & Agras, 1991; Wilfrey et al., 1993). Medications, such as the antidepressants, are sometimes used in combination with psychosocial therapy: They have been found to reduce binging–purging, but long-term follow-ups are limited. A general conclusion about the literature on the treatment of bulimia can be taken from the wide-reaching meta-analytic review of 9 double-blind placebo-controlled medication trials (with a total of 870 participants) and 26 randomized psychosocial studies (with a total of 460 participants) reported by Whittal, Agras, and Gould (1999). These reviewers reported that, based on binge and purge frequency, depression, and self-monitored eating attitudes, cognitive-behavioral therapy produced significantly larger effects than medications for all treatment outcomes.

Considering the pressure placed on women in most cultures (Cohen, Brownell, & Felix, 1990), it is not surprising that many hold a strong desire to be thin. In excess, however, this desire is abnormal. Present approaches to treating and understanding eating disorders implicate family systems, the need for behavior modification, and the relevance of distorted cognitive processing that is in need of reformulation. Multifaceted treatments seem the order of the day.

Summary

Anorexia nervosa is characterized by an intense fear of becoming obese, a distorted self-perception of body image, refusal to maintain minimal body weight, and, in females, a cessation of menses. By far more common among females, anorexia if unchecked can lead to death. Family influences have been implicated in anorexia (each family member lacks a distinct identity, and the child fails to develop a personal sense of autonomy and independence). Family treatment and cognitive-behavioral treatments, as well as medications, have been applied with anorexic patients.

Bulimia nervosa is characterized by the rapid consumption of a large quantity of food in a discrete period of time while feeling out of control over the eating. It is also characterized by self-induced vomiting, use of diuretics, fasting, vigorous exercise, and overconcern with body weight.

Mental retardation and learning disabilities 9

Unlike earlier chapters that focused on disruptive behavior or disturbances in emotion, the focus of this chapter is on two related themes that both have to do with limitations or difficulties in intellectual activities. As we will see in more detail, mental retardation and learning disabilities are childhood disorders that present difficulties for the child in the areas of cognitive functioning. In the UK, both types of problems are listed under the one phrase "learning disabilities," whereas the separate phrase "mental retardation" has been maintained in many other countries. Like the disorders discussed thus far, children with mental retardation or learning disabilities can and do have other childhood disorders as well. It has been estimated that 20–35% of noninstitutionalized children and adults with mental retardation have other diagnoses or behavior problems (Handen, 1998).

Mental retardation

There is an association of professionals—the American Association on Mental Retardation (AAMD)—that has provided an accepted definition (1994) of this disorder: Mental retardation is significantly subaverage general intellectual functioning that exists concurrently with deficits in adaptive behavior. Adaptive behavior is the self-care skills (such as the ability to appropriately dress and groom oneself and hold a simple job) needed to live independently. A person identified as having mental retardation is significantly subaverage in intellectual functioning and is sometimes incapable of self-care or independent living. For a diagnosis of mental retardation, the disorder must be identified before the 18th birthday. Persons older than 18 who, for the first time, display subaverage intellectual functioning and fail to adapt independently are not diagnosed as mentally retarded.

Phenomenology and classification

It is important to keep in mind that the identification of mental retardation requires impairment in both intellectual and adaptive functioning (see Box 9.1). Accordingly, no single test can identify who is mentally retarded: Instead, multiple scores and several criteria are combined to make this judgment. For example, mental retardation is not simply a low score on an IQ test. In fact, some practitioners in the field assess levels of IQ only after deficits in adaptive behavior have already been identified.

To assess adaptive behaviors, psychologists use inventories such as the Adaptive Behavior Scale (Lambert, Nihira, & Leland, 1993), a measure of independent functioning, language development, responsibility, and economic, domestic, and physical activity (for alternate measures see Handen, 1998). Select examples of the areas of competence that are assessed are provided in Box 9.2. To assess intellectual ability, psychologists use well-standardized and recently normed tests such as revised forms of the Wechsler Intelligence Scale for Children (WISC-III) or the Stanford–Binet.

Who are the children with mental retardation?

Several broad studies have been conducted to determine the prevalence of mental retardation. Early estimates were quite varied, ranging from 1% to 13%. When the IQ score is used to assess mental retardation, prevalence rates of 3% are typical, whereas when adaptive behavior is the criterion, prevalence drop to 1% (McLaren & Bryson, 1987). Taking into account adaptive behavior makes a big difference! Using

Reprinted with permission from the Diagnostic and Statistical Manual of Mental Disorders, Fourth Edition. Copyright 1994 American Psychiatric Association.

BOX 9.1   DSM criteria for a diagnosis of mental retardation

- Significantly subaverage intellectual functioning: An IQ of approximately 70 or below on an individually administered IQ test.
- Concurrent deficits or impairments in present adaptive functioning (i.e. the person's effectiveness in meeting the standards expected for his or her age by his or her cultural group) in at least two of the following areas:
  * communication
  * social/interpersonal skills
  * functional academic skills
  * health
  * self-care
  * use of community resources
  * work
  * safety
  * home living
  * self-directiion
  * leisure.
- The onset is before age 18 years.

BOX 9.2 Assessing areas of competence

Determinations of mental retardation require assessments of a persons's adaptive functioning. Some of the areas of competence assessed as part of the evaluation of adaptive behavior among the mentally retarded include:

- independent functioning
- physical development
- economic activity
- language development
- numbers and time
- domestic activity
- vocational ability
- self-direction
- responsibility
- socialization.

only an IQ score could "damn" many more people with a limiting label when, in fact, what is important is whether or not you demonstrate adaptive behavior. Based on a review of studies conducted around the world, a range between 1% and 3% is an accepted prevalence estimate (Handen, 1998; Scott, 1994).

Are IQ test scores "fair"?

As has been mentioned, one of the criteria for mental retardation is an IQ score—more specifically, an IQ score equal to or greater than two standard deviations below the mean. On the WISC, for example, the average score is 100, with a standard deviation of 15; thus, a person with a score of 70 or less would meet one of the criteria for a diagnosis of mental retardation. Keep in mind that a change in the criterion—say 1 or 1.5 standard deviations instead of 2—would have a dramatic effect on the identification of mental retardation. What is normal and what is abnormal, in terms of IQ test scores, is based solely on a chosen criterion and the distribution of scores.

The theoretical distribution of IQ scores closely resembles the normal curve (the bell curve). Because only approximately 2% of the distribution earns an IQ score less than 70, 2% of the population—about 7.5 million people in the US—meet this criterion. But not all persons who score in the retarded range on IQ tests lack adaptive behavior, and vice versa. For example, in a study by Mastenbrook (1978; cited in Handen, 1997), children with IQ scores between 50 and 70 were also assessed for adaptive behavior. Fewer than 35% of these children were classified as mentally retarded based on the two-part definition.

One source of controversy regarding tests of intelligence has to do with their "fairness" or "unfairness," especially when used with disadvantaged individuals. To appraise the issue, we must know who the disadvantaged are. Most conceptualizations of disadvantage are relative: The disadvantaged are those, relative to others, who are hindered in leading productive lives in their society. This group may include low-income families, ethnic minorities, very rural families, and in some cases members of bilingual families. If these disadvantaged groups score lower on IQ tests, does it indicate that the tests are unfair?

Modern IQ tests use standardized samples that include representatives from all types of backgrounds. By so doing, the test strives to remain fair to all groups. Similarly, the content of the test—the actual test questions—aspire to be free from cultural bias. On these counts, many agree that the tests have attained fairness. How the test results are interpreted by human beings, however, is still open to potential unfairness. For example, someone could, in error, attempt to make a statement about a person's ethnic group based on the performance of only one individual from the group, such as saying that all ethnics are unintelligent because one ethnic person performed poorly. Here, the user of the test results is the one who is unfair, not necessarily the test itself.

Mental retardation occurs in varying degrees of severity (see Box 9.3). Although adaptive behavior and intellectual functioning are dual criteria, IQ test scores are often used to differentiate the levels of mental retardation (see Handen, 1998). Nevertheless, different levels of

---

BOX 9.3   Degrees of mental retardation and school-age (6–21) adaptive behavior

IQ scores are often used to determine degrees of retardation. Within the retarded range, there are associated levels of expected adaptive behavior.

Classification	IQ score	Adaptive Behavior
Very superior	130 and above	
Superior	120–129	
High average	110–119	
Average	90–109	
Low average	80–89	
Borderline	70–79	
Intellectually deficient	69 and below	
Mild retardation	55–70	Learn academic skills of 11-year-old by late teens; typically, cannot learn general high school subjects; need special education.
Moderate	40–55	Can learn functional academic skills of 9-year-old by late teens; special education necessary.
Severe	25–40	Can talk and learn to communicate and can be trained in elementary health habits; cannot learn functional academic skills, but do profit from habit training.
Profound	Less than 25	Some motor development is present, but they do not profit from training in self-help; need total care.

adaptive behavior can be expected for individuals with varying levels of retardation. Box 9.3 provides illustrative examples of the variations in potential outcomes for individuals at different ages. Of the total prevalence of mental retardation, approximately 89% are mildly retarded, 7% moderately retarded, 3% severely retarded, and 1% profoundly retarded (Madle, 1990).

The prevalence of mental retardation is affected by factors such as gender, socioeconomic status, and race. Most of the variation takes place within the mildly retarded category, whereas there is a more even distribution within the severe levels of retardation. Somewhat higher prevalence estimates are found among males (2:1), and there is a higher frequency among blacks than whites, although the ethnic variations are likely due to cultural and socioeconomic status factors associated with race. Social class is regularly linked to variations in the prevalence of mental retardation, with low socioeconomic status groups accounting for a disproportionate number of cases, especially mild retardation (Crnic, 1988; Scott, 1994).

Those individuals with mental retardation sometimes have other problems as well. Ambulatory problems, fine motor problems, and speech, hearing, and visual impairments are likely to coexist with mental retardation. Some persons have comorbid epilepsy and cerebral palsy.

Other psychological problems have also been identified among those with mental retardation (Einfeld & Aman, 1995; Johnson, Lubetsky, & Sacco, 1995). Data gathered in the UK reflect that 22% of mentally retarded young adults have problems with anxiety and 20% showed conduct disorder or antisocial behavior (Richardson, Katz, Koller, McLaren, & Rubinstein, 1979). Problems also exist with self-injurious behavior (Scott, 1994), and other reports have suggested that both depression (Matson & Barrett, 1982) and schizophrenia (Romanczyk & Kistner, 1982) can occur among retarded persons. Mental health disorders are three to four times more common in children (and adults) with mental retardation than in the general population (Scott, 1994). There is also a relationship between intellectual level and presence of a mental health disorder: The rates of disorder increase with more severe retardation. How is this explained? One hypothesis is that low intellectual functioning reduces the ability to cope with stress, restricts the environment, and contributes to distress in the family, and that these factors combine to contribute to additional disorder. In contrast, it might be that the presence of disorder not only limits intellectual development but also influences others to place limitations on intellectual development. Less likely, but it could also be the case that the retardation places limits on one's ability to understand and respond to structured diagnostic interviews.

Causes

The influence of genetics on normal as well as abnormal intelligence has been the subject of enormous controversy and a great deal of research. Controversy aside, what do the data tell us? Generally, research has revealed that genes contribute to individual differences in IQ scores (Sternberg & Grigorenko, 1999)—as the degree of genetic relatedness between two people increases, so too does the correlation between their IQ scores (Neisser et al., 1996). For example, the IQ scores of monozygotic (identical) twins are more alike than the scores of dizygotic (fraternal) twins (Plomin, 1989). Similarly, the correlations between IQ scores of adoptees and their biological families are larger than the correlations between scores of adoptees and their adoptive families (Plomin & DeFries, 1980; Scarr & Weinberg, 1976). However, an IQ score is not determined solely by genes—it is influenced by environmental factors as well (Neisser et al., 1996).

In general, mental retardation is a disorder whose cause is generally considered to be multifaceted, with genetic and environmental factors contributing. However, some specific instances of retardation can be attributed to genetics. Biological factors and prenatal and social environmental forces have also been found to be influential.

Biological factors. Certain biological factors are implicated in mental retardation. Chromosomal aberrations, for example, are associated with a specific syndrome of mental retardation first described in 1866 by the British physician, Langdon Down. Down's syndrome is a form of mental retardation caused by the presence of an extra 21st chromosome (Vandenberg & Crowe, 1989). Chromosome 21 emerges as a triplet instead of a pair; all of the other chromosomes are in pairs. The physical characteristics of the Down's syndrome child are usually quite apparent: The neck is short and broad, there is loose skin on the sides and back, height is below average, the head is small and the back of the head is flat, the eyes slant upward and have folds in the corners, muscle tone is poor (floppy), and hands are often short and square with short fingers. Brain anomalies in persons with Down's syndrome include low brain weight, reduced number of cells, and short dendrites (Coyle, Oster-Granite, & Gearhart, 1986). Individuals with this chromosomal abnormality regularly score in the subaverage range on measures of intellectual ability, although there is considerable variability in terms of intelligence scores and adaptive behavior.

Lenny had the physical characteristics of most Down's syndrome children: His face had a flat nose, his square-shaped ears and his mouth were small, his tongue protruded, and his neck was short and broad. Unfortunately, these characteristics, as well as his mental retardation, were the target for teasing by several children in his neighborhood. Although he rarely voiced complaints, Lenny did feel the rejection.

Now in his middle teens, Lenny was enrolled in a special placement class and had made friends with several other children with Down's syndrome in his school. His teacher described him as very likeable, responsive to directions and instructions, and one of the more popular youngsters in his group. One of Lenny's major accomplishments was that he was responsible for his classroom's fish tank—for feeding the fish and cleaning the tank. Prompts were sometimes required, but Lenny was nevertheless very proud of "his tank."

An interesting and important relationship exists between the age of the mother at the time of the child's birth and the incidence of Down's syndrome (Hook, 1987). Risk increases with increased mother's age. For mothers of age 20, the incidence is 1 in 2000. At 35, the rate of occurrence of Down's syndrome has been reported to be 1 in 500 births. At 45, the rate rises to 1 in 20 (Evans & Hammerton, 1985). There has been a report suggesting that the rate of Down's syndrome is also related to the father's age, but this is not widely accepted (Hook, Cross, & Regal, 1990; Steen & Steen, 1989).

Although it has been suggested that adults with Down's syndrome would show a rapid age-related decline in functioning, follow-up studies in the US (e.g. Burt, Loveland, Chen, & Chuang, 1995) and the UK (e.g. Shepperdson, 1995) evidenced minimal changes with age. More recently, a 5-year follow-up study of adults with Down's syndrome (Callocott & Cooper, 1997) reported that, especially for those over the age of 40, there was loss of some adaptive behavior skills with age. Lenny, described earlier, may have abilities as an adult that are best predicted by an initial IQ and that are not likely to show a dramatic decline with age beyond that seen in other adults. Some evidence suggests that, if they live long enough, persons with Down's syndrome will develop memory problems and multiple cognitive deficits (Alzheimer's-like) symptoms.

Other forms of mental retardation, in addition to Down's syndrome, are associated with chromosomal abnormalities. The fragile X syndrome, named for a constricted region at the end of the X chromosome, has associated physical features as well as intellectual deficiencies. Physical features include short stature, prominent forehead, prominent mandible, and large ears, hands, and feet. The fragile X syndrome is more commonly seen in males. Nevertheless, autistic behaviors were reported in girls with fragile X syndrome (Mazzocco, Kates, Baumgardner, Freund, & Reiss, 1997). In one study (Dykens, Hodapp, Ort, & Leckman, 1993), males with fragile X syndrome were found to make positive gains in adaptive behavior over a 2-year period. The participants, especially the older ones, showed strengths in daily living skills. Further changes with development were studied using both longitudinal and cross-sectional approaches, with data coming from six centers. Dykens et al. (1996) reported that boys aged 1 to 10 showed significant gains in adaptive behavior whereas adaptive behavior plateaued and was stable from ages 11 to 20.

Another disorder, phenylketonuria (PKU), is organic and genetically determined. It is a hereditary error of metabolism resulting from an inactive liver enzyme. Infants with PKU are normal at birth but, if untreated, will develop mental retardation during the first year of life. Quite fortunately, research has determined that if identified early and placed on a special diet soon after birth, children with PKU will develop normally.

Carriers of PKU pass on a recessive gene to their children. If these children marry a person who also carries the recessive gene, they may have offspring who are affected (Vandenberg & Crowe, 1989). PKU is rare, occurring only once in approximately 14,000 births (Rubenstein, Lotspeich, & Ciaranello, 1990), and is associated with moderate to profound retardation. This form of retardation is no more prevalent in family members of the affected individual than in the general population, and it occurs equally across the social classes. Unlike many other forces that cause mental retardation, the intellectual deficit associated with PKU can be prevented through early detection and dietary modification. In the US, for example, the law requires postnatal blood testing to promote prevention.

Other organic forces, such as infections, poisons, and malnutrition, are also factors in retardation. Cranial anomalies and head injuries can cause retardation as well. It is certainly easy to recognize that malformed or dysfunctional portions of the brain, as well as injuries to portions of the brain, can have serious detrimental effects on mental functioning.

Prenatal environment. It is widely accepted that unhealthy influences in the prenatal environment can damage the intellectual ability of the offspring. Health problems in the mother have significant effects on the fetus. Maternal conditions such as poor nutrition, tobacco smoking and alcohol consumption, infections, drugs, radiation, and a lack of oxygen contribute to subnormal intelligence in the child. These maternal health behaviors can be monitored and changed, and the outcome can affect the fetus (Streissguth, Barr, Sampson, Darby, & Martin, 1989).

Alcohol readily crosses the placenta of the pregnant woman and exposes the developing fetus to a wide range of harmful effects. Uniformly, because even small amounts of alcohol may not be safe (Jones, 1988), researchers recommend that pregnant women abstain from alcohol during pregnancy. In the most extreme cases, for four to twelve infants per 10,000 births, the mother's drinking during pregnancy causes permanent physical damage to the infant, a condition known as fetal alcohol syndrome (Clarren & Smith, 1978; Jones & Smith, 1973). Fetal alcohol effects include a retardation of physical growth as well as neurological and intellectual retardation (Neisser et al., 1996). Aronson, Hagberg, and Gillberg (1997) reported that children born to mothers who had abused alcohol throughout pregnancy had severe intellectual and behavioral problems that remained at age 11–14 years. Also, there was a correlation between the occurrence and severity of the disorder and the degree of alcohol exposure *in utero*. The exact amount of maternal alcohol consumption necessary to produce fetal alcohol syndrome is not yet known, but increasingly, concerned, health-conscious pregnant women are discontinuing alcohol consumption during pregnancy.

Social environment.   Our minds and mental faculties are sparked by the environments to which we are exposed. Environmental factors, such as extreme psychological and social deprivation, are implicated in the cause of mental retardation. Because it is unethical to manipulate environments in ways that might restrict intellectual development, consider studies done with animals. Animals reared in deprived environments showed behavioral deficits as well as lighter brains, with less cortical depth and fewer synapses (e.g. Rosenzweig, Bennett, & Diamond, 1972). Lack of contact with people of normal intelligence, limited access to books and verbal stimulation, and an absence of educational opportunities do impede intellectual development, and it is not difficult to imagine that individuals raised in a culturally deprived environment—one that lacks learning opportunities—are likely to register lower IQ scores. Poverty also hampers intellectual development—economically disadvantaged youngsters are at risk for intellectually deprived lives. Indeed, poverty can have unwanted effects on many features of psychological adjustment—without available resources, the ability to cope with life's difficulties can be hampered. Large family size, poor nutrition, lack of organization in the home, and low expectations for academic achievement can depress intellectual growth. The following case example described by Repp and Deitz (1983) is worth contemplation.

> Steve's parents were migrant workers, so he has moved numerous times. His mother went back to work shortly after he was born, and an older sister took care of him. His sister wanted him to be quiet and nondemanding, and she yelled at him for most behaviors other than sitting quietly. When his parents came home from work, they were tired and wanted to be left alone. He was again urged to keep quiet and out of trouble. The family's living quarters were always sparsely furnished, and Steve had only a few toys, of which he had tired long ago.
>
> When Steve was enrolled in school, his language level was very low for his age. In addition, he did not possess the academic readiness skills that his peers exhibited. Steve was referred for evaluation and, after being given a battery of standardized tests, he was labeled as retarded and placed in a classroom for the retarded.

Not all cases of mental retardation are the same, and the causal pathways are equally dissimilar. Biological causes of mental retardation are identified more often in children with severe cognitive delays. Some children's retardation may simply reflect the low end of the intellectual distribution and these cases may have had a greater environmental influence. For example, McLaren and Bryson (1987) reported that biological causes were more likely (70% vs 50%) in severe mental retardation than in mild retardation.

Services

Wicks-Nelson and Israel (1991) described three types of services for mental retardation: placement, treatment, and education.

Placement refers to the living arrangements that must be organized for the person. At one time in history, most persons with mental retardation were placed in public institutions that provided nothing more than custodial care. Since the 1960s, this practice has declined in the US and the UK, and the decline can be attributed in part to the criticisms directed at large public institutions. The settings were criticized as being cold and lacking in human interaction, having a shortage of services, and being poorly staffed. Alternative arrangements, such as community centers, provide a more home-like atmosphere and a greater opportunity for the person with mental retardation to interact with people and the local environment. One current trend that appears to be on the rise is not to seek an outside-of-the-home placement, but rather to allow the retarded child to stay at home with the family. Although parents need assistance with daily care, as well as a break from the demands of continuous supervision, an increasing number of mentally retarded youngsters are remaining with the family during childhood.

Treatment for the mentally retarded refers to interventions aimed at the remediation of the associated emotional and behavioral problems. Research reports have indicated that a substantial number of mentally retarded persons also suffer from psychological disorders (Matson & Barrett, 1982). A survey of more than 8000 mentally retarded persons (infants to adolescents) conducted in New York revealed that 9.8% had significant mental health needs (Jacobson, 1982a, 1982b). The identified problems included cognitive (hallucinations), emotional (depression), and behavioral (aggression, self-injury) disorders. Across levels of intellectual functioning, an average of half of the patients were found to have behavior problems (from 38% to 65%). Not surprisingly, those with dual diagnoses were more likely to have behavior problems.

The treatments that are applied for the emotional and behavior problems in the mentally retarded resemble the treatments used with the general population, with some adjustments because of the clients' level of conceptual ability. There is a strong tendency for the treatments to follow the behavioral orientation (Baer, Wolf, & Risley, 1968; Birnbauer, 1976; Huguenin, Weidenman, & Mulick, 1991). Behavioral training programs focus on teaching retarded clients specific skills for more adaptive functioning. These programs emphasize the contingent application of rewards and take many forms. Social reinforcers (such as smiles, verbal praise, or a pat on the back) work particularly well with retarded persons. Behavioral methods have been successfully used, for example, to reduce disruptive behavior (Zimmerman, Zimmerman, & Russell, 1969), control aggressive behavior (Mace, Kratochwill, & Fiello, 1983), improve toileting (Giles & Wolf, 1966), and control public masturbation (Barmann & Murray, 1981) among retarded persons. Other applications have been successful with overcoming food refusal (Handen, Mandell, & Russo, 1986) and sleep problems (e.g. Ashbaugh & Peck, 1998; Piazza & Fisher, 1991).

Family members are increasingly involved in treatments for the mentally retarded (Baker, Landen, & Kashima, 1991; Crnic, Friedrich, & Greenberg, 1983; Crnic & Reid, 1989). Maintaining a behavioral orientation, these treatments focus not only on specific child problems that require change but also on the goals and feelings of the family and the family's learning and use of behavior modification procedures to rear their special needs child. In one sense, when family members are taught behavioral procedures, there is an increased opportunity for the application of these procedures (both in the home and elsewhere) and a corresponding increase in the potential for beneficial effects.

Treatments for retardation do not cure the disorder. That is, mental retardation is not erased by the interventions. The programs do produce desired gains in the targeted behavior problems, and these gains do contribute to a better life for the recipients.

To achieve that "better life," education is important. So too for the mentally retarded. In the US, considerable litigation eventually produced laws aimed at guaranteeing education for the retarded (Katz-Garris, 1978). The Education for All Handicapped Children Act of 1975 (Public Law 94-142) requires that all handicapped children receive a free public education designed to meet their specific needs, that the rights of the handicapped be protected, and that the effectiveness of the educational programs be assessed and evaluated. It also stipulates that the education be provided in the least restrictive environment, which means that retarded children should be placed in classrooms with nonretarded children whenever possible.

Educational interventions with the mentally retarded include using specific teaching strategies to facilitate their learning and programming the learning environment at school and at home to meet their needs. Although the teaching strategies that are used may resemble those used in regular classes, there are adjustments for the pace and level of the learner. Concerns about class size and teacher–student ratios have been addressed in special education classrooms; special education classes have fewer students and a higher teacher–student ratio than regular classes. But special education settings have been criticized for isolating the retarded and limiting their contact with normal children. The movement away from segregated classes to the integration of special needs with regular students has been called *mainstreaming*. Preliminary research suggested that the integrated classroom may offer moderate benefits (Haywood, Meyers, & Switzky, 1982). Although communities have been reported to hold mildly positive attitudes (Eiserman, Shisler, & Healey, 1995) and recommendations for how to facilitate mainstreaming have been offered (Mortimer, 1995), reviews of the research concluded that mainstreaming has not enhanced social development in special needs children, and there is little convincing evidence that they perform any better academically (MacMillan, Keogh, & Jones, 1986). What is your opinion about mainstreaming?

Programs for the home have been designed to enhance the learning environments of children whose environments had inadequate resources for development. Head Start, for instance, is a prevention program designed to increase cognitive and social stimulation for children at risk because of their economic and cultural deprivation.

Medications

Although drug therapy is used with the retarded, it is not intended to be a cure for retardation or to improve intellectual abilities. As with other populations, medications are aimed at reducing behavioral and emotional conditions (see Handen, 1998). Examples of the conditions likely to improve with medication are disruptive behavior, psychotic symptoms, or attentional problems. Surveys of institutionalized persons have indicated that 40–50% are receiving psychotropic medications (Aman & Singh, 1983). Those most likely to be medicated are older individuals with more severe behavior problems. Perhaps because of their distance from mental health services, the overall medication rate is lower for noninstitutionalized individuals.

Anticonvulsant medications are routinely prescribed for the suppression of seizures. Among the retarded, these medications are widely used, although there is not always evidence of seizure disorder. Researchers have suggested that this practice may be the result of the unsupported belief that anticonvulsants reduce behavior problems (Crnic & Reid, 1989).

As was true for ADHD, stimulant medications are used with mentally retarded children who evidence attentional problems— estimated to be 9–18%. Although data have supported the effects of these medications with ADHD children, their effectiveness with retarded children has yet to be fully studied or clearly demonstrated. Preliminary data hint to a relationship between effectiveness and severity: Stimulants are not useful with severe retardation (Gadow, 1992) but can be safe and effective for some hyperactive children with mild to moderate retardation (Handen et al., 1992). Other studies suggest a positive drug response in 60–70% of mildly retarded youngsters, but there is little evidence regarding outcomes for the severe to profound ranges of mental retardation (Aman, Marks, Turbott, Wilsher, & Merry, 1991).

There is a notable lack of well-designed and properly controlled evaluations of the use of medications with mentally retarded individuals, yet there continues to be widespread use. The absence of appropriate control groups and the failure to include a measure of learning are two examples of major weaknesses (Crnic & Reid, 1989). Truly determining the effects of medications is not possible until these methodological problems are corrected.

Learning disabilities

Ethan—an attractive and athletic 12-year-old—was not mentally retarded, but his mathematics ability was severely restricted. Despite the results of intelligence tests indicating that his IQ score was in the normal range, his performance in math was well below age and grade level. As an 11- year-old (in 6th grade in the US), and despite his parents trying to help, Ethan was alone in his struggles with basic subtraction and multiplication. When shopping, for example, Ethan could not determine the total costs of his purchases nor calculate correct change.

Phenomenology and classification

Use of the phrase "learning disability" has become widespread and the number of children identified as learning disabled has increased markedly, with estimates ranging from 5% to 15% (Taylor, 1989). Males are more frequently identified than females, often in a ratio of between 2:1 and 5:1 (Taylor, 1989). Variations in the estimates, however, result from the inconsistency in the definition used to identify children with a learning disability.

One method defines learning disability as a discrepancy between performance on tests of intellectual functioning (e.g. IQ) and performance on tests of educational achievement. For example, a normal IQ score with below-average achievement in a particular academic topic. This criterion has been recorded as "failing in one or more basic achievement skill areas despite normal intelligence" (Kistner & Torgesen, 1987, p. 289).

Below expected age- and grade-level performance is an alternate definition of learning disability. Recall Ethan, whose mathematics learning disorder was based on below expected grade-level performance. Use of age or grade level as a cutoff creates problems: How discrepant must the scores be? One year? Two years? Although a 1- or 2-year discrepancy is often used, the impact of a grade-level discrepancy changes with increasing age. For example, being 2 years behind is more troublesome for a 10-year-old than for a 13-year-old. Keep in mind that the determination of learning disorders is not without problems. Based on a review of the literature, Morris (1988, p. 793) offered a critical conclusion: "The most commonly used classification systems and definitions of learning disabled children do not meet basic empirical criteria for reliability and validity."

The statutory definition of learning disabilities, in the Individuals with Disabilities Education Act (IDEA, 1990, p. 300), states:

> The term, "specific learning disability" means a disorder in one or more of the basic psychological processes involved in understanding or in using language, spoken or written, which may manifest itself in an imperfect ability to listen, speak, read, write, or spell, or to do mathematical calculations.

DSM-IV defines learning disorders (also called academic skills disorders) using a combination of the IQ score–achievement discrepancy approach and the below age- and grade-level approach. DSM-IV diagnoses include reading disorder, mathematics disorder, and disorder of written expression, as well as learning disorder not otherwise specified. In each disorder, specific academic achievement, as measured by an individually administered standardized test, is considered below that expected given the person's chronological age, measured intelligence, and age-appropriate education. In addition, the condition must interfere with academic achievement or activities of daily living. According to Lyon and Cutting (1998), reading disabilities are the most common learning disability, affecting 60–80% of children receiving special education (LD) services (Lerner, 1989).

The need to weigh exclusionary criteria deserves mention. Should a learning disability be independent of emotional or behavioral problems? Research often finds emotional and behavioral complications in children with learning disability (e.g. Lahey, Green, & Forehand, 1980). For instance, ADHD is often associated with learning difficulties. Estimates vary, but approximately 75% of ADHD boys in a sample from the US were underachieving, and about 33% were performing at least one grade below their expected level (Cantwell, 1987). Estimates of the percentage of ADHD children who have learning disabilities vary widely (Wicks-Nelson & Israel, 1991), with some agreement that about 15% of children with ADHD have a formally defined learning disability (Hinshaw, 1992). Learning-disabled children are also less socially competent than their peers (Toro, Weissberg, Guare, & Liebenstein, 1990), more likely to have internalizing disorders (Thompson & Kronenberger, 1990), and more likely to be involved in delinquency (Brier, 1989). Not all learning-disordered children have these or other emotional or behavior problems, but the extent of comorbidity is sufficient to rule out the idea that a learning disorder must be independent of an emotional or behavioral problem.

Nevertheless, in the IDEA (1990), there are statements suggesting exclusions.

> learning disabilities include conditions such as perceptual handicaps, brain injury, and developmental aphasia, but do not include children who have learning difficulties which are primarily the result of visual, hearing or motor handicaps, or mental retardation or emotional disturbance, or of environmental, cultural, or economic disadvantage.

Although the exact operations used to define the exclusion criteria are not provided, it is clear that the statutory definition is delimiting.

Causes

The exact causes of learning disabilities are, at present, unknown. Genetic factors, difficulties in brain function, and cognitive and motivational influences have all been examined as possible links to learning disorders. We do not yet know, for example, if learning disabilities result from cognitive processing deficits or deficits in motivation or achievement.

Research into genetic causes has been reviewed by Smith, Pennington, Kimberling, and Ing (1990). Children of parents with reading difficulties have a greater chance of reading problems than children of parents who read normally, but these data could be viewed as supporting either a genetic or family environment explanation, or both. A 4-year follow-up study of Latin American children found that 17% of children with reading disabilities had become average readers. Improvements are possible.

Brain dysfunction may contribute to learning disorders. According to Taylor (1989), children who have experienced head injury, central nervous system infection, neurological problems, or epilepsy are at higher risk for learning problems than are other children. Not all children with a history of these conditions develop a learning disability, however, and these same conditions can contribute to other emotional and behavioral problems.

Psychological theories have tended to emphasize motivational and cognitive explanations of learning disability. Learning-disabled children may experience an initial degree of failure, come to doubt their abilities, and fail to put forth effort on future tasks. Their expectations for success are lower and, as one study found, they are less likely than nondisabled children to attribute success to their ability, yet more likely to attribute failure to a lack of ability (Tarnowski & Nay, 1989).

Several writers, based on reviews of the literature, have suggested that there is empirical support for differentiating learning-disabled from nondisabled children on the basis of information-processing characteristics (Kistner & Torgesen, 1987; Torgesen, 1986; Wong, 1985). The difficulties in cognitive processing that have been promoted as influential in learning disability have included limited attentional focusing and failure to use effective learning strategies. For example, when learning a list of words, nondisabled readers use memory strategies to enhance recall. Reading-disabled children are less likely to use memory strategies such as rehearsal, clustering, or elaboration.

Treatments

Treatments for learning disability are often consistent with the view that these children have difficulties with cognitive-processing strategies (Lyon & Cutting, 1998). For example, one group of learning-disabled children improved their reading comprehension after they were taught to monitor their performance by asking themselves questions while they read (Wong & Jones, 1982). Interestingly, the same strategy was taught to students who were not learning disabled, and their performance was not as enhanced. Perhaps self-questioning helped the learning-disabled children, but not the nondisabled group, because the learning-disabled group initially lacked self-questioning and self-monitoring.

Torgesen (1979) further documented the effectiveness of strategy training. Pictures of objects from four different categories were shown to good and poor readers in the fourth grade. The children were instructed that they would be asked to recall the pictures and that they could do anything they wanted to help them remember the pictures. The children's behavior was observed through a one-way mirror. Compared with the good readers, the poor readers were less likely to organize the pictures into categories, spent more time off-task, and recalled fewer pictures. When these same poor readers were taught to use a categorical clustering strategy, they were able to recall as well as the good readers. Moreover, the time they spent off-task fell to a level that was comparable to that of the good readers. Apparently, various cognitive strategy training approaches have had some beneficial effects with children identified as learning disabled (Hallahan, Kneedler, & Lloyd, 1983; Wong, Harris, & Graham, 1991). Adolescents with learning disabilities have been found to show improved mathematics ability when interventions using strategy instruction, self-monitoring strategies, and cooperative homework assignments have been applied (Maccini & Hughes, 1997). However, it should be kept in mind that not all children in need have the benefit of receiving proper interventions, and, even among those in some form of remedial program, the effects are not always favorable. One report (Shaywitz, Fletcher, & Shaywitz, 1994) indicated that approximately three-quarters of reading disabled 9-year-old children continued to manifest reading difficulties through their high school years.

Working with the individual child may not be enough, as evident in a recommendation from the National Agenda for improving services for children with needs. Collaboration with families is one target for the improvement of services (Cheney & Osher, 1997). Families can be involved in the planning and implementation of the services, and family support groups can be provided. The latter influence the families' ability to participate in the former.

Summary

Mental retardation is significantly subaverage general intellectual functioning that exists concurrently with deficits in adaptive behavior. Indeed, adaptive behavior is an important component of the determination of mental retardation. In terms of IQ level, scores that are equal to or greater than two standard deviations below the mean are indicative of retardation. Estimates have suggested a 1–3% prevalence of mental retardation, with approximately 89% of these in the mildly retarded range. Gender, race, and socioeconomic factors are involved. The causes of mental retardation include biological (e.g. genetic) as well as environmental forces. Interventions for individuals with mental retardation strive not to cure the problem, but to teach adaptive skills and maximize individual potential.

One definition of learning disability relies on a discrepancy between intellectual ability and achievement. An alternate definition of learning disability is below expected age- and grade-level performance. DSM-IV defines learning disorders (academic skills disorders) using a combination of the IQ-achievement discrepancy approach and the below age- and grade-level approach. Biological and environmental factors are said to contribute to learning disorders, but the exact causes are unknown.

Pervasive developmental disorders 10

"Pervasive developmental disorder" is the phrase presently used to refer to severe psychological problems emerging in infancy. Pervasive developmental disorders involve severe upset in the child's cognitive, social, behavioral, and emotional growth that produces widespread complication of the developmental process (Lord & Rutter, 1994; Rutter & Schopler, 1987). DSM-IV includes several pervasive developmental disorders, although one, autism, has clearly become the dominant pervasive developmental disorder in both the research and clinical realm. Autism affects basic human qualities: interpersonal socialization and complex communication. Children with autism demonstrate severe impairments in social interaction and relationships, interpersonal play, and communication.

Historically, there were two pervasive developmental disorders: autism and childhood schizophrenia. Because childhood schizophrenia has sometimes been viewed as the same as the adult disorder, descriptions of the adult disorder and the diagnostic procedures for adult schizophrenia have been applied to children. Childhood schizophrenia may resemble the adult disorder in the presence of severe withdrawal and an inability to relate to others, but delusions and hallucinations are less common in children. Children with schizophrenia-spectrum disorders have been found to evidence thought disorder within a family interaction context (Tompson, Asarnow, Hamilton, Newell, & Goldstein, 1997). Age of onset is key in differentiating childhood schizophrenia from autism: Children with schizophrenia have a period of relatively normal adjustment followed by the onset of the severe symptoms of schizophrenia, whereas autism is evident very early in life. Recent advances, however, suggest that severe disorders with early onset are different from adult schizophrenia and that a schizophrenic disorder resembling that seen in adults does not appear until after puberty (Newsom & Hovanitz, 1997).

Autism

Nadia, at age six, produced a drawing of a rooster. The drawing was intricate, complex, and remarkably accurate. Nadia possessed genuine artistic talent, but she did not speak. She preferred to be alone, in a room that she kept in a rigid order, where she would sit unresponsive to the presence of others. Nadia was diagnosed as autistic. A pervasive developmental problem, autistic disorder includes a lack of responsiveness to people and severely delayed language development. The problems begin before the child is 36 months old. It is interesting, if sad, to note that when therapy was effective in promoting Nadia's communication with other people, her artistic talents declined.

Phenomenology and classification

As mentioned earlier, children with autism show severe impairments in interpersonal socialization (relationships, play) and complex communication. Kanner (1943) was the first to describe autism. According to Kanner (p. 242), the outstanding, fundamental feature in autism is "the children's inability to relate themselves in the ordinary way to people and situations from the beginning of life." The severity of the disorder is exemplified by Chuck, a child who had many of the characteristic features of autism:

Chuck was an attractive 5-year-old of average height and weight, yet he never seemed to hear or respond to other people. His parents had once thought that he was deaf or severely hearing impaired. Adults could come and go from the room, and there would be no indication that Chuck was aware of their movement. When someone called to him directly by name, there was no answer. Usually, adults had to tap his shoulder before he would show even minimal signs of acknowledgment. Chuck did respond to changes in his environment—when a chair was moved to add a place at the kitchen table, Chuck had a temper outburst. Rearranging living room furniture or adding a new bookcase to a room distressed Chuck, but he was still unlikely to initiate any form of communication. Even in play there was something odd about his behavior. He showed an extreme intensity while playing alone. In one instance, Chuck played with a broken light switch for more than 30 minutes.

Some of the early symptoms of autistic disorder were outlined by Borden and Ollendick (1992). In the newborn, the baby seems different from other babies, seems not to need the mother, is indifferent to being held, has flaccid muscle tone, and cries infrequently but may be intensely irritable. In the first 6 months, the baby fails to notice the mother; is undemanding; has delayed or absent smiling, babbling, or anticipatory responses; and lacks interest in toys. In the second 6 months, the child shows no interest in social games, is unaffectionate, demonstrates an absence of verbal and nonverbal communication, and is underreactive or overreactive to stimulation. Can autism be diagnosed in children before the age of 3? Recent data (Stone et al., 1999) indicate that diagnoses of autism, often using social deficits and delays in spoken language, can be done reliably before the age of 3.

Often, parents of autistic children are the first to have noticed that the children are unresponsive socially. The severely autistic child's imperviousness to the social and physical environment does not lie on a continuum with normal behavior (Wenar, Ruttenberg, Kalish-Weiss, & Wolf, 1986). According to Wenar (1982), the autistic child approaches the world as intrinsically noxious. Descriptions of autistic children often mention their lack of cuddling in the early months of life, an obsessive desire for sameness in the environment, self-stimulatory behaviors (such as rocking, spinning, and arm flapping), self-destructive behaviors (such as head banging, arm banging, and self-biting), lack of eye contact (gaze avoidance) with other people, and fascination with inanimate objects (see also Newsom & Hovanitz, 1997). A research study found that autistic children engaged in more ritualized behavior and initiated interactions with peers much less frequently than retarded youth (Hauck, Fein, Waterhouse, & Feinstein, 1995). Lack of responsiveness to people is a characteristic of autistic children—a characteristic that contributes meaningfully to parental frustration when caregiving.

From the wide array of unusual behavior seen in autism, DSM-IV identifies three key features: (1) qualitative impairment in social interaction, (2) severe impairments in communication, and (3) restricted, repetitive, and stereotyped patterns of behavior. Onset occurs before age three. According to Volkmar (1996), this definition is consistent with the ICD-10 (WHO, 1992). The details of the diagnostic criteria are presented in Box 10.1.

Echolalia is one striking example of the communication difficulties typical of autistic children. Echolalia is the repetition or echoing back of speech, as in the following example:

Reprinted with
permission from the
Diagnostic and
Statistical Manual of
Mental Disorders,
Fourth Edition.
Copyright 1994
American Psychiatric
Association.

BOX 10.1   Criteria for a diagnosis of autism

A child reaches the diagnostic criteria for autism if the child evidences at least 6 items from the categories provided below, with at least 2 from the first category and 1 from each of the second and third categories. The child must evidence onset before the age of 3.

First category: Qualitative impairment in social interaction
- marked impairment in the use of multiple nonverbal behaviors such as eye-to-eye gaze, facial expression, body posture, and gestures to regulate social interaction
- failure to develop peer relationships appropriate to developmental level
- lack of spontaneous seeking to share enjoyment, interests, or achievements with other people
- lack of social or emotional reciprocity.

Second category: Qualitative impairments in communication
- delay in, or total lack of, the development of spoken language in individuals with adequate speech
- in individuals with adequate speech, marked impairments in the ability to initiate or sustain a conversation with others
- stereotyped and repetitive use of language or idiosyncratic language
- lack of varied spontaneous make-believe play or social imitative play appropriate to developmental level.

Third category: Restrictive, repetitive, and stereotyped patterns of behavior, interests, and activities
- encompassing preoccupation with one or more stereotyped and restricted patterns of interest that is abnormal either in intensity or focus
- apparently compulsive adherence to specific, nonfunctional routines or rituals
- stereotypes and repetitive motor mannerisms (e.g. hand- or finger-flapping, complex whole body movements)
- persistent preoccupation with parts of objects.

Therapist:	Can you point to Chuck's shoe?
Chuck:	Can you point to Chuck's shoe?
Therapist:	Use this finger [touches finger] and point like this to your shoe [directs finger pointing].
Chuck:	Point like this to your shoe.

Because communication problems like this occur very early in life, they probably reflect an inherent cognitive defect (Rutter, 1978).

What could this defect be? Much recent research has focused on perceptual and cognitive difficulties that might underlie echolalia and other symptoms of autism (Donnellan, 1985; Litrownik & McInnis, 1986; Prior, 1984). For example, many studies have examined autistic children's tendency to display stimulus overselectivity—responding to only select aspects of stimulus materials (see Lovaas, Koegel, & Schreibman, 1979). For instance, let us suppose that a therapist who is trying to teach language skills shows a picture of a shoe to an autistic child, says the word "shoe," and emphasizes the movements of the mouth to make the sounds. The autistic child might look at the picture, but fail to attend to the sounds. Autistic children seem unable to pay attention to more than one cue (stimulus feature) at a time. What may make matters worse is that they may pay attention to idiosyncratic and often irrelevant stimuli. For example, touching the paper on which the picture is printed, but not attending to the picture or to the sounds. This pattern of attention hinders their ability to communicate and to interact with the social and physical environment.

Processing and integrating information also present as difficulties for autistic children. For example, they do not use the meaning of words to assist in the recall of information nor do they reorganize incoming information to reduce redundancy (Hermelin, 1976). Autistic children have difficulty transforming or manipulating information in their minds (Shulman, Yirmiya, & Greenbaum, 1995). Autism can be described as a disorder of multiple primary deficits (Goodman, 1989).

Recent thinking has suggested that autistic children have a deficit in their understanding of their own and others' mental states. "Theory of mind" has been described as the ability to consider people in terms of internal mental states, such as beliefs, intentions, and emotions, and an understanding of the social environment and the ability to engage in socially competent behavior has been said to be linked to a person's having a "theory of mind." Many studies have examined theory of mind in children with autism (e.g. Baron-Cohen, Leslie, & Frith, 1985; Bauminger & Kasari, 1999), and most studies have indicated that these children do have limited abilities. It is worth noting that the data do not suggest that a limited understanding of others' mental states is the cause of autism. However, although it may be related to general cognitive ability, it does appear that a limited theory of mind is a descriptive feature of children having autism.

Some autistic children achieve IQ scores in the normal range, and some display some remarkable mental abilities (5–10% of autistic persons; O'Connor & Hermelin, 1988), but the majority of persons with autism show intellectual deficits that fall into the retarded range (Bristol et al., 1996; Rutter & Schopler, 1987). Because the lower IQ scores are related to both more severe communication problems and a poorer prognosis, researchers have suggested that children with autistic disorder be divided into high- and low-functioning groups. High-functioning autistic children typically have a better prognosis (Newsom, 1998), but not all studies find meaningful differences between high- and low-functioning cases (Myles, Simpson, & Johnson, 1995).

Perhaps you were wondering about the "remarkable mental abilities" mentioned earlier. With regard to these rare but quite interesting people, recall the character portrayed by Dustin Hoffman in the movie *Rain Man*. The character, whose pattern was that of someone with an autistic disorder, could perform remarkable calendar calculations, determining the day of the week of a date several years in the future. Equally impressive, if not equally puzzling, Nadia's drawing of a rooster mentioned earlier in this chapter illustrated remarkable special talents that are seen in a small percentage of autistic children.

Structured approaches to diagnosing autism (e.g. autism diagnostic interview) have shown international applicability (Lord et al., 1997). Diagnoses can be reached using parent reports of current behavior, but the accuracy is enhanced if a behavioral history is taken into account (Lord et al., 1997). It is important to keep in mind that, although the field has made substantial progress in assessing and classifying autism (e.g. Cohen, Paul, & Volkmar, 1986), there are still sources of uncertainty as well as advocates for other approaches. For example, the classification and study of children with autistic disorder has sometimes followed an approach referred to as "autistic spectrum" (Wing & Attwood, 1987). That is, to learn about the disorder, children with varying degrees of symptoms would be studied. The continuum is one of pervasiveness and severity. At the pervasive end of the continuum fall those children who are profoundly retarded, multiply handicapped, and with profound impairments across intellectual, adaptive, social, language, and motor functioning. At the least pervasive end of the continuum are children with relatively mild impairment in one domain.

Who are the autistic children?

Autistic disorder is relatively rare, occurring in only 5–10 births per 10,000 (Bristol et al., 1996; Lord & Rutter, 1994). For example, recent data from a population-based study of Norwegian children 3–14 years of age (Sponheim & Skjeldal, 1998) indicated a prevalence rate of 4–5 per 10,000. According to Newsom and Hovanitz (1997), the two best studies of the prevalence of autism were conducted in the UK (Lotter, 1966; Wing, Yeates, Brierley, & Gould, 1976) and produced comparable estimates: 4.5 per 10,000.

Autism is seen in both genders, but at a frequency that is three to four times higher in boys than in girls (Bryson, 1996). One study of gender differences among higher-functioning persons with autistic disorder reported that males were rated to be more severely autistic than females in terms of early social development but not on stereotypic behaviors (McLennan, Lord, & Schopler, 1993).

Autism has been found in families throughout the world and in all social classes (Gilberg, 1990; Sponheim & Skjeldal, 1998). Some data, however, suggest different prevalence rates in certain countries. In China, for instance, Kuo-Tai (1987) reported only 5 cases from among 1190 childhood psychiatric clients over a 26-year period. What about the rate of autism relative to all births? Kuo-Tai (1987) set the population of Nanjing, a city in China, at 4.5 million; only two cases of autism came from the entire population of Nanjing. At the other end of the distribution is Japan, where the prevalence rates for autism have been estimated to be higher than elsewhere in the world. One study reported a prevalence of 0.16% (Tanoue, Oda, Asano, & Kawashima, 1988). Another, which examined 12,263 Japanese children, reported a minimum prevalence of 0.13% (Sugiyama & Abe, 1989). What might be an explanation for these differences?

At present there is no apparent explanation for the different prevalence rates. Perhaps, a failure to identify all of the true cases of autism, because of any of a variety of reasons, could explain the very low frequency in China. Other possibilities include methodological dissimilarities (for example, studies of population-based samples versus studies of clinic samples) and diagnostic differences (such as use of different diagnostic criteria). It is also possible that the differences are real, and research is needed to test hypotheses to help explain them. For example, are birthing practices, nutritional variations, or genetic factors contributing to different prevalence rates?

Causes

What could conceivably cause this extremely serious disorder called autism? A historically relevant theory proposed by Bettelheim (1967) was influential for well over a decade. During the 1950s and 1960s, psychoanalytic theory was prevalent, and Bettelheim's notions were in this tradition. He argued that when a child faces an unresponsive world that is frustrating and destructive, the child withdraws from it and from people. Thus, the theory blamed autism on the actions of the caregiver (mother): the cold and unloving *"refrigerator"* parent. But Bettelheim's theory is no longer viable and has not maintained its prominence; both an increased interest in behavioral and biological theories, and the lack of scientific evidence needed to support the theory, contributed to its being largely abandoned. A contrasting explanation was proposed by Ferster (1961). He attempted to untangle autistic behavior using an analysis of each child's reinforcement history. This behavioral theory, too, failed to receive empirical support (Schreibman, 1988), although the behavioral approach has had a favorable impact on the treatment of autistic disorder.

Based on the data it is clear that autistic disorder is not caused by a cold, disinterested, or in some other way pathological parent. Autistic children are not the product of being reared by unemotional and ineffectual mothers, and they do not seem to have experienced any undue stress in the early years of their lives. Moreover, studies of the parents of autistic children have generally failed to find any characteristic pattern of maladjustment in them (McAdoo & DeMeyer, 1978).

Other explanations for autism must be explored. Do these children suffer from a genetically transmitted abnormality? Although studies have been conducted and literature reviews published, disagreements exist in the interpretations of the published research literature. In a thorough review of the research data available at the time, Hansen and Gottesman (1976) concluded that no strong evidence existed implicating genetics in the development of autism. They stated that few siblings are affected and cases of autism did not predict greater incidence among family members. Other researchers have argued, however, that the very rarity of autism and the fact that adult autistic persons are unlikely to have offspring may account for the low rate among relatives (Folstein & Rutter, 1977).

There has been a shift in the beliefs and convictions of researchers in the field—"the view shared in 1998 by most researchers in autism is that genetic factors do play an influential role in the etiology of autism" (Fombonne, 1998, p. 349). Support for a genetic contribution to autism comes from a study of 21 pairs of same-sex twins in which one twin met stringent criteria for autism (Folstein & Rutter, 1978). Of the identical twins, 36% were concordant for autism, as compared to none of the fraternal twins. If the criteria for autism are loosened (autistic spectrum), and concordance is sought in cognitive and linguistic problems, not just in the diagnostic criteria for autistic disorder, 82% of the identical twins and only 10% of the fraternal twins would be considered concordant (see also Bailey, Palferman, Heavey, & Le Couteur, 1998). Rubenstein and associates (1990) argued that these data—the higher concordance for monozygotic twins than for dizygotic twins and a higher than normal incidence among siblings of children with autism—suggested a genetic contribution (see also Bailey, 1993; Bailey et al., 1995). It may be premature to rush to a conclusion, however, as other data (see Smalley, 1991; Smalley & Collins, 1996) are not as clear-cut. Scholars have concluded that although autism is still not known to be an entirely genetic disorder, and although there are some points of uncertainly, there appear to be some causal factors that are genetic (Rutter et al., 1999; Szatmari, Jones, Zwaigenbaum, & MacLean, 1998).

Of course, it is possible that there are other biological factors contributing to the autistic disorder. One such biological component to autism has been identified in recent research, using a wide range of new technologies. In one study, autistic participants exhibited reduced brain activity (Dawson, Klinger, Panagiotides, Lewy, & Castelloe, 1995). In another study, the brains of persons with autism were found to be slightly larger and heavier and the neurons themselves were considered developmentally immature (Minshew, 1996). These anatomical differences are consistent with a developmental curtailment that takes place at some point earlier than 30 weeks gestation—before birth (see Denckla, 1996 cited in Bristol et al., 1996). Certain features of brain function remain unaffected by autism, but the disorder nevertheless involves brain dysfunction consistent with a biological explanation.

A small portion of autistic cases have been said to arise from diseases as diverse as congenital rubella, tuberous sclerosis, and neuro-fibromatosis. Children with congenital rubella (measles existing at birth), for example, are affected with the rubella virus early in prenatal development and, as a result of the infection, are born with a variety of malformations and resulting deafness, blindness, and central nervous system abnormalities, as well as seizures and retardation. In the 1970s, studies reported that 8–13% of children with rubella were autistic (see Chess, 1977). Today, researchers believe that diseases account for a tiny minority of cases of autism.

The possibility remains that prenatal damage or disrupted development contributes to the cause of autism. Autistic persons have been found to evidence central nervous system disorder and show signs of neurological abnormalities (see Gubbay, Lobascher, & Kingerlee, 1970). More recently, Dawson, Warrenburg, and Fuller (1983) have found reduced left hemisphere activity—the area important for communication—in individuals with autistic disorder.

Even today, there is no compelling evidence to fully explain why autistic children behave in their very unusual ways. The consensus among scholars of autism is that the disorder is largely a cognitive and social one that has multiple biological causes that occur sometime between conception and birth. According to Rutter and Schopler (1987), the vast majority of cases of autism have no identifiable medical cause, and it has been estimated that a definite cause can be identified in only 5–10% of cases (Rutter, Bailey, Bolton, & Le Couteur, 1994). Nevertheless, these autistic children do seem to enter the world biologically different. Environmental factors, however, do affect the development of the disorder and the prognosis for later adjustment. For example, the autistic children themselves contribute to the production of an interpersonal environment that is suboptimal, but specially designed educational settings and supportive homes can improve their chances of acquiring skills.

Course

Although some individuals with autistic disorder show improvements, most autistic children continue into adulthood severely handicapped and unable to take full care of themselves. In the absence of early and intensive intervention, only 1–2% of autistic individuals develop to the point that there is no difference between them and children never diagnosed. An estimated 10% achieve adequate functioning in language and social areas but maintain peculiarities, whereas 20% make some school and social progress in spite of a significant handicap such as impoverished speech. About 70% evidence limited progress and evidence continuing major handicaps (Newsom, 1998).

What predicts who will and who will not show some improvement? Language skills and IQ scores are often the best prognostic indicators: Early language development and high IQ score suggest a better prognosis (Lord & Rutter, 1994).

Useful speech develops in only about 50% of autistic persons. During adolescence, behavior and emotional problems emerge: Aggression, oppositional behavior, and tantrums may occur and are quite distressing to parents. Estimates have suggested that approximately 75% of autistic children fall in the moderate range of mental retardation and that 25% develop seizure disorders by adulthood (Crnic & Reid, 1989).

The social deficits in children with autism persist into adulthood. How do these deficits affect the sexual lives of autistic adults? Although this topic has only recently been studied, the data suggest that masturbation was the most common sexual behavior. In one study, one-third of the autistic adults engaged in person-oriented behavior such as touching and holding with some kissing. Known attempts at sexual intercourse are rare (Van Bourgondien, Reichle, & Palmer, 1997).

Programs

Without treatment, the long-term prognosis for persons with autistic disorder is guarded. Generally, autistic persons do not form strong interpersonal relationships nor do they develop the ability to interact socially in ways that are considered "normal." Persons with autistic disorder achieve, however, different levels of functioning. Children who, early in life, have at least some language ability and score near the normal range on nonverbal tests of intelligence have a much better long-term prognosis than children who do not show either of these qualities. In some instances, programs for autistic children teach learning readiness skills (sitting in a chair, attending to the teacher, looking at task materials) to help prepare the child for other programs. But, as noted, even optimistic estimates have suggested that at least two-thirds of autistic children remain severely handicapped into adulthood. Only a small proportion of autistic children live somewhat independent lives without any signs of the disorder. Despite these prognostications, the care of the autistic child can include intervention programs for parents (Schreibman & Koegel, 1996), and programs designed to improve communication (Koegel & Koegel, 1996), reduce disruptive behavior, and enhance socialization (e.g. peer-mediated programs; Strain, Kohler, & Goldstein, 1996).

Over the years, a wide variety of treatments for autism have been employed. When the psychoanalytic explanation of autism was dominant, the treatment followed from the theory. That is, if the disorder is the result of faulty or failed parenting, then the child must be taken from the parents and placed in an environment where the milieu will allow the child to return to more normal development. Reviews of evaluations of such treatment programs find this therapy to be ineffective with autistic children (Levitt, 1963; Rimland, 1974).

Are there medications that benefit autistic children? The use of medications has received some attention, although the evidence has not provided unbridled encouragement (see Campbell, 1988; Conners & Wherry, 1979). Stimulants, antidepressants, and antipsychotics have all been tried, with little or no evidence of beneficial gains. One study (Quintana et al., 1995) found that stimulants improved the hyperactivity of autistic children but did not alter the autistic symptoms, and another study (Gordon, State, Nelson, Hamburger, & Rapoport, 1993) reported that clomipramine reduced compulsive ritualized behaviors in autistic children. The use of vitamins has also been tried and studied, but methodological shortcomings in the studies prevent trustworthy conclusions (Pfeiffer, Norton, Nelson, & Shott, 1995).

At the present time, the majority of psychological programs for autism are based on research evaluations and emphasize the application of behavior modification procedures and parent training. The evidence supports the continued use of these programs (see Newsom, 1998). However, this raises the question, "If autism is a cognitive and social disorder produced by biological causes, why is the treatment a behavioral and parent training program?" As one of many possible answers, consider the case of Helen Keller (after Rimland, 1974). Helen Keller, who was blind and deaf from birth, learned to speak and write, not through treatments for blindness and deafness, but as a result of training like that used in behavioral programs. The cause of a problem need not be behavioral for a behavioral treatment to be useful.

Educational opportunities for autistic youth are a source of debate: Should autistic children be mainstreamed to receive full inclusion—be educated in the same settings as their normally developing peers? Or, are special education classrooms or specialized schools the most appropriate (see Zigmond & Baker, 1995)? According to Mesibov and Shea (1996), advocates of full inclusion mention increased expectations by teachers, modeling of normal development by peers, increased learning, and potentially improved self-esteem as supportive reasons. However, Mesibov and Shea reviewed the literature and also concluded that autistic children benefit from smaller and highly structured environments—situations more likely in the specialized environments created for them.

Autistic children can receive treatment while in a residential setting. However, the trend for autistic children has shifted from institutionalization to providing appropriate treatment in home and regular school settings (Schopler & Hennike, 1990). The trend for autistic adults has shifted toward group homes in the community, thus helping adolescents and adults move toward independence from their families (Van Bourgondien & Schopler, 1990).

The dominant approach to treatment for autism involves behavioral programs that seek to treat behavioral deficits or excesses by applying reinforcements on a contingent basis. Targets may be learning readiness skills, social behavior, or communication skills. Because autistic children are not as social as normal children, they do not respond in the same way to smiles, verbal praise, or peer social events. Consequently, more concrete and sensory rewards are employed, as illustrated in the case of Dicky (see Wolf, Risley, & Mees, 1964):

> Dicky received a behaviorally based treatment beginning at age three. To overcome his refusal to wear his spectacles, a shaping procedure was used. He was rewarded for touching and holding his glass frames, for trying them on, and eventually for wearing them. To control his tantrum behaviors, he was removed from the pleasant environment whenever a tantrum occurred (that is, time out). Similarly, his food plate was removed whenever he ate with his fingers, and he was physically removed for throwing food or taking the food of others. His lack of communication was addressed by a consistent program of showing Dicky a picture, labeling

the object, prompting Dicky to repeat the label, and eventually rewarding him (for example, with apple sauce) for identifying the object in the picture without the therapist's prompting.

Language development is the focus of many behavioral programs. The shaping process is evident in the sequence of the training. First, the child is rewarded for any verbalizations. Second, the reward is provided only when the verbalization follows a prompt by the therapist. Next, the rewards are given only when the child makes closer and closer approximations to the verbalizations of the therapist. Once the child has acquired the word, the therapist provides reward only when the child follows the correct prompt, in spite of the therapist's introducing other sounds. Through this shaping sequence, using modeling and reward, the child gradually learns language skills. The improvements are noteworthy, when judged against initial levels, but the process is painstaking and the end result is not the achievement of "normal" communication. A great deal of time and effort is required for autistic children to respond verbally and to generate sentences.

An example of an intensive and extensive intervention was provided by Lovaas and his colleagues at the University of California at Los Angeles. Lovaas initiated an intensive behavior modification program in which the autistic children received full-time treatment. The children were diagnosed as autistic, younger than 3 years 10 months of age, and evidenced a minimum level of mental ability. Three groups of children were compared: children who received intensive training (19), children who received minimal training (19), and another group received no training at all. The intensive treatment lasted two or more years and involved more than 40 hours of one-to-one treatment per week. Minimal treatment was similar, but with 10 hours of one-to-one treatment per week.

There were several goals for the treatment. In the first year, therapists sought to achieve compliance to verbal commands, imitation, and appropriate play. To reduce self-stimulation or aggression, the therapist ignored these undesirable behaviors. Therapists also used a loud "no" or a slap on the thigh as a last resort. Language growth was emphasized in the second year, and preacademic skills and emotional expression were goals in the third year. An over-arching goal of the entire program was the placement of the children into regular school settings.

Lovaas (1987) reported the results, including that the children in the intensive treatment achieved significantly higher educational placements than the other two groups of children. Specifically, 47% of those in the intensive treatment condition completed the first year of regular elementary school, as compared to 0% and 5% for the other groups. A further study (Lovaas, Smith, & McEachin, 1989) of the intensively treated children at age 13 reported that, in terms of clinical interviews and measures of adaptive behavior, eight of the original nineteen were "indistinguishable" (p. 166) from an age-matched control group of normal children.

Although these results are very encouraging they should be viewed with some caution. Other treatments, though less intense, have not had as great a success rate, and the present study does require replication. Given that a minimum mental age was required for inclusion in the study, these autistic children were probably from the high-functioning end of the continuum, thus limiting generalization to all autistic children. Similarly, the sample was quite a young group. The dramatic effect reported by Lovaas (1987), however, caused others to take notice. Schopler, Short, and Mesibov (1989) offered a more conservative conclusion: Due to methodological factors (such as apparent absence of random assignment to treatment and control groups), it is not possible to truly determine the effects of the intervention. Others (e.g. Gresham & MacMillan, 1997) have identified methodological shortcomings and suggest that the limitations (e.g. school placement as an outcome measure) should give reason for concern. Nevertheless, the study adds to the evidence of the benefits of behavior programs for the autistic child and suggests that intensive and extensive treatments may be necessary to have a meaningful affect on such a pervasive disorder as autism.

Summarizing the years of applying behavior modification to autistic children, the data provide evidence of measurable progress, though progress is often slow. Not all interventions with autistic children produce dramatic success, and, indeed, the prognosis for most autistic children is not optimistic. The highest successes are based on very intensive intervention (40 hours per week) with very young and select patients. However, at least one study has suggested that when parents are trained in the behavioral program and take over as therapists, the results remain stable (see Lovaas, Koegel, Simmons, & Long, 1973). At least one point of current emphasis is on early introduction (Mesibov, 1997), with many professionals agreeing that intervention in the preschool years is critical.

Training parents

The training that was originally provided for parents of autistic children focused on their disruptive and sometimes dangerous behaviors that were evident in the home. More recently, to facilitate generalization to settings outside of the treatment context, parents have become involved in language training as well. Lastly, though no less important, parents can suffer emotional problems linked to parenting an autistic child, and these needs, too, can and should become goals for parent training interventions.

As is true for parent training in general, programs include a variety of procedures, such as lectures and readings, demonstrations and role-playing, and home visits and telephone contacts. The main focus is training in the behavior modification principles used in treatments of autism: shaping, reinforcement, ignoring, and generalization. Parent groups provide opportunities for discussion of difficulties as well as social support (Koegel & Koegel, 1995).

With regard to the shaping of communication skills, a parent would be taught to first reward eye contact as a step toward increased communicativeness. For example, a parent would be told, "When Joanne makes eye contact with you, immediately provide a reward, no matter how busy you might be at the time." Later on, parents can become involved in teaching specific words—saying the word "toy" when pointing to Joanne's toy—and concepts of ownership—pointing to Joanne when saying "your toy" and pointing to oneself when saying "my toy."

Some of the benefits of parent training are illustrated by the work of Koegel, Schreibman, and their colleagues (Koegel, Schreibman, Britten, Burke, & O'Neill, 1982). Their project compared 25–50 hours of parent training in behavior modification procedures with outpatient clinic treatment (4–5 hours a week for a year). Both treatments improved the social behavior, play, and speech, and decreased tantrums and echolalia. Relative to the parent-trained group, the clinic-trained children did not show generalization of their improvements during an assessment in the home. The parent training condition resulted in observable gains in the home environment. In a more recent report, parent training procedures improved the pattern of parent–child interactions—children were happier and parents were more interested and less stressed (Koegel, Bimbela, & Schreibman, 1996).

A program in the UK also produced some illuminating findings. Howlin (1981) and Howlin and Rutter (1987) reported on a home-based parent training program where 16 families with a high-functioning autistic boy (average age 6 years) received treatment over an 18-month period. Comparison groups received outpatient treatment. Mothers in parent training were individually trained to use behavioral procedures and to teach language and manage behavior problems.

Psychologists visited the parents in their home for 2 to 3 hours weekly or biweekly for 6 months and monthly for the final 12 months. There were also instances of counseling regarding other matters and the occasional inclusion of some other services.

The outcomes were favorable, but mixed. For example, the autistic boys whose parents received training showed significantly more social responsiveness to parents, but no more interactive play with peers. There were fewer tantrums and instances of aggression, but no changes in stereotypic behavior or hyperactivity. Based on an examination of audiotapes, the children with trained parents showed improved quantity and communicativeness of speech yet no significant differences in IQ scores. Many of the outcomes were favorable and, where differences were observed, they favored the parent training approach. As Howlin and Rutter (1987) concluded, the results were sufficiently positive to be encouraging, but not so overwhelming as to preclude the need for more intensive intervention. Indeed, their recommendation—for a more comprehensive parent-training intervention—is consistent with the recommendations of others as well (see also Agosta & Melda, 1996).

Parents of children with autistic disorder have their own needs and concerns. Living with a child with a pervasive developmental disorder creates problems in addition to those of interacting with the child. Not the least of these problems is simply facing the life-long task of managing a severely handicapped child. Sandra Harris (1983), of Rutgers University, provided a set of recommendations that include pragmatic issues (dealing with a community that may not have resources), emotional issues (personal distress), and interpersonal problems (withdrawal of the extended family). Parents must address their responsibilities toward the autistic child and recognize their own work and recreational needs as well. Siblings must face the challenge of being a responsible member of the helping family while also maintaining their independent existence. In families in which these issues are met with less than adequate adjustment, depression, guilt, anger, and a sense of inadequacy can become a source for concern. Interventions for parents may not have a direct effect on the behavior of the autistic child, but they are nevertheless valued as they improve the home and general family environment and may prevent parental burnout and distress.

What can be done about self-injury?

The topic of self-injury will be discussed here, but it should not be taken as an indication that autistic children are the only ones who self-injure or that self-injury is solely characteristic of autism. Although it is true that one of the distressing features commonly associated with autism is self-injurious behavior (Newsom & Hovanitz, 1997), a variety of severely handicapped and psychologically disturbed children sometimes engage in self-injurious behavior. Examples of self-injury include head-banging, hair-pulling, self-biting, and eating nonedible substances. At times, the self-injurious behavior is so extreme that it actually poses a threat to the life of the child. Perhaps you recall from Chapter 1 the brief description of Ginger, who engaged in pin-sticking. Pins or needles can travel in the blood stream! Also, other behavior, such as forceful head-banging, can result in extreme brain damage. What should be done when a disabled child engages in uncompromising self-injurious actions?

The use of physical restraints is one approach that is proffered by some: Put the self-injurious child in a restraint and prevent the actions that are harmful. Others recommend medications (Hammock, Schroeder, & Levine, 1995) to restrain the child from self-harm. For example, with adults, risperidone has been reported to reduce aggression and self-injury (Cohen, Ihrig, Lott, & Kerrick, 1998). However, only eight cases were studied, and the absence of proper control conditions reduces the confidence one can place in the reported outcomes. Unfortunately, both physical and chemical restraints, although options in some patients, nevertheless can prevent the individual from participating in other therapeutic, social, and educational programs. What follows next is a discussion of approaches to treatment that have been found to be effective—we later note and discuss a relevant controversy about the use of certain procedures.

In 1982 a monograph on the treatment of self-injurious behavior was prepared by a special task force, and Favell and colleagues commented that self-injurious behavior is repetitious and chronic, and that the incidence and severity of self-injurious behavior is greatest among persons with retardation, autism, and severe disabilities. The task force consisted of 14 preeminent clinicians and researchers who reviewed the research literature and provided recommendations.

Favell and associates (1982) were clear in recommending that whatever intervention is to be used it should be evaluated in terms of its ability to reduce the self-injurious behavior by a clinically significant amount. That is, reduce its frequency and intensity to the extent that the individual refrains from self-injury and is capable of participation in therapeutic activities. Although the need for evaluation may seem obvious, evaluation of treatments for self-injurious behavior is especially important because of the controversy that exists among practitioners and parents about the use of aversive procedures.

Behavioral procedures, such as the removal of reinforcement for self-injury, punishing self-injury, and reinforcing more desirable behavior, have been evaluated as methods to produce clinically significant changes in self-injurious behavior (see Baumeister & Rollings, 1976; Favell & Green, 1981; Russo, Carr, & Lovaas, 1980). One behavioral procedure, differential reinforcement of other behavior (DRO), involves providing reinforcement after periods of time when no self-injury occurs. With DRO, an increase in self-injurious behavior may occur at first, though it is followed by a meaningful reduction of the unwanted behavior. Another procedure, extinction, involves withholding previously given reinforcement after episodes of self-injury. Time-out consists of taking the self-injuring child away from the opportunity to receive reinforcement for self- injury. Each of these procedures have been used both singly and in combination with other approaches to try to reduce self-injury. There are documented cases where the procedures have been successful, but there are also cases where reinforcements are difficult to identify or manipulate, and other cases where the procedures were less than fully effective.

What about the use of aversive procedures, such as mild electric shock, to reduce self-injurious behavior? What does the research say about its effectiveness? And, if it is effective, would you consider using the procedures? According to the Favell task force report, "Aversive electrical stimulation (informally termed shock) is the most widely researched and, within the parameters of shock employed in the research literature, the most generally effective method of initially suppressing self-injury" (Favell et al., 1982, p. 540). Although it is effective, it is considered appropriate only in extreme cases when applied in carefully controlled situations by experienced and trained professionals. When shock is used for treating self-injury, the shock (electrical stimulus) is physically harmless but subjectively noxious and is applied for a brief duration immediately after each occurrence of self-injury. Research demonstrates its effectiveness—clinically significant reductions in self-injury—but there is controversy around its use (Mudford, 1995). In addition to methodologically sound and supportive research, it is apparent that politics and personal beliefs are also factored into decisions about the treatments to be employed when treating self-injurious behavior.

Other pervasive developmental disorders

Although much less common than autism, there are other pervasive developmental disorders. Rett's disorder, Asperger's disorder, and childhood disintegrative disorder are included in DSM-IV among the pervasive developmental disorders. We review these briefly here.

Rett's disorder. There is the development of multiple specific deficits, but the deficits appear after a period of normal motor development (e.g. first 5 months of life). Head size is normal at birth, but head growth decelerates between 5 months and 4 years of age. Noteworthy, too, is the loss of previously purposeful hand movements between 5 months and 2½ years of age. Interest in social activities diminishes, language development is impaired, and there is the appearance of poorly coordinated gait or trunk movements. Rett's disorder, which has only been reported in females, is usually accompanied by severe mental retardation and persists throughout life.

Asperger's disorder. The essential features of Asperger's disorder are severe and sustained impairment in social interaction and the development of repetitive patterns of behavior and activities. These features cause clinically meaningful impairment in functioning, yet there are no clinically meaningful delays in cognitive development of age-appropriate self-help skills. Although similar to autism, cases with Asperger's disorder less frequently exhibit deviance in language and communication than autistic children. More common in males, the majority of cases of the disorder are lifelong (see also Volkmar, Klin, & Pauls, 1998).

Childhood disintegrative disorder. When a child shows 2 years of normal development in communication, social relationships, play, and adaptive behavior followed by a clinically meaningful loss of previously acquired skills before age 10 it may be the very rare childhood disintegrative disorder (recall also the discussion earlier in the chapter about childhood schizophrenia). The essential feature of Childhood Disintegrative disorder is the marked deterioration of functioning following at least two years of apparently normal development. The social and communicative deficits seen in autism, as well as severe retardation, are also seen in childhood disintegrative disorder. Somewhat more common in males, this disorder is relatively constant throughout life.

Much work has been completed since the initial description of autism and the disorder is now better understood and treated. With continued effort, the future is likely to bring a clearer understanding of and treatment for the other pervasive developmental disorders.

Summary

Pervasive developmental disorders involve severe upset in the child's cognitive, social, behavioral, and emotional growth, producing widespread impact on the process of development. One such disorder, autism, affects the basic human qualities of interpersonal socialization and complex communication. Autism is relatively rare, although it does occur worldwide and with no pattern linked to social class or educational background. It is not thought to be caused by the actions of the caregiver nor can it be explained by behavioral learning principles. Data have suggested a biological and potential genetic component.

Programs for autistic persons do not expect to cure the disorder, but are designed and provided to maximize personal adjustment. Psychodynamic programs and medications have not provided effective leads. Intensive behavior modification interventions have shown promising results. Increasingly, interventions focus on the family, providing parent training to address child problems and parent counseling to address the difficulties associated with rearing an autistic

Tics and elimination disorders 11

Our coverage of behavioral, emotional, eating, and pervasive developmental disorders of childhood closes with contemplation of tic disorders and disorders associated with elimination (enuresis and encopresis). Some children with tic or elimination disorders also display other diagnosable conditions, whereas some cases occur in otherwise normal children.

Tic disorders

Tics are involuntary, rapid, recurrent, and stereotyped motor movements or vocalizations. Tics are sudden and nonrhythmic. Usually of brief duration, individual tics rarely last more than a second, but many tics tend to occur in bouts with a brief inter-tic interval (Leckman & Cohen, 1994). The tics occur many times a day, nearly every day or intermittently. In DSM-IV, both motor and verbal tics may be classified as either chronic or transient, depending on the duration. As would be expected, chronic tics have a history of lasting for a period of more than 1 year, whereas the transient tic has been seen for less than 12 consecutive months. Transient tic disorders, which are almost invariably a disorder of childhood, wax and wane over periods of weeks or months (Leckman & Cohen, 1994).

Some common motor tics include neck jerking and facial grimacing, and common verbal tics include grunting and throat-clearing. Some tics can be more complex, such as self-biting, smelling objects, and repeating sounds made by others. Tic behaviors may be exacerbated by stress, diminished during absorbing activities (such as reading), and reduced during sleep.

Of the several tic disorders, Tourette's is perhaps the best known and the most complex. In 1885, Gilles de la Tourette described nine cases of tic disorder characterized by motor incoordinations (or tics) and inarticulate shouts. Known today as Tourette's disorder, this tic disorder involves both multiple motor and one or more verbal tics. The tics can be simultaneous or occur at different times; they may occur daily or intermittently; the location, frequency, and intensity of the tics may change over time. The tics usually involve the head, although complex tics involving other parts of the body are often present. The DSM diagnostic criteria for Tourette's are presented in Box 11.1.

One of the unusual tics is coprolalia. Coprolalia, in which the individual utters, calls, or screams obscenities, is apparent in only about one-third of all patients with Tourette's disorder. Simple swearing when angry is not coprolalia.

Age 7 is the approximately average age of the first appearance of Tourette's disorder (Friedhoff & Chase, 1982). The initial symptoms are often rapid eye-blinking, facial grimacing, and throat-clearing (Comings & Comings, 1985). Although Tourette's tics are markedly reduced when children are asleep, they do not disappear completely (Janovic & Rohaidy, 1987). Many young children are oblivious to their tics, and experience them as entirely involuntary. By the age of 10, most children with tics are aware of any signals or urges that come before the tic (Leckman, Walker, & Cohen, 1993).

Children with Tourette's disorder have difficulty maintaining age-appropriate social skills (Stokes, Bawden, Camfield, Ackman, & Dooley, 1991). One of the recurring themes emerging from interviews of the families of persons with Tourette's disorder is the presence of discipline problems (Comings & Comings, 1985). Parents report that the discipline problems are greater than routine and more severe than for nonaffected siblings. "Overreactive" and "explosive" were typical descriptions used by parents. Of the behavioral and emotional problems that frequently complicate Tourette's, impulsive, disinhibited, and immature behavior and compulsive touching and sniffing are common. At present, there are no clear dividing lines between these disruptive behaviors and complex tics on the one hand and comorbid conditions of ADHD and obsessive-compulsive disorder (OCD) on the other (Leckman & Cohen, 1994).

Reprinted with permission from the Diagnostic and Statistical Manual of Mental Disorders, Fourth Edition. Copyright 1994 American Psychiatric Association.

BOX 11.1   DSM criteria for a diagnosis of Tourette's disorder

- Both multiple motor and one or more vocal tics have been present at some time during the illness, although not necessarily concurrently.
- The tics occur many times a day, nearly every day, intermittently throughout a period of more than one year, and during this period there was never a tic-free period of more than three consecutive months.
- The disturbance causes marked distress or significant impairment in social, occupational, or other important areas of functioning.
- The onset is before 18 years of age.
- The disturbance is not due to the direct physiological effects of a substance (e.g. stimulants) or a general medical condition (e. g. Huntington's disease or postviral encephalitis).

What is thought to be the cause of Tourette's? Because there is an increased incidence of Tourette's disorder in the first-degree relatives of people with the disorder, a genetic factor has been implicated in the etiology. Some researchers believe that it is an inherited disorder (e.g. Comings, Comings, Devor, & Cloninger, 1984), and others have noted an increased frequency among Jewish people (Shapiro, Shapiro, Brunn, & Sweet, 1978). However, the high frequency of Jews reported in earlier studies may simply reflect the high percentage of Jews in the community (New York) where the research was carried out (Nee, Caine, & Polinsky, 1980). One study found that first-degree relatives of patients with Tourette's disorder were at substantially higher risk for developing Tourette's disorder, chronic motor tic disorder, and obsessive-compulsive disorder than were unrelated individuals. Interestingly, risk was gender related: The risk to male first-degree relatives for any tic disorder was 50% (18% for Tourette's disorder, 31% for chronic motor tics, and 7% for OCD) and only 31% for females (5% for Tourette's disorder, 9% for chronic motor tics, and 7% for OCD) (Pauls, Raymond, Stevenson, & Leckman, 1991).

Medications, such as haloperidol, are often prescribed for Tourette's disorder, and 70–80% of patients show some benefit. Because of unwanted side effects, only 20–30% take the drug for extended periods. In lower doses, however, patients may experience a remission of symptoms and few adverse reactions (Leckman & Cohen, 1994).

You might wonder what it would be like to have Tourette's, and to blurt out verbalizations in an involuntary fashion. Bliss (1980) provided a rare self-description of the experience of Tourette's disorder. In his published account he described his 35-year attention to events that preceded, accompanied, and followed his motor and verbal tics. According to Bliss, the tics are actions taken to satisfy unfulfilled sensations and urges. By paying close attention, he claimed to be able to identify when his sensations would be overwhelming and when he needed to substitute a socially appropriate action. Bliss's self-description is not a scientific study, and some researchers have argued that this disorder is not under voluntary control. Bliss did provide a glimpse into the experiential qualities of Tourette's disorder, however, and his report suggests that behavioral management programs and training in self-awareness skills may help some Tourette's patients.

Enuresis and encopresis

Elimination disorders are typically identified during childhood. Enuresis, the occurrence of wetting in the absence of a urologic or

| BOX 11.2 | DSM criteria for a diagnosis of enuresis |

- repeated voiding of urine into bed or clothes (whether involuntary or intentional).
- the behavior is clinically significant as manifested by either the frequency of twice a week for at least three consecutive months or the presence of clinically significant distress or impairment in social, academic (occupational), or other important areas of functioning.
- chronological age is at least five years (or equivalent developmental level).
- the behavior is not due exclusively to the direct physiological effect of a substance (e.g. a diuretic) or a general medical condition (e.g. diabetes, spina bifida, a seizure disorder).

Reprinted with permission from the Diagnostic and Statistical Manual of Mental Disorders, Fourth Edition. Copyright 1994 American Psychiatric Association.

neurologic pathology, can be a source of concern to parents whose child is 3 to 5 years of age or older (DSM criteria are presented in Box 11.2). Some sources estimate that as many as 20% of all 5-year-olds wet their beds a sufficient number of times to qualify as enuretic (Doleys, 1983). Fortunately, the problem is much less frequent among older children—it occurs in less than 2% of 12- to 14-year-olds. There are some gender differences: Bed-wetting is equally common for boys and girls until age 5, but by 11 boys are twice as likely to be wet as girls (Shaffer, 1994).

Encopresis, the fecal parallel to enuresis, is reported in approximately 2–3% of 3- to 5-year-olds with a 3:1 male–female ratio (Hersov, 1994). The DSM diagnostic criteria for encopresis are listed in Box 11.3. By ages 10–12, 1% or fewer children are encopretic.

Research on the elimination disorders has focused mainly on enuresis; encopresis has not been studied extensively. Potential explanations of the cause of enuresis include genetic inheritance, a response to arousal during sleep, the expression of underlying emotional conflicts, smaller bladder capacity, and the failure to learn an adaptive response to the sensation of a full bladder. The research evidence is nonexistent for some of these explanations and equivocal for others, leaving the field to be uncertain of the etiology but to assume that there are potentially multiple causes for the problem.

| BOX 11.3 | DSM criteria for a diagnosis of encopresis |

- repeated passage of feces into inappropriate places (e.g. clothing or floor) whether involuntary or intentional.
- at least one such event a month for at least three months.
- chronological age is at least 5 years (or equivalent developmental level).
- the behavior is not due exclusively to the direct physiological effects of a substance (e.g. laxatives) or a general medical condition except through a mechanism involving constipation.

Reprinted with permission from the Diagnostic and Statistical Manual of Mental Disorders, Fourth Edition. Copyright 1994 American Psychiatric Association.

Although the cause of the problem remains a puzzle, there are well-studied, effective methods for bladder control training. The clear majority of the programs that have been demonstrated to be effective apply behavioral procedures. Medications such as imipramine (a medication used to treat depression in adults) increase bladder control in a reported 85% of patients (Shaffer, 1977), although total continence is achieved in only 30% of the patients. Unfortunately, up to 95% of these children relapse after the medication is withdrawn (Doleys, 1983). Based on a meta-analytic review of several studies, the customary psychological treatment was reported to be superior to medications (Houts, Berman, & Abramson, 1994).

Perhaps the most often used treatment for enuresis is the urine alarm system sometimes called the "bell and pad." The bell and pad system is based on classical conditioning. A urine-sensing device rests between the child and the mattress during sleep hours. Urine that passes onto the device triggers an alarm. Once awake, the child urinates in the toilet and can then return to bed. Doleys (1977), summarizing results over 15 years, concluded that 75% of the more than 600 children treated with the urine alarm showed remission. The average length of treatment with the urine alarm is 5–12 weeks. Relapse remains a problem, however, as 41% of the treated children were unable to maintain the dry state after treatment discontinued.

Two modifications to the urine alarm approach help reduce the relapse rate (Doleys, 1983; Finley, Wansley, & Blenkarn, 1977; Jehu, Morgan, Turner, & Jones, 1977). First, because responses are more persistent under conditions of partial reinforcement, the alarm is set to go off 50–75% of the time that the pad is wet. Second, the child sometimes consumes liquids before bed and after dryness days have been achieved. By so doing, the child learns bladder control when the bladder is full as well as when it is not as full.

Dry-bed training combines other behavioral procedures with the urine alarm (Azrin, Sheed, & Foxx, 1974). Dry-bed training includes opportunities for positive practice, nighttime awakening, practice in retention control, and full cleanliness training. In research reported by Fincham and Spettell (1984), parents who were actually involved in the treatment of enuretic children viewed the urine alarm as more acceptable than the dry-bed training.

Summary

Tics are involuntary, rapid, recurrent, and stereotyped movements or verbalizations. Tics may be motor or verbal, simple or complex, and

Questions for your consideration 12

The psychological disorders of youth are diverse and multifaceted. There is no one single causal agent to explain the disorders and, likewise, although some treatments are more effective than others, there is no one therapeutic approach that is universally most effective. Add to the presence of diverse disorders the fact that there are many social pressures facing both nondisturbed and the less-well-adjusted children and it is apparent that progressing through development is not an easy task for today's youngsters.

Should psychologists take an active stance with regard to the challenges of childhood? Consider that some children are not unaware or unexperienced about the stresses and dangers of life: Numerous examples have been brought to our attention by media exposure of children who are involved in crime, victims of violence and abuse, abandoned and assaulted by their parents, and suffering from poverty and hunger. Consider also that research suggests that problems of childhood do not naturally go away, and that the research data support the benefits of early intervention. All the information combines to alert us to the need, be it with individuals, families, or communities, for action and intervention.

Owing to society's increased awareness of the challenges facing child adjustment, there has been and will continue to be a broadening of the research scope and a flourishing of the research literature that addresses the causes and treatments for the psychological disorders of childhood. In addition, the more we learn about the challenges that face children as a part of their normal development, and about how well-adjusted children cope and adjust, the more we will advance our understanding and be able to enhance our interventions.

That childhood experiences influence adult behavior patterns is a principal theme in several theories of psychopathology. For example, both cognitive and learning approaches accent the important role of early acquired patterns of behavior. The outlook for the future contains continued emphasis on the importance of early experiences, but with greater specificity—advances in theory and treatment regarding the precise role of child experiences and the nature of the cognitive processing style and behavioral pattern of childhood with specific behavioral and emotional disorders.

The family matters, and research on topics within family psychology, has come of age. No longer are family approaches criticized as cult-like, nor are they burdened by sole reliance on nonempirical theories. The increased experimental focus on parent–child interactions, parenting styles, and parent and family interventions combines to promote an evolving and expanding knowledge base about the contribution of family forces to adjustment and maladjustment. The 1990s have been witness to this emerging focus.

A trend in the treatment of mental retardation and pervasive disorders specifically, and childhood disorders in general, is an increased involvement of the family. In particular, the trend is away from custodial care with a corresponding increase in community centers and family programs. Progress in the treatment of behavior problems in individuals with the disorder has been significant, and these advances are now being coordinated with interventions for the family. For example, there is widespread recognition that the family of a retarded or autistic child is a part of the system that influences the child's behavior and adjustment (Baker, 1984).

The appeal of biological models is likely to continue. Advances in genetic research methods will have application to the study of childhood disorders, such as in the study of the cause of autism. Some forms of retardation, too, have an underlying genetic cause and advances in genetic research methods can and will be applied. In contrast to the speculation that genetic and biological forces will receive increased attention in the study of the cause of these disorders, the lack of any meaningful breakthrough in the use of medications suggests that the focus of treatment will not be entirely biological but will continue to employ the effective behavioral interventions. As previously noted, these are likely to be increasingly adapted to include family members as well as the identified child.

What would you do?

In the following specific situations questions are raised pertaining to child adjustment, the psychological disorders of childhood, parenting practices, and societal decisions. The six situations will be described with some details and descriptive information, but they could occur in any of a variety of contexts. The answers, too, are not black and white—

there are many debatable points and a great deal of room for the influence of personal beliefs and opinions. Nevertheless, all of the situations are relevant to how we, as members of society, address the psychological issues and challenges of childhood.

It is suggested that you read and weigh each situation separately—one at a time—and engage in a discussion or self-reflection about the issues and your responses to them. Space is provided for you to list your ideas and arguments and to make related notes and suggestions.

Situation 1: The educated parent

No matter how old you are at the present time, skip either ahead or back to the time in your life soon after you first choose/chose to become a parent. To help set the situation, think about where you might be (were) living at this time and your likely (usual) friends and activities at the time. Think about your aspirations for your child.

Now, move ahead several years and suppose that your 6-year-old son, Dan, has been described by his teacher as wiggly and full of excess energy. You know from your time with him that there are occasions when Dan can be very difficult to manage, but you really didn't expect his teacher to suggest to you and your spouse that he is more active than the other children, that he appears hyperactive, and that he may have ADHD.

What do you think about these comments about Dan? Do you blame the school or the classroom teacher? Do you blame yourselves? Independent of the possible causes, you and your spouse have to consider whether or not to have Dan seen by a psychologist and tested and, if he is diagnosed, whether or not to seek treatment and possibly use medications? Given what you have learned in this book, can you anticipate the issues to weigh up? What data sources would you want the diagnostician to consider?

Use the space below to list (a) the issues and (b) the data sources to be considered.

_____   _____

_____   _____

_____   _____

_____   _____

Situation 2: Advertisers that market to children

Suppose that you have a younger sister and that her name is Darla. Darla is quite athletic and healthy, but she has recently begun to complain about her weight and to follow a strict diet. By the age and height charts she is at the low end of the recommended weight range and no one else thinks she is heavy—but somehow she got the idea in her head and has convinced herself that she is fat. Many cultures praise thinness, so much so that industries have developed around the providing of services to help people with the process of weight loss. Advertisements clearly promote a certain "look."

Is it acceptable for advertisers to use inordinately thin (if not almost "sickly") figures in sexually explicit modeling poses? What are the effects of these advertisements on the developing young teenager? Should advertisers be asked or required to use "healthy" models?

List the pros and cons of regulating advertisements that are geared to sell to children and to influence children.

Pro: _____

_____

_____

_____

Con: _____

_____

_____

_____

Situation 3: Do we legislate the right to reproduce?

You spent most of your childhood in a medium-sized town with many but not all of the niceties of life. Your school was safe, there were playgrounds and parks near your home, and the local recreational facilities included outdoor activities and several regional sports. Suppose also that a neighbor— someone about the same age as yourself—was someone with mental retardation. And suppose further that, as a young adult, he now goes daily to a sheltered workshop where he has met a young woman. Both are mentally retarded, but in otherwise good physical health. They fall in love.

Often held as a basic human privilege, many adults marry and start a family. But, with regard to persons with mental retardation, we know of their limitations in self-care and social functioning, and of the increased risk (both genetic and environmental) of mental retardation among their offspring. Can society impose rules and regulations to govern reproduction among the mentally retarded? Who is to say whether or not a retarded couple can marry and reproduce? Should the couple be given sex education (Shepperdson, 1995)? To what extent should they be counseled about the risks and rewards associated with their particular reproduction situation?

All of these questions and possible answers become especially difficult when one considers the criterion for making decisions about whether or not mental retardation is present: Who would decide? Would a panel of experts decide? The courts? Would an IQ test and IQ score be involved and, if so, what test score would be used? Even more difficult would be a situation in which a person had an IQ that was just one point above or below the cutoff score? Would exceptions be made, and on what basis?

As is apparent, questions of an individual's personal freedoms can be legally complicated and philosophically troublesome—but let's now turn to a more complicated dilemma. The issues and decisions become even more complex when someone else's rights are involved. Although not a frequent problem, how best to address sexual acting-out among persons with mental retardation? Are they to be held responsible?

Document your thinking about both sides of these issues. For one list, assume that you support the position that persons deemed mentally retarded should be restrained from reproducing and list the criteria that you would propose for determinations of the presence and absence of mental retardation. For the second list, assume that you are against regulating the reproductive rights of those with mental retardation and list the reasons to justify this position.

Pro: _____

_____

_____

_____

Con: _____

_____

_____

_____

Situation 4: To use prebirth information?

With scientific investigation comes increased knowledge. For example, there are modern screening tests that can provide early identification of yet-to-be-born children with Down's syndrome. Such early identification also unearths a potential predicament. First, it is clear that there are inordinate benefits to be gained by early identification. In PKU, for example, early identification leads to treatment that prevents the disorder. However, with early identification also comes both personal and professional challenges to ethics. How will the parents of these offspring address prebirth decisions? Advances in science can stimulate social debates, provoke personal challenges, and create new dilemmas as yet unknown to future parents. The real and potential gains associated with early identification merit continued investigation, but there are issues to consider.

Describe and justify your position with regard to the following question. How would you use prebirth information about the nature of your unborn child's health?

_____

_____

_____

_____

_____

Situation 5: Educational tracking?

For this next situation, again suppose that you are a parent. In this case your daughter is an exceptionally bright 9-year-old student who has come home on several occasions complaining that she is totally bored at school. On this particular day you ask a few questions and quickly learn something that you consider a major source of concern—the teacher is spending much of her class time repeating the lessons for some of the slower learners. As you consider this scenario, ask yourself the following questions. Should your daughter be separated from the slower students in the class? Should the bright students, in general, be separated and given more advanced work? Is it an optimal educational strategy to mainstream the slow learners or developmentally delayed children into the regular classroom, or should they be selected out for special education opportunities? Do you see benefits in having a variety of educational levels represented in one class? Are there benefits to classrooms that are stratified by ability levels?

List the pro and con arguments. What problems can you identify for each side of the debate? After you consider the arguments, make a choice for yourself. Then, specify how the benefits of your decision would outweigh the related problems?

Pro: _____

_____

Con: _____

_____

Cost/benefit: _____

_____

_____

_____

Situation 6: Allocating funding

Our knowledge and awareness of autism has mushroomed. Despite this, its exact cause remains unknown and most interventions are of circumscribed success. How should society respond? Although it is severe and quite troubling, it is not at all common. Do we need to spend more time and money on research, and place greater focus on treating autism? With regard to services, should parents be prepared to be the primary providers for autistic youth or should hospital care be provided by society? Attitudes in the US have changed from segregating people who are "inferior" and considered to be a burden to others to viewing these people as having equal rights, making positive contributions to society, and deserving of inclusion. Although attitudes change and answers are not always readily available, mental health professionals and citizens are nevertheless faced with perplexing issues such as these.

Assume that you have a vote in the control of the national budget that was designated for the treatment of childhood disorders. One of your tasks is to assign portions of the money to different problems. How would you distribute the funds? What percentage of the total would be allocated for autism? Given your knowledge of childhood disorders, here are two tasks: First, assign percentages of the total to each of the disorders we have addressed and describe your rationale for the allocations that you made. Second, provide an argument for allocating all of the money to one topic—what topic would it be and why?

1. Conduct disorder _____

2. ADHD_____

3. Anxiety disorder_____

4. Depression _____

5. Eating disorder _____

6. Mental retardation and learning disabilities_____

7. Pervasive developmental disorders _____

8. Tics and elimination _____

Which topic deserves special allocation and why? _____

_____

_____

_____

Summary

Our journey through the disorders of childhood has exposed us to the diverse psychological problems affecting children, to the fact that there are manifold causal ingredients that can lead to psychological distress, and to the assorted interventions that have been developed, evaluated, and provided for children in need. Importantly, however, we also discovered that there is much yet to be learned. For example, we do not have a full appreciation of the biological forces operating in autism, the familial factors that contribute to conduct disorder, or the parenting styles that unwittingly foster anxiety disorders. Similarly, we do not yet have a sufficient grasp of exactly how best to treat specific disorders or how to, in the ideal, prevent them from developing. Moreover, although we have gained a greater appreciation of the steps that need to be taken to further advance our knowledge, we are still faced with many grave and penetrating questions that require careful and serious consideration. It is hoped that the applications of our knowledge about childhood disorders will result in a series of reasoned and well-balanced decisions—decisions that should, in the end, benefit our overall society as well as the specific children.

Suggested readings

There are now several contemporary and advanced edited books that address the nature and treatment of childhood disorders. Although the interested reader can pursue topics by going to the references to specific studies, the following select readings offer collections of chapters, reviews of literatures, and some conceptual and theoretical advances.

Cicchetti, D. (1993). Developmental psychopathology: Reactions, reflections, projections. *Developmental Review, 13*, 471–502.

Crick, N., & Dodge, K. (1994). A review and reformulation of social information-processing mechanisms in children's social adjustment. *Psychological Bulletin, 115*, 74–101.

Hammen, C. (1991). *Depression runs in families: The social context of risk and resilience in children of depressed mothers.* New York: Springer-Verlag.

Hibbs, E., & Jensen, P. (Eds.). (1996). *Psychosocial treatments for child and adolescent disorders: Empirically based strategies for clinical practice.* Washington, DC: American Psychological Association.

Kazdin, A.E., & Weisz, J.R. (1998). Identifying and developing empirically supported child and adolescent treatments. *Journal of Consulting and Clinical Psychology, 66*, 19–36.

Kendall, P.C. (Ed.) (2000). *Child and adolescent therapy: Cognitive-behavioral procedures* (2nd ed.). New York: Guilford Press.

Kendall, P.C., & MacDonald, J.P. (1993). Cognition in the psychopathology of youth, and implications for treatment. In K.S. Dobson & P.C. Kendall (Eds.), *Psychopathology and cognition* (pp. 387–432). San Diego, CA: Academic Press.

Mash, E., & Barkley, R. (Eds.) (1996). *Child psychopathology.* New York: Guilford Press.

Mash, E., & Terdal, L. (Eds.) (1997). *Assessment of childhood disorders* (3rd ed.). New York: Guilford.

Patterson, G.R. (1982). *Coercive family process.* Eugene, OR: Castalia.

Rutter, M., Taylor, E., & Hersov, L. (Eds.) (1994), *Child and adolescent psychiatry.* Oxford, UK: Blackwell Scientific Publications.

References

Abikoff, H. (1985). Efficacy of cognitive training interventions in hyperactive children: A critical review. *Clinical Psychology Review, 5,* 479–512.

Abikoff, H. (1991). Cognitive training in ADHD children: Less to it than meets the eye. *Journal of Learning Disabilities, 24,* 205–209.

Abikoff, H., Ganales, D., Reiter, G., Blum, C., Foley, C., & Klein, R.G. (1988). Cognitive training in academically deficient ADHD boys receiving stimulant medication. *Journal of Abnormal Child Psychology, 16,* 411–432.

Abikoff, H., & Gittelman, R. (1985). Hyperactive children treated with stimulants: Is cognitive training a useful adjunct? *Archives of General Psychiatry, 42,* 953–965.

Abikoff, H., & Hechtman, L. (1996). Multimodal therapy and stimulants in the treatment of children with ADHD. In E. Hibbs & P. Jensen (Eds.), *Psychosocial treatments for child and adolescent disorders: Empirically based strategies for clinical practice* (pp. 341–370). Washington DC: American Psychological Association.

Abramson, L., Metalsky, G., & Alloy, L.B. (1989). Hopelessness depression: A theory-based subtype of depression. *Psychological Review, 96,* 358–372.

Achenbach, T.M. (1982). Assessment and taxonomy of children's behavior disorders. In B.B. Lahey & A.E. Kazdin (Eds.), *Advances in clinical child psychology* (Vol. 5, pp. 2–38). New York: Plenum.

Achenbach, T.M. (1990). Conceptualization of developmental psychopathology. In M. Lewis & S. M. Miller (Eds.), *Handbook of developmental psychopathology.* New York: Plenum Press.

Achenbach, T.M. (1991). *Manual for the child behavior checklist: 4–18 and 1991 profile.* Burlington, VT: University of Vermont.

Achenbach, T.M., & Edelbrock, C. (1978). The classification of child psychopathology: A review and analysis of empirical efforts. *Psychological Bulletin, 85,* 1275–1301.

Achenbach, T.M., & Edelbrock, C. (1983). *Manual for the child behavior checklist and revised child behavior profile.* Burlington, VT: Psychiatry Associates, University of Vermont.

Agosta, J., & Melda, K. (1996). Supporting families who provide care at home for children with disabilities. *Exceptional Children, 62,* 271–282.

Albano, A.M., & Silverman, W. (1996). *Anxiety Disorders Interview Schedule for DSM-IV: Child version.* San Antonio, TX: Psychological Corporation.

Alessandri, S.M. (1992). Attention, play, and social behavior in ADHD preschoolers. *Journal of Abnormal Child Psychology, 20,* 289–302.

Alexander, J.F., Holtzworth-Munroe, A., & Jameson, P. (1994). The process and

outcome of marital and family therapy:
Research review and evaluation. In S.
Garfield & A. Bergin (Eds.), *Handbook of
psychotherapy and behavior change* (4th
ed, pp. 595–630). New York: Wiley.

Alford, B.A., & Norcross, J.C. (1991).
Cognitive therapy as integrative
therapy. *Journal of Psychotherapy
Integration, 1,* 175–190.

Alloy, L., Abramson, L., Murray, L.,
Whitehouse, W., & Hogan, M. (1997).
Self-referrant information processing in
individuals at high and low risk for
depression. *Cognition and Emotion, 11,*
539–568.

Alloy, L.B., & Clements, C.M. (1998).
Hopelessness theory of depression.
Tests of the symptom component.
Cognitive Therapy and Research, 22,
303–336.

Aman, M., Marks, R., Turbott, S., Wilsher,
C., & Merry, S. (1991). Clinical effects
of methylphenidate and thioridazine in
intellectually subaverage children.
*Journal of the American Academy of Child
and Adolescent Psychiatry, 30,* 246–256.

Aman, M.G., & Singh, N.N. (1983).
Pharmacological intervention. In L.
Matson & F. Andrasik (Eds.), *Treatment
issues and innovations in mental
retardation* (pp. 347–372). New York:
Plenum Press.

American Association of Mental
Retardation (1994). *Mental retardation:
Definition, classification, and system
support* (9th ed.), Washington, DC:
AAMR Publications.

American Psychiatric Association. (1952).
*Diagnostic and statistical manual of mental
disorders.* Washington, DC: Author.

American Psychiatric Association. (1994).
*Diagnostic and statistical manual of mental
disorders* (4th ed.). Washington, DC:
Author.

American Psychologist (1992). Reflections
on B.F. Skinner and psychology [Special
Issue], *47*(11).

Anastopoulos, A.D. (1996). Facilitating
parental understanding and
management of attention deficit and
hyperactivity disorder. In M.A.
Reinecke, F.M. Dattilio, & A. Freeman
(Eds.), *Cognitive therapy with children
and adolescents: A casebook for clinical
practice* (pp. 327–343). New York:
Guilford Press.

Anastopoulos, A.D., Barkley, R.A., &
Sheldon, T. (1996). Family based
treatment: Psychosocial intervention
for children and adolescents with
attention deficit hyperactivity disorder.
In E. Hibbs & P. Jensen (Eds.),
*Psychosocial treatments for child and
adolescent disorders: Empirically based
strategies for clinical practice* (pp.
267–284). Washington, DC: American
Psychological Association.

Anastopoulos, A.D., Shelton, T., DuPaul,
G.J., & Gouvremont, D.C. (1993).
Parent training for attention-deficit
hyperactivity disorder: Its impact on
parent functioning. *Journal of Abnormal
Child Psychology, 21,* 581–596.

Anderson, J.C., Williams, S., McGee, R., &
Silva, P.A. (1987). DSM-III disorders in
preadolescent children: Prevalence in a
large sample from the general
population. *Archives of General
Psychiatry, 44,* 69–76.

Aronson, M. Hagberg, B., & Gillberg, C.
(1997). Attention deficits and autistic
spectrum problems in children exposed
to alcohol during gestation: A follow-
up study. *Developmental Medicine and
Child Neurology, 39,* 683–587.

Ashbaugh, R., & Peck, S. (1998).
Treatment of sleep problems in a
toddler: A replication of the faded
bedtime with response cost protocol.
Journal of Applied Behavior Analysis, 31,
127–129.

August, G.J. (1987). Production
deficiencies in free recall: A comparison
of hyperactivity learning-disabled and

normal children. *Journal of Abnormal Child Psychology, 15,* 429–440.

Azrin, N.H., Sheed, T.J., & Foxx, R.M. (1974). Dry bed: Rapid elimination of childhood enuresis. *Behavior Research and Therapy, 12,* 147–156.

Babinski, L.M., Hartsough, C., & Lambert, N.M. (1999). Childhood conduct problems, hyperactivity-impulsivity, and inattention as predictors of adult criminal activity. *Journal of Child Psychology and Psychiatry, 40,* 347–355.

Baer, D., Wolf, M., & Risley, T. (1968). Some current dimensions of applied behavior analysis. *Journal of Applied Behavior Analysis, 1,* 91–97.

Bailey, A. (1993). The biology of autism. *Psychological Medicine, 23,* 7–11.

Bailey, A., Le Couteur, A., Gottesman, L., Bolton, P., Simonoff, E., Yuzda, E., & Rutter, M. (1995). Autism as a strongly genetic disorder: Evidence from a British twin study. *Psychological Medicine, 25,* 63–77.

Bailey, A., Palferman, S., Heavey, L.M., & Le Couteur, A. (1998). Genetics of autism: Overview and new directions. *Journal of Autism and Developmental Disabilities, 28,* 351–368.

Baker, B. (1984). Interventions with families with young severely handicapped children. In J. Blacker (Ed.), *Severely handicapped young children and their families.* New York: Academic.

Baker, B.L., Landen, S.J., & Kashima, K.J. (1991). Effects of parent training on families of children with mental retardation: Increased burden or generalized benefit? *American Journal on Mental Retardation, 96,* 127–136.

Bandura, A. (1969). *Principles of behavior modification.* New York: Holt, Rinehart & Winston.

Bandura, A. (1971). Psychotherapy based upon modeling procedures. In A. Bergin & S. Garfield (Eds.), *Handbook of psychotherapy and behavior change.* New York: Wiley.

Bandura, A. (1986). *Social learning theory.* Englewood Cliffs, NJ: Prentice-Hall.

Barclay, M., & Hoffman, J. (1990). Conduct disorders. In M. Lewis & S. Miller (Eds.), *Handbook of developmental psychopathology.* New York: Plenum Press.

Barkley, R.A., Anastopoulos, A. Guevremont, D., & Fletcher, K. (1992). Adolescents with ADHD: Mother–adolescent interactions, family beliefs and conflicts, and maternal psychopathology. *Journal of Abnormal Child Psychology, 20,* 263–288.

Barkley, R.A. (1990). *Attention deficit hyperactivity disorder: A handbook for diagnosis and treatment.* New York: Guilford Press.

Barkley, R.A. (1996). Attention-deficit/ hyperactivity disorder. In E.J. Mash & R.A. Barkley (Eds.), *Child psychopathology* (pp. 63–112). New York: Guilford Press.

Barkley, R.A. (1997a). Advancing age, declining ADHD. *American Journal of Psychiatry, 154,* 1323–1324.

Barkley, R.A. (1997b). Attention-deficit hyperactivity disorder. In E. Mash & L. Terdal (Eds.), *Assessment of childhood disorders* (3rd ed., pp. 71–129). New York: Guilford.

Barkley, R.A. (1997c). Behavioral inhibition, sustained attention, and executive functions: Constructing a unifying theory of ADHD. *Psychological Bulletin, 121,* 65–94.

Barkley, R.A., Fischer, M., Edelbrock, C., & Smallish, L. (1991). The adolescent outcome of hyperactive children diagnosed by research criteria-III: Mother–child interactions, family conflicts and maternal psychopathology. *Journal of Child Psychology and Psychiatry, 32,* 233–255.

Barkley, R.A., Guevremant, D.C., Anastopoulos, A.D., DuPaul, G.J., & Shelton, T.L. (1993). Driving-related risks and outcomes of attention-deficit hyperactivity disorder in adolescents and young adults: 3- to 5-year follow-up survey. *Pediatrics*, *92*, 212–218.

Barkley, R.A., Guevremant, D.C. Anastopoulos, A.D., & Fletcher, K.E. (1992). A comparison of three family conflicts in adolescents with attention deficit hyperactivity disorder. *Journal of Consulting and Clinical Psychology*, *60*, 450–462.

Barkley, R.A., Karlsson, J., Pollard, S., & Murphy, J.U. (1985). Developmental changes in the mother–child interactions of hyperactive boys: Effects of two dose levels of Ritalin. *Journal of Child Psychology and Psychiatry*, *26*, 705–715.

Barkley, R.A., McMurray, M.B., Edelbrock, C., & Robbins, K. (1990). Side effects of methylphenidate in children with attention-deficit hyperactivity disorder: A systematic, placebo-controlled evaluation. *Pediatrics*, *86*, 184–192.

Barlow, D.H. (1988). *Anxiety and its disorders*. New York: Guilford.

Barmann, B.C., & Murray, W.J. (1981). Suppression of inappropriate sexual behavior by facial screening. *Behavior Therapy*, *12*, 730–735.

Baron-Cohen, S., Leslie, A., & Frith, U. (1985). Does the autistic child have a "theory of mind"? *Cognition*, *21*, 37–46.

Barrett, P.M., Dadds, M., & Rapee, R.M. (1996a). Family treatment of childhood anxiety: A controlled trial. *Journal of Consulting and Clinical Psychology*, *64*, 333–342.

Barrett, P.M., Rapee, R.M., Dadds, M., & Ryan, S.M. (1996b). Family enhancement of cognitive style in anxious and aggressive children. *Journal of Abnormal Child Psychology*, *24*, 187–203.

Barrios, B.A., & Hartmann, D. (1997). Fear and anxieties. In E. Mash & L. Terdal (Eds.), *Assessment of childhood disorders* (3rd ed, pp. 230–327). New York: Guilford Publications.

Bauermeister, J.J., Bird, H.R., Canino, G., Rubio-Stipec, M., Bravo, M., & Algeria, M. (1995). Dimensions of attention deficit hyperactivity disorder: Findings from teacher and parent reports in a community sample. *Journal of Consulting and Clinical Psychology*, *24*, 264–271.

Baumeister, A.A., & Rollings, J.P. (1976). Self-injurious behavior. In N.R. Ellis (Ed.), *International review of research in mental retardation* (Vol. 8, pp. 87–112). New York: Academic.

Bauminger, N., & Kasari, C. (1999). Theory of mind in high-functioning children with autism. *Journal of Autism and Developmental Disabilities*, *29*, 81–87.

Beck, A.T. (1967). *Depression: Clinical, experimental, and theoretical aspects*. New York: Harper & Row.

Beck, A.T. (1976). *Cognitive theory and the emotional disorders*. New York: International University Press.

Beck, A.T. (1987). Cognitive models of depression. *Journal of Cognitive Psychotherapy*, *1*, 5–38.

Beck, A.T., & Emery, G. (1985). *Anxiety disorders and phobias: A cognitive perspective*. New York: Basic Books.

Beidel, D. (1991). Social phobia and overanxious disorder in school-aged children. *Journal of the American Academy of Child and Adolescent Psychiatry*, *30*, 545–552.

Beidel, D., & Randall, J. (1994). Social phobia. In T. Ollendick, N. King, & W. Yule, (Eds.), *International handbook of phobic and anxiety disorders in children and adolescents*. New York: Plenum Press.

Bemis-Vitousek, K., & Orimoto, L. (1993). Cognitive-behavioral models of anorexia nervosa, bulimia nervosa, and obesity. In K.S. Dobson & P.C. Kendall (Eds.), *Psychopathology and cognition* (pp. 193–245). San Diego: Academic Press.

Bettelheim, B. (1967). *The empty fortress.* New York: Free Press.

Bickett, L., & Milich, R. (1990). First impressions formed of boys with learning disabilities and attention deficit disorder. *Journal of Learning Disabilities, 23,* 253–259.

Biederman, J. (1992). New developments in pediatric psychopharmacology. *Journal of the American Academy of Child and Adolescent Psychiatry, 31,* 14–15.

Biederman, J., Milberger, S., Faraone, S.V., Kiely, K., Guite J., Mick, E., Ablon, S., Warburton, R., & Reed, E. (1995). Family-environment risk factors for attention-deficit hyperactivity disorder. *Archives of General Psychiatry, 52,* 464–470.

Biederman, J., Munir, K., Knee, D., Armentano, M., Autor, S., Waternaux, C., & Tsuang, M. (1987). High rate of affective disorders in probands with attention deficit disorder and in their relatives: A controlled family study. *American Journal of Psychiatry, 144,* 330–333.

Biederman, J., Rosenbaum, J.F., Bolduc-Murphy, E.A., Faraone, S.V., Chaloff, J., Hirshfeld, D.R., & Kagan, J. (1993). A 3-year follow-up of children with and without behavioral inhibition. *Journal of American Academy of Child and Adolescent Psychiatry, 32,* 814–821.

Birnbauer, J.S. (1976). Mental retardation. In H. Leitenberg (Ed.), *Handbook of behavior modification and behavior therapy* (pp. 227–249). Englewood Cliffs, NJ: Prentice-Hall.

Blagg, N.R., & Yule, W. (1984). The behavioral treatment of school refusal: A comparative study. *Behaviour Research and Therapy, 22,* 119–127.

Bliss, J. (1980). Sensory experiences of Gilles de la Tourette syndrome. *Archives of General Psychiatry, 37,* 1343–1347.

Bloomquist, M.L. (1996). *Skills training for children with behavior disorders.* New York: Guilford Press.

Bocella, K. (1995, September 24). Use of Ritalin for children is on the rise. *Philadelphia Inquirer,* pp. B1–B4.

Borden, M.C., & Ollendick, T.H. (1992). The development and differentiation of social subtypes in autism. In B. Lahey & A.E. Kazdin (Eds.), *Advances in clinical child psychology* (Vol. 14, pp. 61–106). New York: Plenum Press.

Bouchard, T.J., Lykken, D.T., McGue, M., Segal, N.L., & Tellegen, A. (1990). Sources of human psychological differences: The Minnesota study of twins reared apart. *Science, 250,* 223–250.

Bowlby, J. (1969). *Attention and loss: Attachment.* New York: Basic Books.

Bradley, R., Casey, P., & Wortham, B. (1984). Home environments of low SES nonorganic failure to thrive infants. *Merrill Palmer Quarterly, 30,* 393–402.

Brady, E.U., & Kendall, P.C. (1992). Comorbidity of anxiety and depression in children and adolescents. *Psychological Bulletin, 111,* 244–255.

Braswell, L. (1991). Involving parents in cognitive-behavioral therapy with children and adolescents. In P.C. Kendall (Ed.), *Child and adolescent therapy: Cognitive-behavioral procedures* (pp. 316–351). New York: Guilford Press.

Braswell, L., August, G., Bloomquist, M.L., Realmuto, G.M., Skare, S., & Crosby, R. (1997). School-based secondary prevention for children with disruptive behavior: Initial outcomes. *Journal of Abnormal Child Psychology, 25,* 197–208.

Braswell, L., & Bloomquist, M.L. (1991). *Cognitive-behavioral therapy with ADHD* children: *Child, family, and school interventions.* New York: Guilford Press.

Brennan, C. (1955). *An elementary textbook of psychoanalysis.* New York: International Universities Press.

Brent, D.A., Holder, D., Kolko, D., Birmaher, B., Baugher, M., Roth, C., Iyengar, S., & Johnson, B.A. (1997). A clinical psychotherapy trial for adolescent depression comparing cognitive, family, and supporting therapy. *Archives of General Psychiatry, 54,* 877–885.

Brewin, C.R. (1997). Psychological defenses and the distortion of meaning. In M. Power & C.R. Brewin (Eds.), *The transformation of meaning in psychological therapies* (pp. 107–123). Chichester, UK: Wiley.

Brewin, C.R., Andrews, B., & Gotlib, I.H. (1993). Psychopathology and early experience: A reappraisal of retrospective reports. *Psychological Bulletin, 113,* 82–98.

Brier, N. (1989). The relationship between learning disability and delinquency: A review and reappraisal. *Journal of Learning Disabilities, 22,* 546–553.

Bristol, M.M., Cohen, D.J., Costello, E.J., Denckla, M., Eckberg, T.J., Kallen, R., Kraemer, H.C., Lord, C., Maurer, R., McIlvane, W.J., Minshew, N., Sigman, M., & Spence, M.A. (1996). State of the science in autism: Report to the national institutes of health. *Journal of Autism and Developmental Disorders, 26,* 121–153.

Brown, R.T., Borden, K.A., Wynne, M.E., Schleser, R., & Clingerman, S.R. (1986). Methylphenidate and cognitive therapy with ADD children: A methodological reconsideration. *Journal of Abnormal Child Psychology, 13,* 69–87.

Brown, R.T., Wynne, M.E., & Medenis, R. (1985). Methylphenidate and cognitive therapy: A comparison of treatment approaches with hyperactive boys.

Journal of Abnormal Child Psychology, 13, 69–87.

Brownell, K.D. (1991). Dieting and the search for the perfect body: Where physiology and culture collide. *Behavior Therapy, 22,* 1–12.

Bruch, H. (1973). *Eating disorders: Obesity, anorexia nervosa, and the person within.* New York: Basic Books.

Bruch, H. (1978). *The golden cage: The enigma of anorexia nervosa.* Cambridge, MA: Harvard University Press.

Bryson, S.E. (1996). Brief report: Epidemiology of autism. *Journal of Autism and Developmental Disorders, 26,* 165–167.

Budd, K.S., & Chugh, C. (1998). Common feeding problems in young children. In T. Ollendick & R. Prinz (Eds.), *Advances in clinical child psychology* (Vol. 20, pp. 183–212). New York: Plenum Press.

Budd, K.S., McGraw, T., Farbisz, R., Murphy, T., Hawkins, D., Heilman, N., Werle, M., & Hochstadt, N. (1992). Psychosocial concomitants of children's feeding disorders. *Journal of Pediatric Psychology, 17,* 81–94.

Burt, D.B., Loveland, K., Chen, Y., & Chuang, A. (1995). Aging in adults with Down syndrome: Report from a longitudinal study. *American Journal on Mental Retardation, 100,* 262–270.

Butler, L., Mietzitiz, S., Friedman, R., & Cole, E. (1980). The effects of two school-based intervention programs on depressive symptoms in preadolescents. *American Educational Research Journal, 17,* 111–119.

Cadoret, R.J., Yates, W.R., Troughton, E., Woodworth, G., & Stewart, M.A. (1995). Adoption study demonstrating two genetic pathways to drug abuse. *Archives of General Psychiatry, 52,* 42–52.

Callocott, R., & Cooper, S. (1997). The five year follow-up study of adaptive behavior in adults with Down syndrome. *Journal of Intellectual and Developmental Disability, 22,* 187–197.

Camara, K.A., & Resnick, G. (1988). Interparental conflict and cooperation: Factors moderating children's post-divorce adjustment. In E.M. Hetherington & J.D. Arasteh (Eds.), *Impact of divorce, single parenting, and stepparenting on children* (pp. 169–195). Hillsdale, NJ: Lawrence Erlbaum Associates Inc.

Campbell, M. (1988). Annotation: Fenfluramine treatment of autism. *Journal of Child Psychology and Psychiatry, 29,* 1–10.

Campbell, S.M. (1986). Developmental issues. In R. Gittelman (Ed.), *Anxiety disorders of childhood* (pp. 24–57). New York: Guilford Press.

Cantwell, D.P. (1987, June). *Assessment and invention.* Paper presented at the conference "The nature of ADHD." Minneapolis, MN.

Caplan, M., Weissberg, R.P., Grober, J.S., Sivo, P.J., Grady, K., & Jacoby, C. (1992). Social competence promotion with inner-city and suburban young adolescents: Effects on social adjustment and alcohol use. *Journal of Consulting and Clinical Psychology, 60,* 56–63.

Carlson, C.L., Pelham, W., Milich, R., & Dixon, J. (1992). Single and combined effects of methylphenidate and behavior therapy on the classroom performance of children with attention-deficit hyperactivity disorder. *Journal of Abnormal Child Psychology, 20,* 213–232.

Carter, J.F. (1993). Self-management: Education's ultimate goal. *Teaching Exceptional Children, 28–31.*

Champion, L.A., Goodall, G., & Rutter, M. (1995). Behavior problems in childhood and stressors in early adult life: A 20 year follow-up of London school children. *Psychological Medicine, 25,* 231–246.

Chatoor, I., & Egan, J. (1983). Nonorganic failure to thrive and dwarfism due to food refusal: A separation disorder: *Journal of the American Academy of Child and Adolescent Psychiatry, 22,* 294–301.

Cheney, D., & Osher, T. (1997). Collaborate with families. *Journal of Emotional and Behavioral Disorders, 5,* 36–44.

Cherlin, A.J., Furstenberg, F.F., Chase-Lansdale, P.L., Kiernan, K., Robins, P., Morrison, D., & Teitler, J. (1991). Longitudinal studies of effects of divorce on children in Great Britain and the United States. *Science, 252,* 1368–1389.

Chess, S. (1977). Report on autism in congenital rubella. *Journal of Autism and Childhood Schizophrenia, 7,* 68–81.

Chodorow, N. (1978). *The reproduction of mothering: Psychoanalysis and the sociology of gender.* Berkeley, CA: University of California Press.

Cicchetti, D. (1993). Developmental psychopathology: Reactions, reflections, projections. *Developmental Review, 13,* 471–502.

Clarizio, H.F. (1994). *Assessment and treatment of depression in children and adolescents.* Brandon, VT: Clinical Psychology.

Clarren, S., & Smith, D.W. (1978). The fetal alcohol syndrome. *New England Journal of Medicine, 298,* 1063–1068.

Cohen, D., Paul, R., & Volkmar, F. (1986). Issues in the classification of pervasive and other developmental disorders: Toward DSM-IV. *Journal of the American Academy of Child Psychiatry, 25,* 213–220.

Cohen, R.Y., Brownell, K., & Felix, M.R.J. (1990). Age and sex differences in health habits of school children. *Health Psychology, 9,* 208–224.

Cohen, S., Ihrig, K., Lott, R., & Kerrick, J. (1998). Risperidone for aggression and self-injurious behavior in adults with mental retardation. *Journal of Autism* and *Developmental Disorders, 28,* 229–234.

Comings, D.E., & Comings, B.G. (1985). Tourette syndrome: Clinical and psychological aspects of 250 cases. *American Journal of Human Genetics, 37,* 435–450.

Comings, D.E., Comings, B.G., Devor, E.J., & Cloninger, C.R. (1984). Detection of a major gene for Gilles de la Tourette syndrome. *American Journal of Human Genetics, 37,* 435–450.

Compas, B. (1997). Depression in children and adolescents. In E. Mash & L. Terdal (Eds.), *Assessment of childhood disorders* (3rd ed., pp. 197–229). New York: Guilford Publications.

Conners, C.K. (1980). *Food additives and hyperactive children.* New York: Plenum Press.

Conners, C.K. (1990). *The Conners Rating Scales.* North Tonawanda, NY: Multi-Health Systems.

Conners, C.K., Sitarenios, G., Parker, J.D., & Epstein, J. (1998a). The Revised Conners Parent Rating Scale (CPRS-R): Factor structure, reliability, and criterion validity. *Journal of Abnormal Child Psychology, 26,* 257–268.

Conners, C.K., Sitarenios, G., Parker, J.D., & Epstein, J. (1998b). Revision and standardization of the Conners Teacher Rating Scale (CTRS-R): Factor structure, reliability, and criterion validity. *Journal of Abnormal Child Psychology, 26,* 279–292.

Conners, C.K., & Wherry, J.S. (1979). Pharmacotherapy. In H.C. Quay & J.S. Wherry (Eds.), *Psychopathological disorders of childhood.* New York: Wiley.

Conrad, M., & Hammen, C. (1989). Role of maternal depression in perceptions of child maladjustment. *Journal of Consulting and Clinical Psychology, 57,* 663–667.

Cook, E.H., Stein, M.A., Krasowski, M.D., Cox, N.J., Olkon, D.M., Kieffer, J., &

Leventhal, B. (1995). Association of attention deficit disorder and the dopamine transporter gene. *American Journal of Human Genetics, 56,* 993–998.

Cooper, P.J., & Goodyear, I. (1993). A community study of depression in adolescent girls: Estimates of symptom and syndrome prevalence. *British Journal of Psychiatry, 163,* 369–374.

Coovert, D.L., & Kinder, B. (1989). The psychosexual aspects of anorexia nervosa and bulimia nervosa: A review of the literature. *Clinical Psychology Review, 9,* 169–180.

Costello, E.J. (1989). Child psychiatric disorders and their correlates: A primary care pediatric sample. *Journal of the American Academy of Child and Adolescent Psychiatry, 28,* 851–855.

Costello, E.J., Burns, B., Angold, A., & Leaf, P. (1993). How can epidemiology improve mental health services of children and adolescents? *Journal of the American Academy of Child and Adolescent Psychiatry, 32,* 1106–1117.

Costello, E.J., Costello, A.J., Edelbrock, C., Burns, B.J., Dulcan, M.K., Brent, D., & Janiszewski, S. (1988). Psychiatric disorders in pediatric primary care: Prevalence and risk factors. *Archives of General Psychiatry, 45,* 1107–1116.

Coyle, J.T., Oster-Granite, D., & Gearhart, L. (1986). The neurobiological consequences of Down's syndrome. *Brain Research Bulletin, 16,* 773–787.

Coyne, J.C. (1982). A critique of cognition as causal entities with particular reference to depression. *Cognitive Therapy and Research, 6,* 3–13.

Craighead, L., & Agras, S. (1991). Mechanisms of action in cognitive-behavioral and pharmacological interventions for obesity and bulimia nervosa. *Journal of Consulting and Clinical Psychology, 59,* 115–125.

Craighead, W.E., Meyers, A.W., & Craighead, L.W. (1985). A conceptual model for cognitive-behavior therapy with children. *Journal of Abnormal Child Psychology, 13*, 331–342.

Crick, N., & Dodge, K. (1994). A review and reformulation of social information-processing mechanisms in children's social adjustment. *Psychological Bulletin, 115*, 74–101.

Crnic, K.A. (1988). Mental retardation. In E.J. Mash & L. Terdal (Eds.), *Behavioral assessment of childhood disorders* (2nd ed., pp. 317–354). New York: Guilford Press.

Crnic, K.A., Friedrich, W.N., & Greenberg, M.T. (1983). Adaptation of families with mentally retarded children: A model of stress, coping, and family ecology. *American Journal of Mental Deficiency, 88*, 125–138.

Crnic, K.A., & Reid, M. (1989). Mental retardation. In E. Mash & R. Barkley (Eds.), *Treatment of childhood disorders* (pp. 379–420). New York: Guilford Press.

Crow, R.R., Noyes, R., Pauls, D.L., & Slymen, D.J. (1983). A family study of panic disorder. *Archives of General Psychiatry, 40*, 1065–1069.

Cummings, E.M., & Cicchetti, D. (1990). Attachment, depression, and the transmission of depression. In M.T. Greenberg, D. Cicchetti, & E.M. Cummings (Eds.), *Attachment during the preschool years*. Chicago: University of Chicago Press.

Dalgleish, T., & Watts, F.N. (1990). Biases of attention and memory in disorders of anxiety and depression. *Clinical Psychology Review, 10*, 589–604.

Dawson, G., Klinger, L.G., Panagiotides, H., Lewy, A., & Castelloe, P. (1995). Subgroups of autistic children based on social behavior display distinct patterns of brain activity. *Journal of Abnormal Child Psychology, 23*, 569–583.

Dawson, G., Warrenburg, S., & Fuller, P. (1983). Hemispheric functioning and motor imitation in autistic persons. *Brain and Cognition, 2*, 346–354.

DeRicco, D.A., & Niemann, J.E. (1980). In vivo effects of peer modeling on drinking rate. *Journal of Applied Behavior Analysis, 13*, 149–152.

Deutsch, K. (1987). Genetic factors in attention deficit disorder: Paper presented at symposium on Disorders of Brain and Development and Cognition, Boston, MA. As cited in Barkley, R., & Anastopoulos, A. (1988). Biological factors in attention-deficit hyperactivity disorder. *The Behaviour Therapist, 11*, 47–53.

DiLalla, L.F., & Gottesman, I.I. (1989). Heterogeneity of causes for delinquency and criminality: Lifespan perspectives. *Development and Psychopathology, 1*, 339–349.

Dishion, T., French, D., & Patterson, G. (1995). The development and ecology of antisocial behavior. In D. Cicchetti & D. Cohen (Eds.), *Developmental psychopathology: Risk, disorder, and adaptation* (Vol. 2, pp. 421–471). New York: Wiley.

Dobson, K.S., & Kendall, P.C. (Eds.) (1993). *Psychopathology and cognition*. San Diego: Academic Press.

Dodge, K.A. (1985). Attributional bias in aggressive children. In P.C. Kendall (Ed.), *Advances in cognitive-behavioral research and therapy* (Vol. 4, pp. 75–111). New York: Academic Press.

Dodge, K.A., Pettit, G.S., Bates, J.E. & Valente, E. (1995). Social information-processing patterns partially mediate the effect of early physical abuse on later conduct problems. *Journal of Abnormal Psychology, 104*, 632–643.

Dolan, B. (1991). Cross-cultural aspects of anorexia nervosa and bulimia: A review. *International Journal of Eating Disorders, 10*, 67–79.

Doleys, D.M. (1977). Behavioral treatments for nocturnal enuresis in children: A review of the recent literature. *Psychological Bulletin, 84,* 30–54.

Doleys, D.M. (1983). Enuresis and encopresis. In T.H. Ollendick & M. Hersen (Eds.), *Handbook of child psychopathology* (pp. 291–316). New York: Plenum Press.

Dollard, J., & Miller, N.E. (1950). *Personality and psychotherapy.* New York: McGraw-Hill.

Donnellan, A.M. (Ed.) (1985). *Classic readings in autism.* New York: Teachers College Press.

Dornbusch, S.M., Carlsmith, J.M., Bushwall, S.J., Ritter, P.L., Leiderman, H., Hastorf, A.H., & Gross, R.T. (1985). Single parents, extended households, and the control of adolescents. *Child Development, 56,* 326–341.

Douglas, V.I. (1983). Attention and cognitive problems. In M. Rutter (Ed.), *Developmental neuropsychiatry* (pp. 280–329). New York: Guilford Press.

Down, J.L. (1866). Observations of an ethnic classification of idiots. *Clinical Lectures and Reports (London Hospital), 3,* 259–262.

Dumas, J.E. (1989). Treating antisocial behavior in children: Child and family approaches. *Clinical Psychology Review, 9,* 197–222.

Dunant, Y., & Israel, M. (1985). The release of acetylcholine. *Scientific American, 252,* 58–83.

DuPaul, G.J., Barkley, R.A., & McMurray, M.B. (1994). Response of children with ADHD to methylphenidate: Interaction with internalizing symptoms. *Journal of the American Academy of Child and Adolescent Psychiatry, 33,* 894–903.

Dykens, E., Hodapp, R.M., Ort, S., & Leckman, J.F. (1993). Trajectory of adaptive behavior in males with fragile X syndrome. *Journal of Autism and Developmental Disorders, 26,* 287–301.

Dykens, E., Ort, S., Cohen, I., Spiridigliozzi, G., Lachiewicz, A., Reiss, A., Freund, L., Hagerman, R., & O'Connor, R. (1996). Trajectories and profiles of adaptive behavior in males with fragile X syndrome: Multicenter studies. *Journal of Autism and Developmental Disorders, 26,* 287–301.

Earls, F. (1994). Oppositional-defiant and conduct disorders. In M. Rutter, E. Taylor, & L. Hersov (Eds.), *Child and adolescent psychiatry* (pp. 308–329). Oxford, UK: Blackwell Scientific Publications.

Edelbrock, C., & Costello, A.J. (1988). Structured psychiatric interviews for children. In M. Rutter, A.H. Tuma, & I.S. Lann (Eds.), *Assessment and diagnosis in child psychopathology.* New York: Guilford Press.

Einfeld, S.L., & Aman, M. (1995). Issues in the taxonomy of psychopathology in mental retardation. *Journal of Autism and Developmental Disorders, 25,* 143–167.

Eiserman, W.D., Shisler, L., & Healey, S. (1995). A community assessment of preschool providers' attitudes toward inclusion. *Journal of Early Intervention, 19,* 149–167.

Ellis, A., & Harper, R. (1975). *A new guide to rational living.* New York: Wilshire Books.

Eme, R.F., & Kavanaugh, L. (1995). Sex differences in conduct disorder. *Journal of Consulting and Clinical Psychology, 24,* 406–426.

Emslie, G.J., Rush, A., Weinberg, A., Kowatch, R., Hughes, C., Carmody, T., & Rintelmann, J. (1997). A double-blind, randomized, placebo-controlled trial of fluoxetine in children and adolescents with depression. *Archives of General Psychiatry, 54,* 1031–1037.

Erdelyi, M.H. (1985). *Psychoanalysis: Freud's cognitive psychology.* New York: Freeman.

Erhardt, D., & Hinshaw, S.P. (1994). Initial sociometric impressions of ADHD and comparison boys: Predictions from social behaviors and from nonbehavioral variables. *Journal of Consulting and Clinical Psychology, 62,* 833–842.

Eron, L.D., & Huesmann, L.R. (1990). The stability of aggressive behavior—even unto the third generation. In M. Lewis & S.M. Miller (Eds.), *Handbook of developmental psychopathology* (pp. 110–136). New York: Plenum Press.

Evans, J.A., & Hammerton, J.L. (1985). Chromosomal anomalies. In A.M. Clarke, A.D. Clark, & J.M. Berg (Eds.), *Mental deficiency: The changing outlook* (pp. 74–92). New York: Free Press.

Eyberg, S. (1988). Parent–child interaction therapy: Integration of traditional and behavioral concerns. *Child and Family Behaviour Therapy, 10,* 33–46.

Fairburn, C.G., & Beglin, S.J. (1990). Studies of the epidemiology of bulimia nervosa. *American Journal of Psychiatry, 147,* 401–408.

Fairburn, C.G., & Cooper, P.J. (1984). The clinical features of bulimia nervosa. *British Journal of Psychiatry, 144,* 238–246.

Fairburn, C.G., Jones, R., Peveler, R.C., Hope, R.A., & O'Connor, M. (1993). Psychotherapy and bulimia nervosa: Longer-term effects of interpersonal psychotherapy, behavior therapy, and cognitive-behavior therapy. *Archives of General Psychiatry, 50,* 419–428.

Fauber, R., & Kendall, P.C. (1992). Children and families: Integrating the focus of interventions. *Journal of Psychotherapy Integration, 2,* 107–124.

Fauber, R., & Long, N. (1991). Children in context: The role of the family in child psychotherapy. *Journal of Consulting and Clinical Psychology, 59,* 813–820.

Fava, M., Copeland, P., Schweiger, U., & Herzog, D.B. (1989). Neurochemical abnormalities of anorexia nervosa and bulimia nervosa. *American Journal of Psychiatry, 146,* 963–971.

Favell, J.E., Azrin, N.H., Baumeister, A.A., Carr, E.G., Dorsey, M.F., Forehand, R., Foxx, R.M., Lovaas, O.I., Rincover, A., Risley, T.R., Romanczyk, R.G., Russo, D.C., Schroeder, S.R., & Solnick, J.V. (1982). The treatment of self-injurious behavior. *Behavior Therapy, 13,* 529–554.

Favell, J.E., & Green, J.W. (1981). *How to treat self-injurious behavior.* Lawrence, KS: H & H Enterprises.

Feingold, B.F. (1975). *Why your child is hyperactive.* New York: Random House.

Fergusson, D., Lynskey, M., & Horwood, L. (1997). Attentional difficulties in middle childhood and psychosocial outcomes in young adulthood. *Journal of Child Psychology and Psychiatry, 38,* 633–644.

Ferster, C.B. (1961). Positive reinforcement and behavioral deficits in autistic children. *Child Development, 32,* 437–456.

Finch, A.J., Lipovsky, J., & Casat, C. (1989). Anxiety and depression in children and adolescents: Negative affectivity or separate constructs. In P.C. Kendall & D. Watson (Eds.), *Anxiety and depression: Distinctive and overlapping features* (pp. 171–204). New York: Academic Press.

Fincham, F., & Spettell, C. (1984). The acceptability of dry bed training and urine alarm training as treatments of nocturnal enuresis. *Behavior Therapy, 15,* 388–394.

Finley, W.W., Wansley, R.A., & Blenkarn, M.M. (1977). Conditioning treatment of enuresis using a 70% intermittent reinforcement schedule. *Behaviour Research and Therapy, 15,* 419–427.

Fischer, M., Barkley, R.A., Edelbrock, C.S., & Smallish, L. (1990). The adolescent outcome of hyperactive children diagnosed by research criteria: Academic, attentional, and neuropsychological status. *Journal of Consulting and Clinical Psychology, 58,* 580–588.

Fischler, G., & Kendall, P.C. (1988). Social cognitive problem-solving and childhood adjustment: Qualitative and topological analyses. *Cognitive Therapy and Research, 12,* 133–154.

Folstein, S., & Rutter, M. (1977). Autism: Familial aggregation and genetic implications. *Journal of Autism and Developmental Disorders, 18,* 3–30.

Folstein, S., & Rutter, M. (1978). A twin study of individuals with infantile autism. In M. Rutter & E. Schopler (Eds.), *Autism: A reappraisal of concepts and treatment.* New York: Plenum Press.

Fombonne, E. (1998). Preface to the Special Issue on the genetics of autism. *Journal of Autism and Developmental Disabilities, 28,* 349–451.

Foote, R., Eyberg, S., & Schuhmann, E. (1998). Parent–child interaction approaches to the treatment of child behavior problems. In T. Ollendick & R. Prinz (Eds.), *Advances in clinical child psychology* (Vol. 20). New York: Plenum Press.

Forehand, R., & McMahon, R.J. (1981). *Helping the noncompliant child: A clinician's guide to parent training.* New York: Guilford Press.

Foreyt, J.P., & McGavin, J.K. (1988). Anorexia nervosa and bulimia. In E.J. Mash & L.G. Terdal (Eds.), *Behavioral assessment of childhood disorders* (2nd ed., pp. 776–805). New York: Guilford Press.

Foreyt, J.P., & Mikhail, C. (1997). Anorexia nervosa and bulimia nervosa. In E. Mash & L. Terdal (Eds.), *Assessment of childhood disorders* (3rd ed., pp. 683–716). New York: Guilford Press.

Freud, S. (1913). *The interpretation of dreams* (A.A. Brill, Trans.). London: Allen & Unwin.

Freud, S. (1914). *Psychopathology of everyday life.* London: Fischer Unwin.

Freud, S. (1943). *A general introduction to psychoanalysis.* Garden City, NY: (Original work published 1917 in German).

Freud, S. (1984). *The Pelican Freud Library: Vol 11. A note on the unconscious in psychoanalysis.* Harmondsworth, UK: Penguin. (Original work published 1912).

Freud, S. (1984). *The Pelican Freud Library: Vol 11. The unconscious.* Harmondsworth, UK: Penguin. (Original work published 1917).

Friedhoff, A.J., & Chase, T.N. (Eds.). (1982). *Gilles de la Tourette syndrome.* New York: Raven Press.

Furstenberg, F.F. (1988). Child care after divorce and remarriage. In E.M. Hetherington & J.D. Arasteh (Eds.), *Impact of divorce, single parenting, and stepparenting on children.* Hillsdale, NJ: Lawrence Erlbaum Associates Inc.

Fyer, A.J., Mannuzza, S.,Gallops, M.S., Martin, L.Y, Aaronson, C., Gorman, J.M., Liebowitz, M.R., & Klein, D.F. (1990). Familial transmission of simple phobias and fears. *Archives of General Psychiatry, 47,* 252–256.

Gadow, K.D. (1992). Pediatric psychopharmacology: A review of recent research. *Journal of Child Psychology and Psychiatry, 33,* 153–195.

Gadow, K.D., Sverd, J., Sprafkin, J., Nolan, E.E., & Ezor, S.N. (1995). Efficacy of methylphenidate for attention-deficit hyperactivity disorder in children with tic disorder. *Archives of General Psychiatry 52,* 444–455.

Garber, J., Braafladt, N., & Zeman, J. (1991). The regulation of sad affect: An information processing perspective. In J. Garber & K. Dodge (Eds.), *The development of emotion regulation and dysregulation* (pp. 208–240). New York: Cambridge University Press.

Garber, J., Kriss, M.R., Koch, M., & Lindholm, L. (1988). Recurrent depression in adolescents: A follow-up study. *Journal of the American Academy of Child and Adolescent Psychiatry, 27,* 49–54.

Garner, D.M., & Bemis-Vitousek, K.M. (1985). Cognitive therapy for anorexia nervosa. In D.M. Garner & P.E. Garfinkel (Eds.), *Handbook of psychotherapy for anorexia nervosa and bulimia* (pp. 107–146). New York: Guilford Press.

Gewirtz, J.L., & Peláez-Nogueras, M. (1992). B.F. Skinner's legacy to human infant behavior and development. *American Psychologist, 47,* 1411–1422.

Gilberg, C. (1990). Autism and pervasive developmental disorders. *Journal of Child Psychology and Psychiatry, 31,* 99–119.

Giles, D.K., & Wolf, M.W. (1966). Toilet training institutionalized, severe retardates: An application of operant behavior modification techniques. *American Journal of Mental Deficiency, 70,* 766–780.

Gilger, J.W., Pennington, B.F., & DeFries, J.C. (1992). A twin study of the etiology of comorbidity: Attention-deficit hyperactivity disorder and dyslexia. *Journal of the American Academy of Child and Adolescent Psychiatry, 31,* 343–348.

Gill, M., Daly, G., Heron, S., Hawi, Z., & Fitzgerald, M. (1997). Confirmation of an association between attention deficit disorder hyperactivity disorder and a dopamine transporter polymorphism. *Molecular Psychiatry, 2,* 311–313.

Gittelman, R., Mannuzza, S., Shenker, R., & Bonagura, N. (1985). Hyperactive boys almost grown up. *Archives of General Psychiatry, 42,* 937–947.

Gladstone, T.R.G., Kaslow, N.J., Seeley, J.R., & Lewinsohn, P.M. (1997). Sex differences, attributional style, and depressive symptoms among adolescents. *Journal of Abnormal Child Psychology, 25,* 297–305.

Goldstein, S., & Goldstein, M. (1998). *Managing attention deficit hyperactivity disorder in children: A guide for practitioners.* New York: John Wiley & Sons.

Goodman, R. (1989). Infantile autism: A syndrome of multiple primary deficits? *Journal of Autism and Developmental Disorders, 19,* 409–429.

Gordon, C.T., State, R.C., Nelson, J.E., Hamburger, S.D., & Rapoport, J.L. (1993). A double-blind comparison of clomipramine, desipramine, and placebo in the treatment of autistic disorder. *Archives of General Psychiatry, 50,* 441–447.

Gottesman, I.I., McGuffin, P., & Farmer, A.E. (1987). Clinical genetics as clues to the "real" genetics of schizophrenia. *Schizophrenia Bulletin, 13,* 23–47.

Gottesman, I.I., & Shields, J. (1972). *Schizophrenia and genetics: A twin study vantage point.* New York: Academic Press.

Greene, R., Biederman, J., Faraone, S., Sienna, M., & Garcia-Jetton, J. (1997). Adolescent outcome of boys with ADHD and social disability: Results from a 4-year longitudinal follow-up study. *Journal of Consulting and Clinical Psychology, 65,* 758–767.

Gresham, F., & MacMillan, D. (1997). Denial and defensiveness in the place of fact and reason: Rejoinder to Smith and Lovaas. *Behavioral Disorders, 22,* 219–230.

Gubbay, S.S., Lobascher, M., & Kingerlee, P. (1970). A neurological appraisal of autistic children: Results of a Western Australian survey. *Developmental Medicine and Child Neurology, 12,* 424–429.

Hagan, J.W., & Hale, G.H. (1973). The development of attention in children. In A. Pick (Ed.), *Minnesota Symposium on*

Child Psychology (Vol. 7). Minneapolis, MN: University of Minnesota Press.

Hallahan, D.P., Kneedler, R.D., & Lloyd, J.W. (1983). Cognitive behavior modification techniques for learning disabled children. In J.D. McKinney & L. Feagans (Eds.), *Current topics in learning disabilities* (Vol. 1). New York: Ablex.

Hammen, C. (1991). *Depression runs in families: The social context of risk and resilience in children of depressed mothers.* New York: Springer-Verlag.

Hammen, C. (1997). *Depression.* Hove, UK: Psychology Press.

Hammock, R.G., Schroeder, S.R., & Levine, W.R. (1995). The effect of clozapine on self-injurious behavior. *Journal of Autism and Developmental Disorders, 25,* 611–626.

Handen, B. (1998). Mental retardation. In E. Mash & R. Barkley (Eds.), *Treatment of childhood disorders* (2nd ed., pp. 369–415). New York: Guilford Press.

Handen, B., Mandell, F., & Russo, D. (1986). Feeding induction in children who refuse to eat. *American Journal of Diseases of Children, 140,* 52–54.

Handen, B.L., Breaux, A.M., Janosky, J., McAuliffe, S., Feldman, S., & Gosling, A. (1992). Effects and noneffects of methylphenidate in children with mental retardation and ADHD. *Journal of the American Academy of Child and Adolescent Psychiatry, 31,* 455–461.

Hansen, C., Weiss, D., & Last, C. (1999). ADHD boys in young adulthood: Psychosocial adjustment. *Journal of the American Academy of Child and Adolescent Psychiatry, 38,* 165–171.

Hansen, D.R., & Gottesman, I.I. (1976). The genetics, if any, of infantile autism and childhood schizophrenia. *Journal of Autism and Childhood Schizophrenia, 6,* 209–234.

Harrington, R.C. (1994). Affective disorders. In M. Rutter, E. Taylor, & L. Hersov (Eds.), *Child and adolescent psychiatry* (pp. 330–350). Oxford, UK: Blackwell Scientific Publications.

Harrington, R.C., Fudge, H., Rutter, M., Pickles, A., & Hill, J. (1990). Adult outcomes of childhood and adolescent depression: I. Psychiatric status. *Archives of General Psychiatry, 47,* 465–473.

Harris, S.L. (1983). *Families of the developmentally disabled: A guide to behavioral intervention.* New York: Pergamon Press.

Hauck, M., Fein, D., Waterhouse, L., & Feinstein, C. (1995). Social initiations by autistic children to adults and other children. *Journal of Autism and Developmental Disorders, 25,* 579–595.

Hawkins, J.D, Arthur, M., & Olson, J. (1997). Community interventions to reduce risks and enhance protection against antisocial behavior. In D. Stoff, J. Breiling, & J. Maser (Eds.), *Handbook of antisocial behavior* (pp. 365–374). New York: Wiley.

Haywood, H.C., Meyers, C.E., & Switzky, H.N. (1982). Mental retardation. In M. Rosenzweig & L. Porter (Eds.), *Annual review of psychology.* Palo Alto, CA: Annual Reviews, Inc.

Heimberg, R.G., Dodge, C.S., Hope, D.A., Kennedy, C.R., Zollo, L.J., & Becker, R.J. (1990). Cognitive behavioral group treatment for social phobia: Comparison with a credible placebo control. *Cognitive Therapy and Research, 14,* 1–23.

Henggeler, S., & Borduin, C. (1990). *Family therapy and beyond: A multisystemic approach to treating the behavior problems of children and adolescents.* Pacific Grove, CA: Brooks/Cole.

Henggeler, S., Melton, G., Brondino, M., Scherer, D., & Hanley, J. (1997). Multisystemic therapy with violent and chronic juvenile offenders and their families: The role of treatment fidelity in successful dissemination. *Journal of Consulting and Clinical Psychology, 65,* 821–833.

Henin, A., & Kendall, P.C. (1997). Obsessive-compulsive disorder in childhood and adolescence. In T. Ollendick & R. Prinz (Eds.), *Advances in clinical child psychology* (Vol. 19, pp. 75–132), New York: Plenum Press.

Herjanic, B., & Reich, W. (1982). Development of a structured psychiatric interview for children: Agreement between child and parent on individual symptoms. *Journal of Abnormal Child Psychology, 10,* 307–324.

Hermelin, B. (1976). Coding and the sense modalities. In L. Wing (Ed.), *Early childhood autism* (2nd ed.). Oxford, UK: Pergamon.

Hersov, L. (1994). Fecal soiling. In M. Rutter, E. Taylor, & L. Hersov (Eds.), *Child and adolescent psychiatry* (pp. 520–528). Oxford, UK: Blackwell Scientific Publications.

Hetherington, E.M. (1987). Family relations six years after divorce. In K. Pasley & M. Ihinger-Tallman (Eds.), *Remarriage and stepparenting: Current research and theory.* New York: Guilford Press.

Hetherington, E.M., Law, T., & O'Connor, T. (1993). Divorce: Challenges, changes, and new chances. In F. Walsh (Ed.), *Normal family processes* (2nd ed., pp. 208–234). New York: Guilford Press.

Hetherington, E.M., Stanley-Hagan, M., & Anderson, E.R. (1989). Marital transitions: A child's perspective. *American Psychologist, 44,* 303–312.

Hibbs, E., & Jensen, P. (Eds.). (1996). *Psychosocial treatments for child and adolescent disorders: Empirically based strategies for clinical practice.* Washington DC: American Psychological Association.

Hill, J., & Schoener, E. (1997). Advancing age, declining ADHD: Reply. *American Journal of Psychiatry, 154,* 1324–1325.

Hinshaw, S.P. (1987). On the distinction between attentional deficits/hyperactivity and conduct problems/aggression in child psychopathology. *Psychological Bulletin, 101,* 443–463.

Hinshaw, S.P. (1992). Externalizing behavior problems and academic underachievement in children and adolescence: Causal relationships and underlying mechanisms. *Psychological Bulletin, 111,* 127–155.

Hinshaw, S.P. (1996). Enhancing social competence: Integrating self-management strategies with behavioral procedures for children with ADHD. In E. Hibbs & P. Jensen (Eds.), *Psychosocial treatments for child and adolescent disorders: Empirically based strategies for clinical practice.* Washington DC: American Psychological Association.

Hinshaw, S.P., & Erhardt, D. (1991). Attention-deficit hyperactivity disorder. In P.C. Kendall (Ed.), *Child and adolescent therapy: Cognitive-behavioral procedures* (pp. 98–128). New York: Guilford Press.

Hinshaw, S.P., Henker, B., & Whalen, C.K. (1984a). Cognitive-behavioral and pharmacologic interventions for hyperactive boys: Comparative and combined effects. *Journal of Consulting and Clinical Psychology, 52,* 739–749.

Hinshaw, S.P., Henker, B., & Whalen, C.K. (1984b). Self-control in hyperactive boys in anger-inducing situations: Effects of cognitive-behavioral training and of methylphenidate. *Journal of Abnormal Child Psychology, 12,* 55–77.

Hinshaw, S.P., & Zupan, B. (1997). Assessment of antisocial behavior in children and adolescents. In D. Stoff, J. Breiling, & J. Maser (Eds.), *Handbook of antisocial behavior* (pp. 36–50). New York: Wiley.

Hoek, H.W. (1991). The incidence and prevalence of anorexia nervosa and bulimia nervosa in primary care. *Psychological Medicine, 21,* 455–460.

Holland, A.J., Sicotte, N., & Treasure, J. (1988). Anorexia nervosa—evidence for a genetic basis. *Journal of Psychosomatic Research, 32,* 561–572.

Homatidis, S., & Konstantareas, M.M. (1981). Assessment of hyperactivity: Isolating measures of high discriminant validity. *Journal of Consulting and Clinical Psychology, 49,* 533–541.

Hook, E.B. (1987). Issues in analysis of data on parental age: Implications for genetic counseling for Down's syndrome. *Human Genetics, 77,* 303–306.

Hook, E.B., Cross, P.K., & Regal, R.R. (1990). Factual, statistical and logical issues in the search for a paternal age effect for Down syndrome. *Human Genetics, 85,* 387–388.

Hopper, M., & Garner, D. (1986). Applicatons of the eating disorder inventory to a sample of black, white, and mixed-race schoolgirls in Zimbabwe. *International Journal of Eating Disorders, 5,* 161–168.

Houts, A.C., Berman, J.S., & Abramson, H. (1994). The effectiveness of psychological and pharmacologic treatments for nocturnal enuresis. *Journal of Consulting and Clinical Psychology.*

Howlin, P.A. (1981). The effectiveness of operant language training with autistic children. *Journal of Autism and Developmental Disorders, 11,* 89–105.

Howlin, P.A., & Rutter, M. (1987). *Treatment of autistic children.* New York: Wiley.

Huguenin, N., Weidenman, L., & Mulick, J. (1991). Programmed instruction. In J. Matson & J. Mulick (Eds.), *Handbook of*

mental retardation (2nd ed., pp. 250–277). New York: Pergamon Press.

Humphrey, L.L., Apple, R.F., & Kirschenbaum, D.S. (1986). Differentiating bulimic-anorexic from normal families using interpersonal and behavioral observational systems. *Journal of Consulting and Clinical Psychology, 54,* 190–195.

Iaboni, F., Douglas, V.I., & Baker, A.G. (1995). Effects of reward and response costs on inhibition in ADHD children. *Journal of Abnormal Psychology, 104,* 232–240.

IDEA (1991). *Individuals with Disabilities Education Act* (Vol. 34, p. 300).

Individuals with Disabilities Education Act (IDEA). (1990). Public Law No. 101-476, 20, U.S.C. 1400.

Ingram, R.E. (1984). Toward an information processing analysis of depression. *Cognitive Therapy and Research, 8,* 443–478.

Ingram, R.E. (Ed.). (1986). *Information processing approaches to clinical psychology.* New York: Academic Press.

Ingram, R.E. (1998). Cognitive processes and vulnerability to affective problems. *Cognitive Therapy and Research, 22,* 301–303.

Ingram, R.E., Miranda, J., & Segal, Z.V. (1998). *Cognitive vulnerability to depression.* New York: Guilford Press.

Jacobson, J.W. (1982a). Problem behavior and psychiatric impairment within a developmentally disabled population: I. Behavior frequency. *Applied Research in Mental Retardation, 3,* 369–381.

Jacobson, J.W. (1982b). Problem behavior and psychiatric impairment within a developmentally disabled population: II. Behavior severity. *Applied Research in Mental Retardation, 3,* 369–381.

Janovic, J., & Rohaidy, H. (1987). Motor, behavioral and pharmacologic findings in Tourette's syndrome. *Canadian*

Journal of Neurological Science, 14, 541–546.

Jayson, D., Wood, A., Kroll, L., Fraser, J., & Harrington, R. (1998). Which depressed patients respond to cognitive-behavioral treatment? *Journal of the American Academy of Child and Adolescent Psychiatry, 37,* 35–39.

Jehu, D., Morgan, R.T.T., Turner, R.K., & Jones, A. (1977). A controlled trial of the treatment of nocturnal enuresis in residential homes for children. *Behavior Research and Therapy, 15,* 1–16.

Jennings, J., Van der Molen, M., Pelham, W., Brock, K., & Hoza, B. (1997). Psychophysiology of inhibition in boys with attention deficit disorder. *Developmental Psychology, 33,* 308–318.

Jerome, L., & Segal, A. (1997). ADHD and dangerous driving. *Journal of the American Academy of Child and Adolescent Psychiatry, 36,* 13–25.

Jersild, A.T., & Holmes, F.B. (1935). *Children's fears.* New York: Teachers College, Columbia University.

Johnson, C.R., Lubetsky, M.J., & Sacco, K.A. (1995). Psychiatric and behavioral disorders in hospitalized preschoolers with developmental disabilities. *Journal of Autism and Developmental Disorders, 25,* 169–182.

Jones, D.J., Fox, M.M., Babigian, H., & Hutton, H. (1980). Epidemiology of anorexia nervosa in Monroe County, New York: 1960–1976. *Psychosomatic Medicine, 42,* 551–558.

Jones, K.L. (1988). *Smith's recognizable patterns of human malformation* (4th ed.). Philadelphia: Saunders.

Jones, K.L., & Smith, B.W. (1973). Recognition of the fetal alcohol syndrome in early infancy. *Lancet, 2,* 999–1001.

Jones, R.L. (1996, August 21). Sharp rise reported in teenagers' drug use. *Philadelphia Inquirer,* pp. A1–A15.

Jouriles, E.N., Bourg, W.J., & Farris, A.M. (1991). Marital adjustment and child conduct problems: A comparison of the correlation across subsamples. *Journal of Consulting and Clinical Psychology, 59,* 354–357.

Jouriles, E.N., McDonald, R., Norwood, W., Ware, H., Spiller, L., & Swank, P. (1998). Knives, guns, and interparental violence: Relations with child behavioral problems. *Journal of Family Psychology, 12,* 178–194.

Kagan, J. (1966). Reflection-impulsivity: The generality and dynamics of conceptual tempo. *Journal of Abnormal Psychology, 59,* 354–357.

Kalat, J.W. (1995). *Biological psychology* (5th ed.). Pacific Grove, CA: Brooks/Cole.

Kalucy, R.S., Crisp, A.H., & Harding, B. (1977). A study of 56 families with anorexia nervosa. *British Journal of Medical Psychology, 50,* 381–395.

Kanner, L. (1943). Autistic disturbances of affective contact. *Nervous Child, 21,* 217–250.

Kashani, J.H., & Carlson, G.A. (1987). Seriously depressed preschoolers. *American Journal of Psychiatry, 144,* 348–350.

Kashani, J.H., & Orvaschel, H. (1988). Anxiety disorders in midadolescence: A community sample. *American Journal of Psychiatry, 145,* 960–964.

Kaslow, N., Brown, R., & Mees, L. (1994). Cognitive and behavioral correlates of childhood depression: A developmental perspective. In W.M. Reynolds & H. Johnston (Eds.), *Handbook of depression in children and adolescents* (pp. 97–122). New York: Plenum Press.

Kaslow, N., & Thompson, M. (1998). Applying the criteria for empirically supported treatments to studies of psychosocial interventions for child and adolescent depression. *Journal of Clinical Child Psychology, 27,* 146–155.

Katz-Garris, L. (1978). The right to education. In J. Wortis (Ed.), *Mental retardation and developmental disabilities* (Vol. 10). New York: Bruner/Mazel.

Kazdin, A.E. (1981). Assessment techniques for childhood depression: A critical appraisal. *Journal of the American Academy of Child and Adolescent Psychiatry*, 20, 358–375.

Kazdin, A.E. (1990). Conduct disorder in childhood. In M. Hersen & C. Last (Eds.), *Handbook of adult and child psychopathology: A longitudinal perspective* (pp. 295–306). New York: Pergamon Press.

Kazdin, A.E. (1994). Psychotherapy for children and adolescents. In S. Garfield & A. Bergin (Eds.), *Handbook of psychotherapy and behavior change* (4th ed., pp. 543–594). New York: Wiley.

Kazdin, A.E. (1996). Problem solving and parent management in treating aggressive and antisocial behavior. In E. Hibbs & P. Jensen (Eds.), *Psychosocial treatments for child and adolescent disorders: Empirically based strategies for clinical practice* (pp. 377–408). Washington, DC: American Psychological Association.

Kazdin, A.E., Esveldt-Dawson, K., Unis, A.S., & Rancurello, M.D. (1983). Child and parent evaluations of depression and aggression in psychiatric inpatient children. *Journal of Abnormal Child Psychology*, 11, 401–413.

Kazdin, A.E., & Kendall P.C. (1998). Current progress and future plans for developing effective treatments: Comments and perspectives. *Journal of Clinical Child Psychology*, 27, 217–226.

Kazdin, A.E., Siegel, T.C., & Bass, D. (1992). Cognitive-behavioural problem-solving skills training and parent management training in the treatment of antisocial child behavior. *Journal of Consulting and Clinical Psychology*, 60, 733–747.

Kazdin, A.E., & Weisz, J.R. (1998). Identifying and developing empirically supported child and adolescent treatments. *Journal of Consulting and Clinical Psychology*, 66, 19–36.

Keel, P.K., Mitchell, J., Miller, K., Davis, T., & Crow, S. (1999). Long-term outcome of bulimia nervosa. *Archives of General Psychiatry*, 56, 63–69.

Keller, M.B., Lavori, P., Wunder, J. Beardslee, W.R., Schwartz, C.E., & Roth, J. (1992). Chronic course of anxiety disorders in children and adolescents. *Journal of the American Academy of Child and Adolescent Psychiatry*, 31, 595–599.

Kendall, P.C. (Ed.) (1991). *Child and adolescent therapy: Cognitive-behavioral procedures*. New York: Guilford Press.

Kendall, P.C. (1992). *Coping cat workbook*. Ardmore, PA: Workbook Publishing.

Kendall, P.C. (1993). Cognitive-behavioral therapies with youth: Guiding theory current status, and emerging developments. *Journal of Consulting and Clinical Psychology*, 61, 235–247.

Kendall, P.C. (1994). Treating anxiety disorders in youth: Results of a randomized clinical trial. *Journal of Consulting and Clinical Psychology*, 62, 100–110.

Kendall, P.C. (1998). Empirically supported psychological therapies. *Journal of Consulting and Clinical Psychology*, 66, 3–7.

Kendall, P.C. (Ed.) (2000). *Child and adolescent therapy: Cognitive-behavioral procedures* (2nd ed.). New York: Guilford Press.

Kendall, P.C., & Braswell, L. (1993). *Cognitive behavioral therapy for impulsive children* (2nd ed.). New York: Guilford Press.

Kendall, P.C., Cantwell, D., & Kazdin, A.E. (1989). Depression in children and adolescents: Assessment issues and recommendations. *Cognitive Therapy and Research, 13,* 109–146.

Kendall, P.C., Flannery-Schroeder, E., Panichelli-Mindel, S.M., Southam-Gerow, M., Henin, A., & Warman, M.J. (1997). Therapy for youth with anxiety disorders: A second randomized clinical trial. *Journal of Consulting and Clinical Psychology, 65,* 366–380.

Kendall, P.C., & Hollon, S.D. (Eds.) (1979). *Cognitive-behavioral interventions: Theory, research and procedures.* New York: Academic Press.

Kendall, P.C., Howard, B.L., & Epps, J. (1988). The anxious child: Cognitive-behavioral treatment strategies. *Behavior Modification, 12,* 281–310.

Kendall, P.C., Kane, M., Howard, B., & Siqueland, L. (1990). *Cognitive-behavioral therapy for anxious children: Treatment manual.* Ardmore, PA: Workbook Publishing.

Kendall, P.C., Kortlander, E., Chansky, T.E., & Brady, E.U. (1992). Comorbidity of anxiety and depression in youth: Treatment implications. *Journal of Consulting and Clinical Psychology, 60,* 869–880.

Kendall, P.C., & MacDonald, J.P. (1993). Cognition in the psychopathology of youth, and implications for treatment. In K.S. Dobson & P.C. Kendall (Eds.), *Psychopathology and cognition* (pp. 387–432). San Diego: Academic Press.

Kendall, P.C., MacDonald, J.P., & Treadwell, K.R.H. (1995). The treatment of anxiety disorders in youth: Future directions. In A.R. Eisen, C.A. Kearney, & C.E. Schaefer (Eds.), *Clinical handbook of anxiety disorder in children and adolescents* (pp. 6–17). New York: Jason Aronson.

Kendall, P.C., Reber, M., McLeer, S., Epps, J., & Ronan, K.R. (1990). Cognitive-behavioral treatment of conduct-disordered children. *Cognitive Therapy and Research, 14,* 279–197.

Kendall, P.C., Stark, K.D., & Adam, T. (1990). Cognitive deficit or cognitive distortion in childhood depression. *Journal of Abnormal Child Psychology, 18,* 255–270.

Kendall, P.C., & Watson, D. (Eds.) (1989). *Anxiety and depression: Distinctive and overlapping features.* New York: Academic Press.

Kendler, K.S., Neale, M.C., Kessler, R.C., Heath, A.C., & Eaves, L.J. (1992). Generalized anxiety disorder in women: A population–based twin study. *Archives of General Psychiatry, 49,* 267–272.

Kerig, P. (1998). Moderators and mediators of the effects of interparental conflict on children's adjustment. *Journal of Abnormal Child Psychology, 26,* 199–212.

Kernberg, O.F. (1976). *Object relations theory and clinical psycho-analysis.* New York: Jason Aronson.

Kihlstrom, J.F. (1987). The cognitive unconscious. *Science, 237,* 1445–1452.

Kistner, J.A., & Torgesen, J.K. (1987). Motivational and cognitive aspects of learning disabilities. In B. Lahey & A.E. Kazdin (Eds.), *Advances in clinical child psychology* (Vol. 10). New York: Plenum.

Klerman, G.L., & Weissman, M.M. (1989). Increasing rates of depression. *Journal of the American Medical Association, 261,* 2229–2235.

Klorman, R., Brumaghim, J.T., Fitzpatrick, P.A., Borgstedt, A.D., & Strauss, J. (1994). Clinical and cognitive effects of methylphenidate on children with attention deficit disorder as a function of aggression/oppositionality and age. *Journal of Abnormal Psychology, 103,* 206–221.

Koegal, R.L., Bimbela, A., & Schreibman, L. (1996). Collateral effects of parent training on family interactions. *Journal of Autism and Developmental Disorders, 26,* 347–359.

Koegal, R.L., Koegal, L. (Eds.) (1995). *Teaching children with autism: Strategies for initiating positive interactions and improving learning opportunities.* Baltimore: Paul H. Brooks.

Koegal, R.L., Schreibman, L., Britten, K.R., Burke, J., & O'Neill, R.E. (1982). A comparison of parent training to direct child treatment. In R.L. Koegel, A. Rincover, & A.L. Egel (Eds.), *Educating and understanding autistic children* (pp. 86–109). San Diego, CA: College Hill Press.

Kohut, H. (1977). *The restoration of the self.* New York: International Universities Press.

Kovacs, M. (1981). Rating scales to assess depression in school aged children. *Acta Paedopsychiatrica, 46,* 305–315.

Kovacs, M. (1991). *The children's depression inventory (CDI).* North Tonawanda, NY: Multi-health Systems.

Kovacs, M., Feinberg, T.L., Crouse-Novak, M.A., Paulauskas, S.L., & Finkelstein, R. (1984). Depressive disorders in childhood: I. A longitudinal prospective study of characteristics and recovery. *Archives of General Psychiatry, 41,* 229–237.

Kratochwill, T.R., & Morris, R.J. (Eds.) (1993). *Handbook of psychotherapy with children and adolescents.* Boston: Allyn & Bacon.

Kuo-Tai, T. (1987). Infantile autism in China. *Journal of Autism and Developmental Disorders, 17,* 289–296.

Lahey, B.B., Green, K., & Forehand, R. (1980). On the independence of ratings of hyperactivity, conduct problems, and attention deficits in children: A multiple regression analysis. *Journal of Consulting and Clinical Psychology, 48,* 566–574.

Lahey, B.B., Loeber, R., Hart, E.L., Frick, P.J., Applegate, B., Zhang, Q., Green, S.M., & Russo, M.F. (1995). Four-year longitudinal study of conduct disorder in boys: Patterns and predictors of persistence. *Journal of Abnormal Psychology, 104,* 83–93.

Lambert, M.C., Weisz, J.R., Knight, F., Desrosiers, M., Overly, K., & Thesiger, C. (1992). Jamaican and American adult perspectives on child psychopathology: Further exploration of the threshold model. *Journal of Consulting and Clinical Psychology, 60,* 146–149.

Lambert, N., Nihira, K., & Leland, O. (1993). *Manual for the adaptive behavior scale—school* (2nd ed.) Austin, TX: Pro-Ed.

Lapouse, R., & Monk, M.A. (1958). An epidemiologic study of behavior characteristics in children. *American Journal of Public Health, 48,* 1134–1144.

Last, C.G. (1992). Anxiety disorders in childhood and adolescence. In W.M. Reynolds (Ed.), *Internalizing disorders in children and adolescents* (pp. 61–106). New York: Wiley.

Last, C.G., Hersen, M., Kazdin, A., Francis, G., & Grubb, H. (1987). Psychiatric illness in mothers of anxious children. *American Journal of Psychiatry, 144,* 1580–1583.

Last, C.G., & Perrin, S. (1993). Anxiety disorders in African-American and white children. *Journal of Abnormal Child Psychology, 21,* 153–164.

Leckman, J.F., & Cohen, D.J. (1994). Tic disorders. In M. Rutter, E. Taylor, & L. Hersov (Eds.), *Child and adolescent psychiatry* (pp. 455–466). Oxford, UK: Blackwell Scientific Publications.

Leckman, J.F., Walker, D.E., & Cohen, D.J. (1993). Premonitory urges in Tourette's syndrome. *American Journal of Psychiatry, 150,* 98–102.

Lee, S., & Chiu, H.F. (1989). Anorexia nervosa in Hong Kong: Why not more in Chinese? *British Journal of Psychiatry, 154,* 683–688.

Leitenberg, H., Agras, W.S., & Thomson, L.E. (1968). A sequential analysis of the effect of selective positive reinforcement in modifying anorexia nervosa. *Behaviour Research and Therapy*, 6, 211–218.

Leon, G.R., & Phelan, P.W. (1985). Anorexia nervosa. In B. Lahey & A.E. Kazdin (Eds.), *Advances in clinical child psychology* (Vol. 8, pp. 81–113). New York: Plenum Press.

Leonard, H. Swedo, S., Allen, A., & Rapoport, J. (1994). Obsessive-compulsive disorder. In T. Ollendick, N. King, & W. Yule (Eds.), *International handbook of phobic and anxiety disorders in children and adolescents* (pp. 207–222). New York: Plenum Press.

Leonard, H., Swedo, S., Rapoport, J., Koby, E., Lenane, M., Cheslow, D., & Hamburger, S. (1989). Treatment of obsessive-compulsive disorder with clomipramine and desipramine in children and adolescents: A double-blind crossover comparison. *Archives of General Psychiatry*, 46, 1088–1092.

Lerner, J. (1989). Educational interventions in learning disabilities. *Journal of the American Academy of Child and Adolescent Psychiatry*, 28, 326–331.

Lerner, R.M., Hess, L.E., & Nitz, K. (1990). A developmental perspective on psychopathology. In M. Hersen & C. Last (Eds.), *Handbook of child and adult psychopathology: A longitudinal perspective* (pp. 9–32). New York: Pergamon Press.

Leung, P., & Wong, M. (1998). Can cognitive distortions differentiate between internalizing and externalizing problems? *Journal of Child Psychology and Psychiatry*, 39, 263–269.

Levitt, E.E. (1963). Psychotherapy with children: A further evaluation. *Behaviour Research and Therapy*, 21, 326–329.

Lewinsohn, P.M. (1974). A behavioral approach to depression. In R.J. Friedman & M.M. Katz (Eds.), *The psychology of depression: Contemporary theory and research* (pp. 157–184). Washington DC: Winston-Wiley.

Lewinsohn, P.M., Clarke, G.N., Hops, H., & Andrews, J. (1990). Cognitive-behavioral group treatment of depression in adolescents. *Behavior Therapy*, 21, 385–401.

Lewinsohn, P.M., Clark, G.N., & Rohde, P. (1994). Psychological approaches to the treatment of depression in adolescents. In W.M. Reynolds & H.F. Johnston (Eds.), *Handbook of depression in children and adolescents* (pp. 309–344). New York: Plenum Press.

Lewinsohn, P.M., Clark, G.N., Rohde, P., Hops, H., & Seeley, J.R. (1996). A course in coping: A cognitive-behavioral approach to the treatment of adolescent depression. In E.D. Hibbs & P.S. Jensen (Eds.), *Child and adolescent disorders: Empirically based strategies for clinical practice* (pp. 109–135). Washington DC: American Psychological Association.

Lewinsohn, P.M., Rohde, P., Hops, H., & Clarke, G. (1991). *Leader's manual for parent groups: Adolescent coping with depression.* Eugene, OR: Castalia Preso.

Lewinsohn, P.M., Rohde, P., Klein,, D., & Seeley, J. (1999). Natural course of adolescent major depressive disorder: I. Continuity into young adulthood. *Journal of the American Academy of Child and Adolescent Psychiatry*, 38, 56–63.

Lewinsohn, P.M., Rohde, P., Seeley, J.R., & Fischer, S.A. (1993). Age-cohort changes in the lifetime occurrence of depression and other mental disorders. *Journal of Abnormal Psychology*, 102, 110–120.

Lips, H.M. (1988). *Sex and gender.* Mountain View, CA: Mayfield.

Litrownik, A.J., & McInnis, E.T. (1986). Information processing and autism. In R.E. Ingram (Ed.), *Information processing approaches to clinical psychology*. New York: Academic.

Lochman, J.E. (1992). Cognitive-behavioral intervention with aggressive boys: Three–year follow-up and preventive effects. *Journal of Consulting and Clinical Psychology*, 60, 426–434.

Lochman, J.E., Burch, P.R., Curry, J.F., & Lampron, L.B. (1984). Treatment and generalization effects of cognitive-behavioral and goal-setting interventions with aggressive boys. *Journal of Consulting and Clinical Psychology*, 52, 915–916.

Lochman, J.E., White, K.J., & Wayland, K.K. (1991). Cognitive–behavioral assessment and treatment with aggressive children. In P.C. Kendall (Ed.), *Child and adolescent therapy: Cognitive–behavioral procedures* (pp. 25–65). New York: Guilford Press.

Loeber, M., Van Kammen, W.B., & Maughan, B. (1993). Developmental pathways in disruptive child behavior. *Development and Psychopathology*, 5, 103–133.

Loeber, R. (1990). Development and risk factors of juvenile antisocial behavior and delinquency. *Clinical Psychology Review*, 10, 1–41.

Loeber, R., & Keenen, K. (1994). Interaction between conduct disorder and its comorbid conditions: Effects of age and gender. *Clinical Psychology Review*, 14, 497–523.

Lombroso, P.J., Pauls, D., & Leckman, J. (1994). Genetic mechanisms in childhood psychiatric disorders. *Journal of the American Academy of Child and Adolescent Psychiatry*, 33, 921–938.

Lonigan, C., Elbert, J., & Johnson, S.B. (1998). Empirically supported psychosocial interventions for children: An overview. *Journal of Clinical Child Psychology*, 27, 138–145.

Lord, C., Pickles, A., McLennan, J., Rutter, M., Bregman, J., Folstein, S., Fombone, E., Leboyer, M., & Minshew, N. (1997). Diagnosing autism: Analyses of data from the autism diagnostic interview. *Journal of Autism and Developmental Disorders*, 27, 501–518.

Lord, C., & Rutter, M. (1994). Autism and pervasive developmental disorders. In M. Rutter, E. Taylor, & L. Hersov (Eds.), *Child and adolescent psychiatry* (pp. 569–593). Oxford, UK: Blackwell Scientific Publications.

Lotter, V. (1966). Epidemiology of autistic conditions on young children: Prevalence. *Social Psychiatry*, 1, 124–137.

Lovaas, O.I. (1987). Behavioral treatment and normal educational and intellectual functioning in young autistic children. *Journal of Consulting and Clinical Psychology*, 55, 3–9.

Lovaas, O.I., Koegel, R.L., & Schreibman, L. (1979). Stimulus overselectivity in autism: A review of research. *Psychological Bulletin*, 86, 1236–1254.

Lovaas, O.I., Koegel, R.L., Simmons, J.Q., & Long, J.S. (1973). Some generalization and follow-up measures on autistic children in behavior therapy. *Journal of Consulting and Clinical Psychology*, 55, 3–9.

Lovaas, O.I., Smith, T., & McEachin, J.J. (1989). Clarifying comments on the Young autism study: Reply to Schopler, Short, and Mesibov. *Journal of Consulting and Clinical Psychology*, 57, 165–167.

Lucas, A.R., Beard, C.M., O'Fallon, W., & Kurland, L. (1991). Fifty year trends in the incidence of anorexia nervosa in Rochester, Minnesota: A population-based study. *American Journal of Psychiatry*, 148, 917–922.

Luk, S., & Leung, P.W. (1989). Conners' teachers' rating scale: A validity study in Hong Kong. *Journal of Child Psychology and Psychiatry, 30,* 785–794.

Lyon, G.R., & Cutting, L. (1998). Learning disabilities. In E. Mash & R. Barkley (Eds.), *Treatment of childhood disorders* (2nd ed., pp. 488–500). New York: Guilford Press.

Maccini, P., & Hughes, C. (1997). Mathematics interventions for adolescents with learning disabilities. *Learning Disabilities Research and Practice, 12,* 168–176.

Mace, F., Kratochwill, T.R., & Fiello, R.A. (1983). Positive treatment of aggressive behavior in a mentally retarded adult: A case study. *Behavior Therapy, 14,* 689–696.

MacMillan, D.L., Keogh, B., & Jones, R.L. (1986). Special education research on mildly handicapped learners. In M.C. Wittrock (Ed.), *Handbook of research on teaching* (pp. 90–111), New York: Macmillan.

Madle, R. (1990). Mental retardation in adulthood. In M. Hersen & C. Last (Eds.), *Handbook of child and adult psychopathology: A longitudinal perspective.* New York: Pergamon Press.

Mahoney, M.J. (1977). Reflections in the cognitive-learning trend in psychotherapy. *American Psychologist, 32,* 5–18.

Mahoney, M.J. (1993). Theoretical developments in the cognitive psychotherapies. *Journal of Consulting and Clinical Psychology, 61,* 187–193.

Manchi, M., & Cohen, P. (1990). Early childhood eating behaviour and adolescent eating disorders. *Journal of the American Academy of Child and Adolescent Psychiatry, 29,* 112–117.

Mann, B.J., & MacKenzie, E.P. (1996). Pathways among marital functioning, parental behaviors, and child behavior problems in school-age boys. *Journal of Consulting and Clinical Psychology, 25,* 183–191.

Mann, J.J., McBride, P.A., Brown, R.P., Linnoila, M., Leon, A.C., DeMeo, M., Mieczkowski, T., Myers, J.E., & Stanley, M. (1992). Relationship between central and peripheral serotonin indexes in depressed and suicidal psychiatric inpatients. *Archives of General Psychiatry, 49,* 442–446.

Mannuzza, S., & Klein, R. (1992). Predictors of outcome of children with attention-deficit hyperactivity disorder. In G. Weiss (Ed.), *Child and adolescent psychiatric clinics of North America: attention-deficit hyperactivity disorder* (pp. 567–578). Philadelphia: Saunders.

Mannuzza, S., Klein, R.G., Bonagura, N., Malloy, P., Giampino, T.L., & Addalli, K.A. (1991). Hyperactive boys almost grown up: V. Replication of psychiatric status. *Archives of General Psychiatry, 48,* 77–83.

March, J. (1995). Behavioral psychotherapy for children and adolescents with obsessive-compulsive disorder: A review of the literature and recommendation for treatment. *Journal of the American Academy of Child and Adolescent Psychiatry, 34,* 7–18.

March, J., & Albano, A.M. (1998). New developments in assessing pediatric anxiety disorders. In T. Ollendick & R. Prinz (Eds.), *Advances in clinical child psychology* (Vol. 20, pp. 213–242). New York: Plenum Press.

March, J., & Mulle, K. (1998). *OCD in children and adolescents: A cognitive-behavioral treatment manual.* New York: Guilford Press.

March, J., Parker, J., Sullivan, K., Stallings, P., & Conners, C. (1997). The Multidimensional Anxiety Scale for Children (MASC): Factor structure, reliability and validity. *Journal of the American Academy of Child and Adolescent Psychiatry, 36,* 554–565.

Martin, B., & Hoffman, J.A. (1990). Conduct disorders. In M. Lewis & S.M.

Miller (Eds.), *Handbook of developmental psychopathology.* New York: Plenum Press.

Mash, E., & Terdal, L. (1997). Assessment of child and family disturbance: A behavioral-systems approach. In E. Mash & L. Terdal (Eds.), *Assessment of childhood disorders* (3rd ed., pp. 3–70). New York: Guilford Publications.

Mash, E.J. (1998). Treatment of child and family disturbance: A behavioral systems perspective. In E.J. Mash & R.A. Barkley (Eds.), *Treatment of childhood disorders* (2nd ed.). New York: Guilford Press.

Mash, E.J., Terdal, L.G., & Anderson, K. (1973). The response-class matrix: A procedure for recording parent–child interactions. *Journal of Consulting and Clinical Psychology, 40,* 163–164.

Mastenbrook, J. (1978). Future directions in adaptive behavior assessment: Environmental adaptation measures. In A.T. Fisher (Chair), *Impact of adaptive behavior: ABIC and the environmental adaptation measure.* Symposium conducted at the meeting of the American Psychological Association, Toronto.

Masters, J., Burish, T., Hollon, S.D., & Rimm, D. (1987). *Behavior therapy: Techniques and empirical findings.* San Diego, CA: Harcourt Brace Jovanovich.

Matson, J., & Barrett, R. (Eds.). (1982), *Psychopathology in the mentally retarded.* New York: Grune & Stratton.

Maughan, B., & Rutter, M. (1998). Continuities and discontinuities in antisocial behavior from childhood to adult life. In T. Ollendick & R. Prinz (Eds.), *Advances in clinical child psychology* (Vol. 20, pp. 1–47). New York: Plenum Press.

Mayron, L.M., Ott, J.N., Nations, R., & Mayron, E.L. (1974). Light, radiation, and academic behavior: Initial studies on the effects of full-spectrum lighting and radiation shielding on behavior and academic performance of school children. *Academic Therapy, 10,* 33–47.

Mazur, E., Wolchik, S.A., & Sandler, I. (1992). Negative cognitive errors and positive illusions for negative divorce events: Predictors of children's psychological adjustment. *Journal of Abnormal Child Psychology, 20,* 523–542.

Mazzocco, M., Kates, W., Baumgardner, T., Freund, L., & Reiss, A. (1997). Autistic behaviors among girls with fragile X syndrome. *Journal of Autism and Developmental Disabilities, 27,* 415–435.

McAdoo, W.G., & DeMeyer, M.K. (1978). Personality characteristics of parents. In M. Rutter & E. Schopler (Eds.), *Autism: A reappraisal of concepts and treatment.* New York: Plenum Press.

McArdle, P., O'Brien, G., & Kolvin, I. (1995). Hyperactivity: Prevalence and relationship with conduct disorder. *Journal of Child Psychology and Psychiatry, 36,* 279–303.

McFarlane, J.W., Allen, L., & Honzik, M.P. (1954). *A developmental study of the behavior problems of normal children between 21 months and 14 years.* Berkeley, CA: University of California Press.

McGee, R., Silva, P.A., & Williams, S. (1984). Behavior problems in a population of seven-year-old children: Prevalence, stability, and types of disorder—a research report. *Journal of Child Psychology and Psychiatry, 25,* 251–259.

McLaren, J., & Bryson, S.E. (1987). Review of recent epidemiological studies of mental retardation: Prevalence, associated disorders, and etiology. *American Journal of Mental Retardation, 92,* 243–254.

McLennan, J.M., Lord, C., & Schopler, E. (1993). Sex differences in higher functioning people with autism. *Journal of Autism and Developmental Disorders, 23,* 217–228.

McMahon, R., & Estes, A. (1997). Conduct problems. In E. Mash & L. Terdal (Eds.), *Assessment of childhood disorders* (3rd ed., pp. 130–196). New York: Guilford Press.

McMahon, R.C. (1980). Genetic etiology in the hyperactive child syndrome: A critical review. *American Journal of Orthopsychiatry, 50,* 145–150.

Meehl, P. (1962). Schizotaxia, schizotypy, schizophrenia. *American Psychologist, 17,* 827–838.

Meichenbaum, D. (1977). *Cognitive behavior modification: An integrative approach.* New York: Plenum Press.

Meichenbaum, D. (1985). *Stress inoculation training.* New York: Pergamon Press.

Meichenbaum, D. (1993). Changing conceptions of cognitive behavior modification: Retrospect and prospect. *Journal of Consulting and Clinical Psychology, 61,* 202–205.

Mesibov, G.B. (1997). Preschool issues in autism: Introduction. *Journal of Autism and Developmental Disorders, 27,* 637–640.

Mesibov, G.B., & Shea, V. (1996). Full inclusion and students with autism. *Journal of Autism and Developmental Disorders, 26,* 337–346.

Milich, R., Loney, J., & Landau, S. (1982). The independent dimensions of hyperactivity and aggression: A validation with playroom observation data. *Journal of Abnormal Psychology, 91,* 183–198.

Milich, R., Loney, J., & Roberts, M. (1986). Playroom observations of activity level and sustained attention: Two-year stability. *Journal of Consulting and Clinical Psychology, 54,* 272–274.

Miller, L.C., Barrett, C.L., & Hampe, E. (1974). Phobias of childhood in a prescientific era. In S. David (Ed.), *Child personality and psychopathology* (pp. 89–134). New York: Wiley.

Minshew, N.J. (1996). Brief report: Brain mechanisms in autism—functional and structural abnormalities. *Journal of Autism and Developmental Disorders, 26,* 205–209.

Minuchin, S., Roseman, B.L., & Baker, L. (1978). *Psychosomatic families: Anorexia nervosa in context.* Cambridge, MA: Harvard University Press.

Mitchell, S.A. (1988). *Relational concepts in psychoanalysis.* Cambridge, MA: Harvard University Press.

Moffit, T.E. (1993a). Adolescence-limited and life-course-persistent antisocial behavior: A developmental taxonomy. *Psychological Review, 100,* 674–701.

Moffit, T.E. (1993b). The neuropsychology of conduct disorder. *Development and Psychopathology, 5,* 135–151.

Morris, R.D. (1988). Classification of learning disabilities: Old problems and new approaches. *Journal of Consulting and Clinical Psychology, 56,* 789–794.

Mortimer, H. (1995). Welcoming young children with special needs into mainstream education. *Support for Learning, 10,* 87–99.

Mudford, O.C. (1995). An intrusive and restrictive alternative to contingent shock. *Behavioral Interventions, 10,* 87–99.

Myles, B.S., Simpson, R.L., & Johnson, S. (1995). Students with higher functioning autistic disorder: Do we know who they are? *Focus on Autistic Behavior, 9,* 1–12.

Neal, A.M., & Knisley, H. (1995). What are African American children afraid of? II. A twelve-month follow-up. *Journal of Anxiety Disorders, 9,* 151–161.

Neal, A.M., Lilly, R.S., & Zakis, S. (1993). What are African American children afraid of: A preliminary study. *Journal of Anxiety Disorders, 9,* 151–161.

Nee, L.E., Caine, E.D., & Polinsky, R.J. (1980). Gilles de la Tourette syndrome: Clinical and family study in 50 cases. *Annals of Neurology, 7,* 41–49.

Neisser, U., Boodoo, G., Bouchard, T.J., Boykin, A.W., Brody, N., Ceci, S.J., Halpern, D.F., Loehlin, J.C., Perloff, R., Sternberg, R.J., & Urbina, S. (1996). Intelligence: Knowns and unknowns. *American Psychologist, 51,* 77–101.

Nelson, C.A., & Bloom, F.E. (1997). Child development and neuroscience. *Child Development, 68,* 970–987.

Nelson, W.M., & Finch, A.J. (1996). *"Keeping your cool": The anger management workbook.* Ardmore, PA: Workbook Publishing.

Newsom, C. (1998). Autistic disorder. In E. Mash & R. Barkley (Eds.), *Treatment of childhood disorders* (2nd ed., pp. 416–467). New York: Guilford Press.

Newsom, C., & Hovanitz, C. (1997). Autistic disorder. In E. Mash & L. Terdal (Eds.), *Assessment of childhood disorders* (3rd ed.). New York: Guilford Press.

Nwaefuna, A. (1981). Anorexia nervosa in a developing country. *British Journal of Psychiatry, 138,* 270–271.

O'Connor, N., & Hermelin, B. (1988). Annotation: Low intelligence and special abilities. *Journal of Child Psychology and Psychiatry, 29,* 391–396.

O'Connor, T., Neiderhiser, J., Reiss, D., Hetherington, E.M., & Plomin, R. (1998). Genetic contributions to continuity, change, and co-occurrence of antisocial and depressive symptoms in adolescence. *Journal of Child Psychology and Psychiatry, 39,* 323–336.

Offord, D.R., Boyle, M.C., & Racine, Y. (1991). The epidemiology of antisocial behavior in childhood and adolescence. In D. Pepler & K.H. Rubin (Eds.), *The development and treatment of childhood aggression.* Hillsdale, NJ: Lawrence Erlbaum Associates Inc.

O'Leary, K.D. (1980). Pills or skills for hyperactive children. *Journal of Applied Behavior Analysis, 13,* 191–204.

O'Leary, K.D., Pelham, W.E., Rosenbaum, A., & Price, G.H. (1976). Behavioral treatment of hyperkinetic children: An experimental evaluation of its usefulness. *Clinical Pediatrics, 15,* 510–515.

O'Leary, K.D., Rosenbaum, A., & Hughes, P.C. (1978). Fluorescent lighting: A purported source of hyperactive behavior. *Journal of Abnormal Child Psychology, 6,* 285–289.

O'Leary, K.D., & Wilson, G.T. (1987). *Behavior therapy: Application and outcome* (2nd ed.). Englewood Cliffs, NJ: Prentice-Hall.

Olivardia, R., & Pope, H.G. (1995). Eating disorders in college men. *American Journal of Psychiatry, 152,* 1279–1285.

Ollendick, T.H., & King, N. (1991). Origins of childhood fears. *Behavior Research and Therapy, 29,* 117–123.

Ollendick, T.H., & King, N. (1998). Empirically supported treatments for children with phobic and anxiety disorders. *Journal of Clinical Child Psychology, 27,* 156–167.

Ollendick, T.H., King, N., & Yule, W. (Eds.) (1994). *International handbook of phobic and anxiety disorders in children and adolescents.* New York: Plenum Press.

Ollendick, T.H., & Mayer, J.A. (1984). School phobia. In S. Turner (Ed.), *Behavioral theories and treatment of anxiety.* New York: Plenum Press.

Patterson, G.R. (1974). Interventions for boys with conduct problems: Multiple settings, treatments, and criteria. *Journal of Consulting and Clinical Psychology, 42,* 471–481.

Patterson, G.R. (1982). *A social learning approach to family intervention: Vol. 3. Coercive family process.* Eugene, OR: Castalia.

Patterson, G.R., & Bank, L. (1989). Some amplifying mechanisms for pathologic processes in families. In M. Gunnar & E. Thelen (Eds.), *Minnesota symposium* on child psychology: Systems and development (pp. 167–209). Hillsdale, NJ: Lawrence Erlbaum Associates Inc.

Patterson, G.R., Chamberlain, P., & Reid, J.B. (1982). A comparative evaluation of a parent-training program. *Behavior Therapy*, *13*, 638–650.

Pauls, D.L, Raymond, C.L., Stevenson, J.F., & Leckman, J.F. (1991). A family study of Gilles de la Tourette. *American Journal of Human Genetics*, *48*, 154–163.

Pavlov, I.P. (1928). *Lectures on conditioned reflexes*. New York: Liveright.

Paykel, E. (Ed.). (1992). *Handbook of affective disorders*. New York: Guilford Press.

Pelham, W., Carlson, C., Sams, S., Vallano, G., Dixon, M., & Hoza, B. (1993). Separate and combined effects of methylphenidate and behavior modification on boys with attention-deficit hyperactivity disorder in the classroom. *Journal of Consulting and Clinical Psychology*, *61*, 506–515.

Pelham, W., & Hoza, B. (1996). Intensive treatment: Summer treatment programs for children with ADHD. In E. Hibbs & P. Jensen (Eds.), *Psychosocial treatments for child and adolescent disorders: Empirically based strategies for clinical practice* (pp. 311–340). Washington DC: American Psychological Association.

Pelham, W., & Sams, S. (1992). Behavior modification. *Child and Adolescent Psychiatric Clinics of North America*, *1*(2).

Pfeiffer, S.I., Norton, J., Nelson, L., & Shott, S. (1995). Efficacy of vitamin B6 and magnesium in the treatment of autism: A methodology review and summary of outcomes. *Journal of Autism and Developmental Disorders*, *25*, 481–493.

Piacentini, J., Gitow, A., Jaffer, M., Graae, F., & Whitaker, A. (1994). Outpatient behavioral treatment of child and adolescent obsessive compulsive disorder. *Journal of Anxiety Disorders*, *8*, 277–289.

Piazza, C., & Fisher, W. (1991). A faded bedtime with response cost protocol for treatment of multiple sleep problems in children. *Journal of Applied Behavior Analysis*, *24*, 129–140.

Plomin, R. (1989). Environment and genes: Determinants of behavior. *American Psychologist*, *42*, 105–111.

Plomin, R., & DeFries, J. (1980). Genetics and intelligence: Recent data. *Intelligence*, *4*, 15–24.

Plomin, R., Nitz, K., & Rowe, D.C. (1990). Behavioral genetics and aggressive behavior in childhood. In M. Lewis & S.M. Miller (Eds.), *Handbook of developmental psychopathology*. New York: Plenum Press.

Polivy, J., & Herman, C. (1985). Dieting and binging. *American Psychologist*, *40*, 193–210.

Polivy, J., & Herman, C. (1987). Diagnosis and treatment of normal eating. *Journal of Consulting and Clinical Psychology*, *55*, 635–644.

Pollock, V., Schneider, L., Gabrielli, W., & Goodwin, D. (1986). Sex of parent and offspring in the transmission of alcoholism: A meta-analysis. *Journal of Nervous and Mental Disease*, *175*, 668–673.

Pope, H.G., Jr., Hudson, J.I., & Yurgelun-Tudd, D. (1984). Anorexia nervosa and bulimia among 300 suburban women shoppers. *American Journal of Psychiatry*, *141*, 292–294.

Power, M., & Brewin, C. (1991). From Freud to cognitive science: A contemporary account of the unconscious. *British Journal of Clinical Psychology*, *30*, 289–310.

Prior, M. (1984). Developing concepts of childhood autism: The influence of experimental cognitive research. *Journal of Consulting and Clinical Psychology*, *52*, 4–16.

Quay, H.C. (1965). Conduct disorders. In H.C. Quay & J.S. Wherry (Eds.),

Psychopathological disorders of childhood. New York: Wiley.

Quay, H.C. (1986). Conduct disorders. In H.C. Quay & J.S. Wherry (Eds.), *Psychopathological disorders of childhood.* New York: Wiley.

Quintana, H., Birmaher, B., Stedge, D., Lennon, S., Freed, J., Bridge, J., & Greenhill, L. (1995). Use of methylphenidate in the treatment of children with autistic disorder. *Journal of Autism and Developmental Disorders, 25,* 283–294.

Rachman, S. (1998). *Anxiety.* Hove, UK: Psychology Press

Rapee, R. (1997). The potential role of childrearing practices in the development of anxiety and depression. *Clinical Psychology Reivew, 17,* 47–67.

Rapee, R. (1991). Generalized anxiety disorder: A review of clinical features and theoretical concepts. *Clinical Psychology Review, 11,* 419–440.

Rapee, R., Barrett, P., Dadds, M., & Evans, L. (1994). Reliability of the DSM-III-R childhood anxiety disorders using structured interviews: Interrater and parent–child agreement. *Journal of the American Academy of Child and Adolescent Psychiatry, 33,* 984–992.

Rapoport, J.L., Buchsbaum, M.S., Zahn, T.P., Weingartner, H., Ludlow, C., & Mikkelsen, E.J. (1978). Dextroamphetamine: Cognitive and behavioral effect in normal prepubertal boys. *Science, 199,* 560–563.

Rapport, M.D., & Kelly, K.L. (1991). Psychostimulant effects on learning and cognitive function in children with attention deficit hyperactivity disorder: Findings and implications. In J.L. Matson (Ed.), *Hyperactivity in children: A handbook.* New York: Pergamon Press.

Rehm, L.P., & Sharp, R.N. (1996). Strategies for childhood depression. In M.A. Reineke, F.M. Dattilio, & A. Freeman (Eds.), *Cognitive therapy with children and adolescents: A casebook for clinical practice* (pp. 103–123). New York: Guilford Press.

Reinecke, M.A., Ryan, N., & DuBois, D. (1998). Cognitive-behavioral therapy of depression and depressive symptoms during adolescence: A review and meta-analysis. *Journal of the American Academy of Child and Adolescent Psychiatry, 37,* 26–34.

Reiss, D., Hetherington, E.M., Plomin, R., Howe, G.W., Simmens, S.J., Henderson, S.H., O'Connor, T.J., Bussell, D.A., Anderson, E.R., & Law, T. (1995). Genetic questions for environmental studies. *Archives of General Psychiatry, 52,* 925–936.

Repp, A.C., & Deitz, D.E.D. (1983). Mental retardation. In T. Ollendick & M. Hersen (Eds.), *Handbook of child psychopathology.* New York: Plenum Press.

Resnicow, K., Ross-Gaddy, D., & Vaughan, R.D. (1995). Structure of problem and positive behaviors in African American youths. *Journal of Consulting and Clinical Psychology, 63,* 594–603.

Reynold, W.M. (1992). The study of internalizing disorders in children and adolescents. In W.M. Reynolds (Ed.), *Internalizing disorders in children and adolescents.* New York: Wiley

Reynolds, C.R., & Paget, K.D. (1982, March). *National normative and reliability data for Revised Children's Manifest Anxiety Scale.* Paper presented at the meeting of the National Association of School Psychologists, Toronto, Ontario, Canada.

Reynolds, C.R., & Richmond, B.O. (1985). *Revised children's manifest anxiety scale (RCMAS): Manual* (pp. 6–9). Los Angeles: Western Psychological Services.

Richardson, M.A., Haugland, G., & Craig, T.J. (1991). Neuroleptic use,

Parkinsonian symptoms, tardive dyskinesia, and associated factors in child and adolescent psychiatric patients. *American Journal of Psychiatry, 148*, 1322–1328.

Richardson, S.A., Katz, M., Koller, H., McLaren, L., & Rubinstein, B. (1979). Some characteristics of a population of mentally retarded young adults in a British city: A basis for estimating service needs. *Journal of Mental Deficiency Research, 23*, 275–283.

Rimland, B. (1974). Infantile autism: Status and research. In A. Davids (Ed.), *Child personality and psychopathology: Current topics* (pp. 137–168). New York: Wiley.

Roberts, R.E., Lewinsohn, P.M., & Seeley, J.R. (1991). Screening for adolescent depression: A comparison of depression scales. *Journal of the American Academy of Child and Adolescent Psychiatry, 30*, 58–66.

Robins, L.N. (1966). *Deviant children grown up.* Baltimore: Williams & Wilkins.

Robins, L.N. (1978). Sturdy childhood predictors of antisocial behavior: Replications from longitudinal studies. *Psychological Medicine, 8*, 611–622.

Robins, L.N., & Price, R.K. (1991). Adult disorders predicted by childhood conduct problems. Results from the NIMH Epidemiologic Catchment Area project. *Psychiatry, 54*, 116–132.

Romanczyk, R., & Kistner, J. (1982). Psychosis and mental retardation: Issues of coexistence. In J. Matson & R. Barrett (Eds.), *Psychopathology in the mentally retarded* (pp. 147–194). New York: Grune & Stratton.

Rosenzweig, M.R., Bennett, E.L., & Diamond, M.C. (1972). Brain changes in response to experience. *Scientific American, 226*, 22–29.

Rosenzweig, M.R., Leiman, A.L., & Breedlove, S.M. (1996). *Biological psychology.* Sunderland, MA: Sinauer Associates.

Rubenstein, J.L.R., Lotspeich, L., & Ciaranello, R.D. (1990). The neurobiology of developmental disorders. In B. Lahey & A.E. Kazdin (Eds.), *Advances in clinical child psychology* (Vol. 13, pp. 1–52). New York: Plenum Press.

Rudolph, K.D., Hammen, C., & Burge, D. (1997). A cognitive-interpersonal approach to depressive symptoms in preadolescent children. *Journal of Abnormal Child Psychology, 25*, 33–45.

Russo, D.C., Carr, E.G., & Lovaas, O.I. (1980). Self-injury in pediatric populations. In J. Ferguson & C.B. Taylor (Eds.), *Comprehensive handbook of behavioral medicine.* New York: Spectrum.

Rutter, M. (1977). Brain damage syndromes in childhood: Concepts and findings. *Journal of Child Psychology and Psychiatry, 139*, 21–33.

Rutter, M. (1978). Language disorder and infantile autism. In M. Rutter & E. Schopler (Eds.), *Autism: A reappraisal of concepts and treatment.* New York: Plenum Press.

Rutter, M., Bailey, A., Bolton, P., & Le Couteur, A. (1994). Autism and known medical conditions: Myth and substance. *Journal of Child Psychology and Psychiatry, 35*, 311–322.

Rutter, M., & Quinton, D. (1984). Parental psychiatric disorder: Effects on children. *Psychological Medicine, 14*, 853–880.

Rutter, M., & Schopler, E. (1987). Autism and pervasive developmental disorders: Concepts and diagnostic issues. *Journal of Autism and Developmental Disabilities, 17*, 159–186.

Rutter, M., Silberg, J., O'Connor, T., & Simonoff, E. (1999). Genetics and child psychiatry: II. Empirical research findings. *Journal of Child Psychology and Psychiatry, 40*, 19–55.

Rutter, M., Tizard, J., Yule, W., Graham, P., & Whitmore, K. (1976). Research report: Isle of Wight studies, 1964–1974. *Psychological Medicine, 6*, 313–332.

Safer, D.J., & Krager, J.M. (1988). A survey of medication treatment for hyperactive/inattentive students. *Journal of the American Medical Association, 260*, 2256–2259.

Santrock, J.W., & Warshak, R.A. (1986). Development of father custody relationships and legal/clinical considerations in father-custody families. In M.E. Lamb (Ed.), *The father's role: Applied perspectives*. New York: Wiley.

Saylor, C.F., Finch, A.J., J.Jr., Baskin, C.H., Furey, W., & Kelly, M.M. (1984). Construct validity for measures of childhood depression: Application of multitrait-multimethod methodology. *Journal of Consulting and Clinical Psychology, 52*, 977–985.

Saylor, C.F., Finch, A.J., J.Jr., Spirito, A., & Bennett, B. (1984). The Children's Depression Inventory: A systematic evaluation of psychometric properties. *Journal of Consulting and Clinical Psychology, 52*, 955–967.

Scarr, S., & Weinberg, R.A. (1976). The IQ performance of black children adopted by white families. *American Psychologist, 31*, 726–739.

Schachar, R., Tannock, R., Marriott, M., & Logan, G. (1995). Deficient inhibitory control in ADHD. *Journal of Abnormal Child Psychology, 23*, 411–437.

Schopler, E., & Hennike, J.M. (1990). Past and present trends in residential treatment. *Journal of Autism and Developmental Disorders, 20*, 291–298.

Schopler, E., Short, A., & Mesibov, G. (1989). Relation of behavioral treatment to "normal functioning": Comment on Lovaas. *Journal of Consulting and Clinical Psychology, 57*, 162–164.

Schreibman, L. (1988). *Autism*. Newbury Park, CA: Sage.

Schreibman, L., & Koegel, R. (1996). Fostering self-management: Parent delivered pivotal response training for children with autistic disorder. In E. Hibbs & P. Jensen (Eds.), *Psychosocial treatments for child and adolescent disorders: Empirically based strategies for clinical practice* (pp. 525–554). Washington DC: American Psychological Association.

Scott, D.W. (1986). Anorexia nervosa: A review of possible genetic factors. *International Journal of Eating Disorders, 5*, 1–20.

Scott, S. (1994). Mental retardation. In M. Rutter, E. Taylor, & L. Hersov (Eds.), *Child and adolescent psychiatry* (pp. 616–646). Oxford, UK: Blackwell.

Seguin, J.R., Pihl, R.O., Harden, P.W., Tremblay, R.E., & Boulerice, B. (1995). Cognitive and neuropsychological characteristics of physically aggressive boys. *Journal of Abnormal Psychology, 104*, 614–624.

Sejnowski, T.J., Koch, C., & Churchland, P.S. (1988). Computational neuroscience. *Science, 99*, 1299–1306.

Shaffer, D. (1977). Enuresis. In M. Rutter & L. Herzov (Eds.), *Child psychiatry: Modern approaches*. Philadelphia: Blackwell.

Shaffer, D. (1994). Enuresis. In M. Rutter, E. Taylor, & L. Hersov (Eds.), *Child and adolescent psychiatry*. Oxford, UK: Blackwell.

Shapiro, A.K., Shapiro, E.S., Brunn, R.D., & Sweet, R.D. (1978). *Gilles de la Tourette syndrome*. New York: Raven Press.

Shaywitz, B.A., Shaywitz, S.E., Byrne, T., Cohen, D.J., & Rothman, S. (1983). Attention deficit disorder: Quantitative analysis of CT. *Neurology, 33*, 1500–1503.

Shaywitz, S., Fletcher, J., & Shaywitz, B. (1994). Issues in the definition and classification of attention deficit disorder. *Topics in Language Disorders, 14*, 1–25.

Shepperdson, B. (1995). The control of sexuality in young people with Down's syndrome. *Child Care, Health and Development, 21*, 333–349.

Shirk, S.R., & Russell, R. (1996). *Change processes in child psychotherapy: Revitalizing treatment and research.* New York: Guilford Press.

Shulman, C., Yirmiya, N., & Greenbaum, C.W. (1995). From categorization to classification: A comparison among individuals with autism, mental retardation, and normal development. *Journal of Abnormal Psychology, 104*, 601–609.

Silove, D., Harris, M., Morgan, A., Boyce, P., Manicavasagar, V., Hadzi-Pavlovic, D., & Wilhelm, K. (1995). Is early separation anxiety a specific precursor of panic disorder-agoraphobia? A community study. *Psychological Medicine, 25*, 405–411.

Silverman, W.K., & Albano, A.M. (1998). *Anxiety Disorders Interview Schedule for Children (ADIS-C).* San Antonio, TX: Psychological Corporation.

Silverman, W.K., & Rabian, B. (1994). Specific phobias. In T. Ollendick, N. King, & W. Yule (Eds.), *International handbook of phobic and anxiety disorders in children and adolescents* (pp. 87–109). New York: Plenum Press.

Silverman, W.K., & Rabian, B. (1995). Test–retest reliability of DSM-III-R childhood anxiety disorders and symptoms using the anxiety disorders interview schedule for children. *Journal of Anxiety Disorders, 9*, 139–150.

Siqueland, L., Kendall, P.C., & Steinberg, L. (1996). Anxiety in children: Perceived family environments and observed family interaction style. *Journal of Clinical Child Psychology, 25*, 225–237.

Skinner, B.F. (1953). *Science and human behavior.* New York: Macmillan.

Skoog, G., & Skoog, I. (1999). A 40-year follow-up of patients with obsessive-compulsive disorder. *Archives of General Psychiatry, 56*, 121–127.

Smalley, S.L. (1991). Genetic influences in autism. *Psychiatric Clinics of North America, 14*, 125–139.

Smalley, S.L., & Collins, F. (1996). Brief report: Genetic, prenatal, and immunologic factors. *Journal of Autism and Developmental Disorders, 26*, 195–203.

Smith, D. (1982). Trends in counseling and psychotherapy. *American Psychologist, 37*, 802–809.

Smith, S.D., Pennington, B.F., Kimberling, W.J., & Ing, P. (1990). Familial dyslexia: Use of genetic linkage data to define subtypes. *Journal of the American Academy of Child and Adolescent Psychiatry, 29*, 204–213.

Smith, T.W., & Allred, K.D. (1986). Rationality revisited: A reassessment of the empirical support for the rational-emotive model. In P.C. Kendall (Ed.), *Advances in cognitive-behavioral research and therapy* (Vol. 5, pp. 63–88). New York: Academic Press.

Smucker, M., Craighead, W.E., Craighead, L., & Green, B.J. (1986). Normative and reliability data for the children's depression inventory. *Journal of Abnormal Child Psychology, 14*, 25–39.

Sommers-Flanagan, J., & Sommers-Flanagan, R. (1996). Efficacy of antidepressant medication with depressed youth: What psychologists should know. *Professional Psychology: Research and Practice, 27*, 145–153.

Sonuga-Barke, E.J. (1998). Categorical models of childhood disorder: A conceptual and empirical analysis.

Journal of Child Psychology and Psychiatry, *39*, 115–123.

Southam-Gerow, M.A., Henin, A., Chu, B., Marrs, A., & Kendall, P.C. (1997). Cognitive-behavioral therapy with children and adolescents. *Psychotherapy*, *6*, 111–136.

Southam-Gerow, M.A., & Kendall, P.C. (1997). Parent-focused and cognitive-behavioral treatments of antisocial youth. In D. Stoff, J. Breiling, & J.D. Maser (Eds.), *Handbook of antisocial behavior.* New York: Wiley.

Southam-Gerow, M.A., & Kendall, P.C. (in press). Emotion understanding in youth referred for treatment for anxiety disorders. *Journal of Clinical Psychology.*

Spencer, T., Biederman, J., Wilens, T., & Faraone, S. (1994). Is attention deficit hyperactivity disorder in adults a valid disorder? *Harvard Review of Psychiatry*, *1*, 326–335.

Spencer, T., Biederman, J., Wilen, T., Harding, M., O'Donnell, D., & Griffin, S. (1996). Pharmacotherapy of attention-deficit hyperactivity disorder across the life cycle. *Journal of the American Academy of Child and Adolescent Psychiatry*, *35*, 409–432.

Spencer, T., Wilens, T., Biederman, J., Faraone, S.V., Ablon, S., & Lapey, K. (1995). A double-bind crossover comparison of methylphenidate and placebo in adults with childhood-onset attention-deficit hyperactivity disorder. *Archives of General Psychiatry*, *52*, 434–443.

Spielberger, C., Gorsuch, R., & Lushene, R. (1970). *STAI manual.* Palo Alto, CA: Consulting Psychologists Press.

Spivack, G., & Shure, M.B. (1982). The cognition of social adjustment: Interpersonal cognitive problem-solving thinking. In B.B. Lahey & A.E. Kazdin (Eds.), *Advances in clinical child psychology* (Vol. 5, pp. 323–372). New York: Plenum Press.

Sponheim, E., & Skjeldal, O. (1998). Autism and related disorders: Epidemiological findings in a Norwegian study using ICD-10 diagnostic criteria. *Journal of Autism and Developmental Disabilities, 28,* 217–228.

Sroufe, A., & Rutter, M. (1984). The domain of developmental psychopathology. *Child Development*, *55*, 17–29.

Stark, K., & Kendall, P.C. (1996). *Treating depressed children: Therapist manual for "ACTION."* Ardmore, PA: Workbook Publishing.

Stark, K.D. (1990). *The treatment of depression during childhood: A school-based program.* New York: Guilford Press.

Stark, K.D., Kendall, P.C., McCarthy, M., Stafford, M., Barron, R., & Thomeer, M. (1996). *Taking action: A workbook for overcoming depression.* Ardmore, PA: Workbook Publishing.

Stark, K.D., Reynolds, W.M., & Kaslow, N. (1987). A comparison of the relative efficacy of self-control therapy and behavioral problem-solving therapy for depression in children. *Journal of Abnormal Child Psychology*, *15*, 91–113.

Stattin, H., & Magnusson, D. (1998). Onset of official delinquency. *British Journal of Criminology*, *35*, 417–449.

Steen, E., & Steen, J. (1989). Controversy concerning parental age effect in Down's syndrome. *Human Genetics*, *81*, 300–301.

Steinberg, L. (1987). Single parents, stepparents, and the susceptibility of adolescents to antisocial peer pressure. *Child Development*, *58*, 269–275.

Steinhausen, H.C. (1994). Anorexia and bulimia nervosa. In M. Rutter, E. Taylor, & I. Hersov (Eds.), *Child and adolescent psychiatry* (pp. 425–440). Oxford, UK: Blackwell Scientific Publications.

Sternberg, R.J., & Grigorenko, E. (1999). Genetics of childhood disorders: I.

Genetics and intelligence. *Journal of the American Academy of Child and Adolescent Psychiatry, 38*, 486–488.

Stokes, A., Bawden, H., Camfield, P., Ackman, J., & Dooley, J. (1991). Peer problems in Tourette's disorder. *Pediatrics, 87*, 936–942.

Stone, W., Lee, E., Ashford, L., Brisse, J., Hepburn, S., Coonrod, E., & Weiss, B. (1999). Can autism be diagnosed in children under 3 years of age? *Journal of Child Psychology and Psychiatry, 40*, 219–226.

Strain, P., Kohler, F., & Goldstein, H. (1996). Learning experiences ... an alternative program: Peer-mediated interventions for young children with autism. In E. Hibbs & P. Jensen (Eds.), *Psychosocial treatments for child and adolescent disorders: Empirically based strategies for clinical practice* (pp. 573–590). Washington DC: American Psychological Association.

Strauss, C. (1994). Overanxious disorder. In T. Ollendick, N. King, & W. Yule (Eds.), *International handbook of phobic and anxiety disorders in children and adolescents* (pp. 80–97). New York: Plenum Press.

Streissguth, A.P., Barr, H.M., Sampson, P.D., Darby, B.L., & Martin, D. (1989). IQ at age 4 in relation to maternal alcohol use and smoking during pregnancy. *Developmental Psychology, 25*, 3–11.

Strober, M. (1992). Relevance of early age-of-onset in genetic studies of affective disorder. *Journal of the American Academy of Child and Adolescent Psychiatry, 31*, 505–510.

Suematsu, H., Kuboki, T., & Itoh, T. (1985). Statistical studies on the prognosis of anorexia nervosa. *Psychosomatics, 43*, 104–112.

Sugiyama, T., & Abe, T. (1989). The prevalence of autism in Nagoya, Japan: A total population study. *Journal of Autism and Developmental Disorders, 19*, 87–96.

Swanson, J., & Kinsbourne, M. (1980). Artificial color and hyperactive children. In R.M. Knights & D.J. Bakker (Eds.), *Treatment of hyperactive and learning disabled children*. Baltimore: University Park Press.

Swedo, S., Rapoport, J., Leonard, J., Lenane, M., & Cheslow, D. (1989). Obsessive-compulsive disorder in children and adolescents: Clinical phenomenology of 70 consecutive cases. *Archives of General Psychiatry, 46*, 335–341.

Szatmari, P., Jones, M.B., Zwaigenbaum, L., & MacLean, J. (1998). Genetics of autism: Overview and new directions. *Journal of Autism and Developmental Disabilities, 28*, 369–342.

Szatmari, P., Offord, D.R., & Boyle, M.H. (1989). Ontario child health study: Prevalence of attention deficit disorder with hyperactivity. *Journal of Child Psychology and Psychiatry, 30*, 219–230.

Tanoue, Y., Oda, S., Asano, F., & Kawashima, K. (1988). Epidemiology of infantile autism in Southern Ibaraki, Japan: Differences in prevalence rates in birth cohorts. *Journal of Autism and Developmental Disorders, 18*, 155–166.

Target, M., & Fonagy, P. (1994). Efficacy of psychoanalysis for children with emotional disorder. *Journal of the American Academy of Child and Adolescent Psychiatry, 33*, 361–371.

Tarnowski, K.J., & Nay, S.M. (1989). Locus of control in children with learning disabilities and hyperactivity: A subgroup analysis. *Journal of Learning Disabilities, 22*, 381–383.

Taylor, E. (1994). Syndromes of attention deficit and overactivity. In M. Rutter, E. Taylor, & L. Hersov (Eds.), *Child and adolescent psychiatry* (pp. 285–307). Oxford, UK: Blackwell Scientific Publications.

Taylor, H.G. (1989). Learning disabilities. In E.J. Mash & R.A. Barkley (Eds.), *Treatment of childhood disorders*. New York: Guilford Press.

Thompson, R.J., & Kronenberger, W. (1990). Behavior problems in children with learning problems. In H.L. Swanson & B. Keogh (Eds.),

Thorndike, E.L. (1898). Animal intelligence: An experimental study of the associative processes in animals. *Psychological Monographs, 2*(8).

Timmerman, M.G., Wells, L.A., & Chen, S. (1990). Bulimia nervosa and associated alcohol abuse among secondary school students. *Journal of the American Academy of Child and Adolescent Psychiatry, 29*, 118–222.

Tompson, M., Asarnow, J., Hamilton, E., Newell, L., & Goldstein, M. (1997). Children with schizophrenia-spectrum disorders: Thought disorder and communication problems in a family interactional context. *Journal of Child Psychology and Psychiatry, 38*, 421–429.

Toone, B., & van der Linden, G. (1997). Attention deficit hyperactivity disorder or hyperkinetic disorder in adults. *British Journal of Psychiatry, 170*, 489–491.

Torgersen, S. (1983). Genetic factors in anxiety disorders. *Archives of General Psychiatry, 40*, 1085–1089.

Torgesen, J.K. (1979). What shall we do with psychological processes? *Journal of Learning Disabilities, 12*, 6–23.

Torgesen, J.K. (1986). Learning disabilities theory: Its current state and future prospects. *Journal of Learning Disabilities, 19*, 399–407.

Toro, P.A., Weissberg, R.P., Guare, J., & Liebenstein, N.L. (1990). A comparison of children with and without learning disabilities on social cognitive-problem solving skills, social behavior, and family background. *Journal of Learning Disabilities, 23*, 115–120.

Treadwell, K., Flannery, E., & Kendall, P.C. (1995). Ethnicity and gender in relation to adaptive functioning, diagnostic status, and treatment outcome in children from an anxiety clinic. *Journal of Anxiety Disorders, 9*, 373–384.

Tremblay, R.E., McCord, J., Boileau, H., LeBlanc, M., Gagnon, C., Charlesbois, P., & Larivee, S. (1990). *The Montreal experiment: School adjustment and self-reported delinquency after three-years of follow-up*. Paper presented at the annual meeting of the American Society of Criminology, Baltimore.

Tuma, J.M. (1989). Mental health services for children: The state of the art. *American Psychologist, 44*, 188–199.

Van Bourgondien, M.E., Reichle, N., & Palmer, A. (1997). Sexual behavior in adults with autism. *Journal of Autism and Developmental Disabilities, 27*, 113–125.

Van Bourgondien, M.E., & Schopler, E. (1990). Critical disuses in the residential care of people with autism. *Journal of Autism and Developmental Disorders, 20*, 291–298.

Vandenberg, S.G., & Crowe, L. (1989). Genetic factors in childhood psychopathology. In B. Lahey & A.E. Kazdin (Eds.), *Advances in clinical child psychology* (Vol. 12, pp. 139–179). New York: Plenum Press.

Vernberg, E.M., LaGreca, A.M., Silverman, W., & Prinstein, M. (1996). Prediction of post-traumatic stress symptoms in children after hurricane Andrew. *Journal of Abnormal Psychology, 105*, 237–248.

Vitousek, K.B., & Orimoto, L. (1993). Cognitive-behavioral models of anorexia nervosa, bulimia nervosa, and obesity. In K.S. Dobson & P.C. Kendall (Eds.), *Psychopathology and cognition* (pp. 193–245). Orlando, FL: Academic Press.

Volkmar, F.R. (1996). Brief report: Diagnostic issues in autism: Results of the DSM-IV field trial. *Journal of Autism and Developmental Disorders, 26,* 155–157.

Volkmar, F.R., Klin, A., & Pauls, D. (1998). Autism: The phenotype in relatives. *Journal of Autism and Developmental Disabilities, 28,* 457–463.

Vuchinich, S., Wood, B., & Angelelli, J. (1996). Coalitions and family problem solving in the psychosocial treatment of preadolescents. In E. Hibbs & P. Jensen (Eds.), *Psychosocial treatments for child and adolescent disorders: Empirically based strategies for clinical practice* (pp. 497–520). Washington DC: American Psychological Association.

Wadden, T., Brown, G., Foster, G., & Linowitz, J. (1991). Salience of weight related worries in adolescent males and females. *International Journal of Eating Disorders, 10,* 407–414.

Wahler, R.G., & Dumas, J.E. (1989). Attentional problems in dysfunctional mother–child interactions. *Psychological Bulletin, 105,* 116–130.

Waldman, I.D., Rowe, D.C., Abramowitz, A., Kozel, S., Mohr, J., Sherman, S., Cleveland, H., Sanders, M., Gard, J., & Stever, C. (1998). Association and linkage of the dopamine transporter gene and attention-deficit hyperactivity disorder in children: Heterogeneity owing to diagnostic subtype and severity. *American Journal of Human Genetics, 63,* 1767–1776.

Wallerstein, J.S., & Kelly, J. (1974). The effects of parental divorce: The adolescent experience. In E. Anthony & C. Koupernick (Eds.), *The child in his family* (Vol. 3). New York: Wiley.

Wallerstein, J.S., & Blakeslee, S. (1989). *Second chances.* New York: Ticknor & Fields.

Wallerstein, J.S., Corbin, S.B., & Lewis, J.M. (1988). Children of divorce: A 10-year study. In E.M. Hetherington & J.D. Arasteh (Eds.), *Impact of divorce, single parenting, and stepparenting on children.* Hillsdale, NJ: Lawrence Erlbaum Associates Inc.

Webster-Stratton, C. (1996). Early intervention with videotape modeling: Programs for families of children with oppositional defiant disorder or conduct disorder. In E. Hibbs & P. Jensen (Eds.), *Psychosocial treatments for child and adolescent disorders: Empirically based strategies for clinical practice* (pp. 435–474). Washington DC: American Psychological Association.

Weiner, H. (1985). The physiology of eating disorders. *International Journal of Eating Disorders, 4,* 347–388.

Weingartner, H., Rapaport, J., Buchsbaum, M., Bunney, W., Ebert, M., Mikkelsen, E., & Caine, E. (1980). Cognitive processes in normal and hyperactive children and their responses to amphetamine treatment. *Journal of Abnormal Psychology, 89,* 25–37.

Weiss, B., & Weisz, J. (1995). Relative effectiveness of behavioral versus nonbehavioral child psychotherapy. *Journal of Consulting and Clinical Psychology 63,* 317–320.

Weiss, G., & Hechtman, L. (1986). *Hyperactive children grown up.* New York: Guilford Press.

Weiss, G., Hechtman, L., Milroy, T., & Perlman, T. (1985). Psychiatric status of hyperactivities as adults: A controlled prospective 15-year follow-up of 63 hyperactive children. *Journal of the American Academy of Child and Adolescent Psychiatry, 24,* 211–220.

Weiss, R.S. (1979). Growing up a little faster: The experience of growing up in a single parent household. *Journal of Social Issues, 35,* 97–111.

Weisz, J., Weiss, B., Hans, S., Granger, D., & Morton, T. (1995). Effects of psychotherapy with children and adolescents revisited: A meta-analysis of treatment outcome studies. *Psychological Bulletin, 117*, 450–468.

Wells, K.C., & Forehand, R. (1985). Conduct and oppositional disorders. In P.H. Bornstein & A.E. Kazdin (Eds.), *Handbook of clinical behavior therapy with children* (pp. 190–209). Homewood, IL: Dorsey.

Wenar, C. (1982). *Psychopathology from infancy through adolescence: A developmental approach.* New York: Random House.

Wenar, C., Ruttenberg, B.A., Kalish-Weiss, B., & Wolf, E.G. (1986). The development of normal and autistic children: A comparative study. *Journal of Autism and Developmental Disorders, 16*, 317–323.

Werry, J. (1997). Severe conduct disorder: Some key issues. *Canadian Journal of Psychiatry, 42*, 577–583.

West, D.J. (1982). *Delinquency: Its roots, careers, and prospects.* Cambridge, MA: Harvard University Press.

Whalen, C.K., & Henker, B. (1991). Therapies for hyperactive children: Comparisons, combinations, and compromises. *Journal of Consulting and Clinical Psychology, 59*, 126–137.

Whitaker, A., Johnson, J., Shaffer, D., Rapoport, J.L., Kalikow, K., Walsh, B.T., Davies, M., Braiman, S., & Dolinsky, A. (1990). Uncommon troubles in young people: Prevalence estimates of selected psychiatric disorders in a nonreferred adolescent population. *Archives of General Psychiatry, 47*, 487–496.

Whittal, M., Agras, S., & Gould, R. (1999). Bulimia nervosa: A meta-analysis of psychosocial and pharmacological treatments. *Behavior Therapy, 30*, 117–136,

Wicks-Nelson, R., & Israel, A.C. (1991). *Behavior disorders of childhood* (2nd ed.). Englewood Cliffs, NJ: Prentice-Hall.

Widom, C.S. (1997). Child abuse, neglect, and witnessing violence. In D. Stoff, J. Breiling, & J. Maser (Eds.), *Handbook of antisocial behaviour* (pp. 159–179). New York: Wiley.

Wilfrey, D., Agras, S., Telch, C., Rossiter, E., Schneider, J., Cole, A., Sifford, L., & Raeburn, S. (1993). Group cognitive-behavioral therapy and group interpersonal psychotherapy for the nonpurging bulimic individual: A controlled comparison. *Journal of Consulting and Clinical Psychology, 61*, 296–305.

Williams, P., & King, M. (1987). The "epidemic" of anorexia nervosa: Another medical myth? *Lancet* (January), 205–208.

Williamson, D.F., Kahn, H.S., Remington, P.I., & Anda, R.F. (1990). The 10-year incidence of overweight and major weight gain in US adults. *Archives of Internal Medicine, 150*, 665–672.

Wilson, T. (1999). *Eating disorders.* Manuscript in preparation.

Wing, L., & Attwood, A. (1987). Syndromes of autism and atypical development. In D.J. Cohen & A.M. Donnellan (Eds.), *Handbook of pervasive developmental disorders.* New York: Wiley.

Wing, L., Yeates, S., Brierley, L., & Gould, J. (1976). The prevalence of early childhood autism: Comparison of administrative and epidemiologic studies. *Psychological Medicine, 6*, 89–100.

Wolf, M.M., Risley, T., & Mees, H. (1964). Application of operant conditioning procedures to the behavior problems of an autistic child. *Behavioral Research and Therapy, 1*, 305–312.

Wolfe, V.V., Finch, A.J., Saylor, C.F., Blount, R.L., Pallmeyer, T.P., & Carek, D.J. (1987). Negative affectivity in children: A multitrait-multimethod investigation.

Journal of Consulting and Clinical Psychology, 55, 245–250.

Wong, B.Y.I. (1985). Issues in cognitive-behavioral interventions in academic skill areas. *Journal of Abnormal Child Psychology, 13,* 425–442.

Wong, B.Y.I., Harris, K., & Graham, S. (1991). Academic applications of cognitive-behavioral programs with learning disabled students. In P.C. Kendall (Ed.), *Child and adolescent therapy: Cognitive-behavioral procedures* (pp. 245–275). New York: Guilford Press.

Wong, B.Y.I., & Jones, W. (1982). Increasing metacomprehension in learning disabled and normally achieving students through self questioning training. *Learning Disabilities Quarterly, 5,* 228–240.

World Health Organization (WHO). (1992). *International classification of diseases* (10th ed.). Geneva: Author.

Zametkin, A.J., Liebenauer, L.L., Fitzgerald, G.A., King, A.C., Minkunas, D.V., Herscovitch, P., Yamada, F.M., & Cohen, R.M. (1993). Brain metabolism in teenagers with attention-deficit hyperactivity disorder. *Archives of General Psychiatry, 50,* 333–340.

Zigmond, N., & Baker, J.M. (1995). Concluding comments: Current and future practices in inclusive schooling. *Journal of Special Education, 29,* 245–250.

Zill, N. (1988). Behavior, achievement, and health problems among children in stepfamilies: Findings from a national survey of child health. In M. Heatherington & J. Arasteh (Eds.), *Impact of divorce, single parenting, and stepparenting on children* (pp. 325–368). Hillsdale, NJ: Lawrence Erlbaum Associates Inc.

Zimmerman, E.H., Zimmerman, J., & Russell, C.D. (1969). Differential effects of token reinforcement in instruction-following behavior in retarded students instructed in a group. *Journal of Applied Behavior Analysis, 2,* 101–112.

Zoccolillo, M. (1993). Gender and the development of conduct disorder. *Development and Psychopathology, 5,* 65–78.

Author index

Aaronson, C., 90
Abe, T., 141
Abikoff, H., 77, 80, 81
Ablon, S., 70, 77
Abramowitz, A., 71
Abramson, H., 159
Abramson, L., 21, 99
Achenbach, T.M., 34, 40, 41, 46
Ackman, J., 156
Adam, T., 99
Addalli, K.A., 76
Agosta, J., 150
Agras, W.S., 107, 113
Albano, A.M., 40, 43, 89
Alessandri, S.M., 66
Alexander, J.F., 61
Alford, B.A., 23
Algeria, M., 65
Allen, A., 92
Allen, L., 84
Alloy, L.B., 21, 22, 99
Allred, K.D., 22
Aman, M.G., 119, 127, 128
American Association of Mental Retardation, 115
American Psychiatric Association (APA), 44, 45
American Psychologist, 16
Anastopoulos, A.D., 72, 74, 77, 79
Anda, R.F., 108
Anderson, E.R., 36, 59

Anderson, J.C., 86, 97
Anderson, K., 40, 43
Andrews, B., 1, 100
Andrews, J., 101
Angelelli, J., 61
Angold, A., 33
Apple, R.F., 111
Applegate, B., 60
Armentano, M., 71
Aronson, M., 123
Arthur, M., 60
Asano, F., 141
Asarnow, J., 135
Ashbaugh, R., 126
Ashford, L., 137
Attwood, A., 140
August, G.J., 61, 71
Autor, S., 71
Azrin, N.H., 151, 152, 159

Babigian, H., 106
Babinski, L.M., 76
Baer, D., 125
Bailey, A., 142, 143
Baker, A.G., 65
Baker, B., 162
Baker, B.L., 126
Baker, J.M., 146
Baker, L., 29, 107, 112
Bandura, A., 19
Bank, L., 29
Barclay, M., 55
Barkley, R.A., 46, 65, 67, 68, 69, 72, 74, 75, 76, 77, 78, 79

Barlow, D.H., 86, 93
Barmann, B.C., 125
Baron-Cohen, S., 139
Barr, H.R., 123
Barrett, C.L., 84
Barrett, P.M., 44, 91, 93, 94
Barrett, R., 119, 125
Barrios, B.A., 83
Barron, R., 102
Baskin, C.H., 98
Bass, D., 63
Bates, J.E., 58
Bauermeister, J.J., 65
Baugher, M., 102
Baumeister, A.A., 151, 152
Baumgardner, T., 122
Bauminger, N., 139
Bawden, H., 156
Beard, C.M., 106
Beardslee, W.R., 83
Beck, A.T., 21, 22, 99
Becker, R.J., 92
Beglin, S.J., 110
Beidel, D., 86, 92
Bemis-Vitousek, K.M., 108, 109
Bennett, B., 41
Bennett, E.L., 123
Berman, J.S., 159
Bettelheim, B., 141
Bickett, L., 67
Biederman, J., 49, 70, 71, 74, 76, 77
Bimbela, A., 149
Bird, H.R., 65

Birmaher, B., 102, 145
Birnbauer, J.S., 125
Blagg, N.R., 93
Blakeslee, S., 37
Blenkarn, M.M., 159
Bliss, J., 157
Bloom, F.E., 14
Bloomquist, M.L., 29, 61, 72, 79
Blount, R.L., 98
Blum, C., 81
Bocella, K., 78
Boileau, H., 63
Bolduc-Murphy, E.A., 76
Bolton, P., 142, 143
Bonagura, N., 74, 76
Boodoo, G., 120, 123
Borden, K.A., 81
Borden, M.C., 137
Borduin, C., 61
Borgstedt, A.D., 77
Bouchard, T.J., 13, 120, 123
Boulerice, B., 56
Bourg, W.J., 57, 58
Bowlby, J., 88
Boyce, P., 88
Boykin, A.W., 120, 123
Boyle, M.C., 55
Boyle, M.H., 67
Braafladt, N., 99
Bradley, R., 104
Brady, E.U., 93, 97
Braiman, S., 97
Braswell, L., 29, 61, 72, 79
Bravo, M., 65
Breaux, A.M., 127
Breedlove, S.M., 12
Bregman, J., 140
Brennan, C., 26
Brent, D.A., 97, 102
Brewin, C.R., 1, 24, 25, 28, 100
Bridge, J., 145
Brier, N., 130
Brierley, L., 140

Brisse, J., 137
Bristol, M.M., 139, 140, 143
Britten, K.R., 149
Brock, K., 66
Brody, N., 120, 123
Brondino, M., 62
Brown, G., 108
Brown, R., 99
Brown, R.P., 70
Brown, R.T., 80, 81
Brownell, K.D., 108, 113
Bruch, H., 105, 107, 112
Brumaghim, J.T., 77
Brunn, R.D., 157
Bryson, S.E., 116, 124, 140
Buchsbaum, M.S., 77
Budd, K.S., 103, 104
Bunney, W., 77
Burch, P.R., 61
Burge, D., 102
Burish, T., 15
Burke, J., 149
Burns, B.J., 33, 97
Burt, D.B., 121
Bushwall, S.J., 37
Bussell, D.A., 59
Butler, L., 101
Byrne, T., 71

Cadoret, R.J., 57
Caine, E.D., 77, 157
Callocott, R., 121
Camara, K.A., 37
Camfield, P., 156
Campbell, M., 145
Campbell, S.M., 35
Canino, G., 65
Cantwell, D.P., 41, 78, 74, 129
Caplan, M., 61
Carek, D.J., 98
Carlsmith, J.M., 37
Carlson, C.L., 80
Carlson, G.A., 97
Carmody, T., 101
Carr, E.G., 151, 152

Carter, J.F., 79
Casat, C., 98
Casey, P., 104
Castelloe, P., 143
Ceci, S.J., 120, 123
Chaloff, J., 76
Chamberlain, P., 58, 61
Champion, L.A., 33
Chansky, T.E., 93
Charlesbois, P., 63
Chase, T.N., 156
Chase-Lansdale, P.L., 38
Chatoor, I., 104
Chen, S., 110
Chen, Y., 121
Cheney, D., 132
Cherlin, A.J., 38
Cheslow, D., 86, 93
Chess, S., 143
Chiu, H.F., 106
Chodorow, N., 28
Chuang, A., 121
Chugh, C., 103
Churchland, P.S., 13
Ciaranello, R.D., 122, 142
Cicchetti, D., 34, 100
Clarizio, H.F., 102
Clark, G.N., 97, 100, 101
Clarren, S., 123
Clements, C.M., 22
Cleveland, H., 71
Clingerman, S.R., 81
Cloninger, C.R., 157
Cohen, D., 140
Cohen, D.J., 71, 139, 140, 143, 155, 156, 157
Cohen, I., 122
Cohen, P., 107
Cohen, R.M., 71
Cohen, R.Y., 113
Cohen, S., 151
Cole, A., 113
Cole, E., 101
Collins, F., 142
Comings, B.G., 156, 157

Comings, D.E., 156, 157
Compas, B., 40, 41, 97
Conners, C.K., 68, 72, 89, 145
Conrad, M., 98
Cook, E.H., 71
Coonrod , E., 137
Cooper, P.J., 97, 110
Cooper, S., 121
Coovert, D.L., 106
Copeland, P., 108
Corbin, S.B., 36, 37
Costello, A.J., 44, 97
Costello, E.J., 33, 86, 97, 139, 140, 143
Cox, N.J., 71
Coyle, J.T., 120
Coyne, J.C., 22
Craig, T.J., 49
Craighead, L.W., 23, 41, 113
Craighead, W.E., 23, 41
Crick, N., 171
Crisp, A.H., 107
Crnic, K.A., 119, 126, 127, 128, 144
Crosby, R., 61
Cross, P.K., 121
Crouse-Novak, M.A., 100
Crow, R.R., 90
Crow, S., 112
Crowe, L., 120, 122
Cummings, E.M., 100
Curry, J.F., 61
Cutting, L., 129, 131

Dadds, M., 44, 91, 93, 94
Dalgleish, T., 28
Daly, G., 71
Darby, B.L., 123
Davies, M., 97
Davis, T., 112
Dawson, G., 143
DeFries, J., 120
DeFries, J.C., 70
Deitz, D.E.D., 124
DeMeo, M., 70

DeMeyer, M.K., 142
Denckla, M., 139, 140, 143
DeRicco, D.A., 19
Desrosiers, M., 85
Deutsch, K., 70
Devor, E.J., 157
Diamond, M.C., 123
DiLalla, L.F., 57
Dishion, T., 60
Dixon, J., 80
Dixon, M., 80
Dobson, K.S., 21
Dodge, C.S., 92
Dodge, K.A., 56, 58, 171
Dolan, B., 106
Doleys, D.M., 158, 159
Dolinsky, A., 97
Dollard, J., 31
Donnellan, A.M., 138
Dooley, T., 156
Dornbusch, S.M., 37
Dorsey, M.F., 151, 152
Douglas, V.I., 65, 71
Down, J.L., 120
DuBois, D., 102
Dulcan, M.K., 97
Dumas, J.E., 62, 72
Dunant, Y., 12
DuPaul, G.J., 74, 77, 79
Dykens, E., 122

Earls, F., 54, 57
Eaves, L.J., 90
Ebert, M., 77
Eckberg, T.J., 139, 140, 143
Edelbrock, C.S., 40, 44, 46, 74, 75, 78, 97
Egan, J., 104
Einfeld, S.L., 119
Eiserman, W.D., 127
Elbert, J., 48
Ellis, A., 20
Eme, R.F., 54
Emery, G., 21
Emslie, G.J., 101
Epps, J., 63

Epstein, J., 68
Erdelyi, M.H., 25
Erhardt, D., 67, 79
Eron, L.D., 60
Estes, A., 52, 54
Esveldt-Dawson, K., 98
Evans, J.A., 121
Evans, L., 44
Eyberg, S., 61
Ezor, S.N., 77

Fairburn, C.G., 110, 113
Faraone, S.V., 70, 74, 76, 77
Farbisz, R., 104
Farmer, A.E., 14
Farris, A.M., 57, 58
Fauber, R., 48
Fava, M., 108
Favell, J.E., 151, 152
Fein, D., 137
Feinberg, T.L., 100
Feingold, B.F., 72
Feinstein, C., 137
Feldman, S., 127
Felix, M.R.J., 113
Fergusson, D., 74
Ferster, C.B., 141
Fiello, R.A., 125
Finch, A.J., 41, 62, 98
Fincham, F., 159
Finkelstein, R., 100
Finley, W.W., 159
Fischer, M., 74, 75
Fischer, S.A., 97
Fischler, G., 56
Fisher, W., 126
Fitzgerald, G.A., 71
Fitzgerald, M., 71
Fitzpatrick, P.A., 77
Flannery, E., 84
Flannery-Schroeder, E., 44, 84, 92, 93
Fletcher, J., 132
Fletcher, K.E., 72
Foley, C., 81
Folstein, S., 140, 142

Fombone, E., 140, 142
Fonagy, P., 47
Foote, R., 61
Forehand, R., 29, 54, 62, 79, 129, 151, 152
Foreyt, J.P., 105, 110
Foster, G., 108
Fox, M.M., 106
Foxx, R.M., 151, 152, 159
Francis, G., 33
Fraser, J., 102
Freed, J., 145
French, D., 60
Freud, S., 23, 27
Freund, L., 122
Frick, P.J., 60
Friedhoff, A.J., 156
Friedman, R., 101
Friedrich, W.N., 126
Frith, U., 139
Fudge, H., 100
Fuller, P., 143
Furey, W., 98
Furstenberg, F.F., 37, 38
Fyer, A.J., 90

Gabrielli, W., 58
Gadow, K.D., 49, 77, 127
Gagnon, C., 63
Gallops, M.S., 90
Ganales, D., 81
Garber, J., 99, 100
Garcia-Jetton, J., 74
Gard, J., 71
Garner, D.M., 108, 110
Gearhart, L., 120
Gewirtz, J.L., 17
Giampino, T.L., 76
Gilberg, C., 140
Giles, D.K., 125
Gilger, J.W., 70
Gill, M., 71
Gillberg, C., 123
Gitow, A., 92
Gittelman, R., 74, 80
Gladstone, T.R.G., 97

Goldstein, H., 145
Goldstein, M., 79, 135
Goldstein, S., 79
Goodall, G., 33
Goodman, R., 139
Goodwin, D., 58
Goodyear, I., 97
Gordon, C.T., 145
Gorman, J.M., 90
Gorsuch, R., 89
Gosling, A., 127
Gotlib, I.H., 1, 100
Gottesman, I.I., 14, 57, 142
Gould, J., 140
Gould, R., 113
Graae, F., 92
Grady, K., 61
Graham, P., 55
Graham, S., 132
Granger, D., 47
Green, B.J., 41
Green, J.W., 152
Green, K., 129
Green, S.M., 60
Greenbaum, C.W, 139.
Greenberg, M.T., 126
Greene, R., 74
Greenhill, L., 145
Gresham, F., 148
Griffin, S., 77
Grigorenko, E., 120
Grober, J.S., 61
Gross, R.T., 37
Grubb, H., 33
Guare, J., 130
Gubbay, S.S., 143
Guevremont, D.C., 72, 74, 79
Guite J., 70

Hadzi-Pavlovic, D., 88
Hagan, J.W., 73
Hagberg, B., 123
Hagerman, R., 122
Hale, G.H., 73
Hallahan, D.P., 132
Halpern, D.F., 120, 123

Hamburger, S.D., 93, 145
Hamilton, E., 135
Hammen, C., 95, 98, 100, 102
Hammerton, J.L., 121
Hammock, R.G., 151
Hampe, E., 84
Handen, B.L., 115, 116, 117, 118, 126, 127
Hanley, J., 62
Hanna, 78
Hans, S., 47
Hansen, C., 74
Hansen, D.R., 142
Harden, P.W., 56
Harding, B., 107
Harding, M., 77
Harper, R., 20
Harrington, R.C., 95, 100, 102
Harris, K., 132
Harris, M., 88
Harris, S.L., 150
Hart, E.L., 60
Hartmann, D., 83
Hartsough, C., 76
Hastorf, A.H., 37
Hauck, M., 137
Haugland, G., 49
Hawi, Z., 71
Hawkins, D., 104
Hawkins, J.D., 60
Haywood, H.C., 126
Healey, S., 127
Heath, A.C., 90
Heavey, L.M., 142
Hechtman, L., 74, 76, 77
Heilman, N., 104
Heimberg, R.G., 92
Henderson, S.H., 59
Henggeler, S., 61, 62
Henin, A., 44, 87, 92, 93
Henker, B., 78, 80, 81
Hennike, J.M., 146
Hepburn, S., 137

Herjanic, B., 40, 44
Herman, C., 111
Hermelin, B., 139
Heron, S., 71
Herscovitch, P., 71
Hersen, M., 33
Hersov, L., 158
Herzog, D.B., 109
Hess, L.E., 35
Hetherington, E.M., 36, 37, 57, 59, 98
Hibbs, E., 9, 47
Hill, J., 74, 100
Hinshaw, S.P., 52, 67, 68, 77, 79, 80, 130
Hirshfeld, D.R., 76
Hochstadt, N., 104
Hodapp, R.M., 122
Hoek, H.W., 106
Hoffman, J.A., 53, 55
Hogan, M., 21
Holder, D., 102
Holland, A.J., 109
Hollon, S.D., 15, 23
Holmes, F.B., 84
Holtzworth-Munroe, A., 61
Homatidis, S., 68, 71
Honzik, M.P., 84
Hook, E.B., 121
Hope, D.A., 92
Hope, R.A., 113
Hopper, M., 110
Hops, H., 97, 101
Horwood, L., 74
Houts, A.C., 159
Hovanitz, C., 135, 137, 140, 151
Howard, B., 92
Howe, G.W., 59
Howlin, P.A., 149, 150
Hoza, B., 66, 77, 80
Hudson, J.I., 106
Huesmann, L.R., 60
Hughes, C., 101, 132
Hughes, P.C., 73

Huguenin, N., 125
Humphrey, L.L., 111
Hutton, H., 106

Iaboni, F., 65
IDEA (Individuals with Disabilities Education Act), 129, 130
Ihrig, K., 151
Ing, P., 130
Ingram, R.E., 21, 22
Israel, A.C., 57, 124, 130
Israel, M., 12
Itoh, T., 106
Iyengar, S., 102

Jacobson, J.W., 125
Jacoby, C., 61
Jaffer, M., 92
Jameson, P., 61
Janiszewski, S., 97
Janosky, J., 127
Janovic, J., 156
Jayson, D., 102
Jehu, D., 159
Jennings, J., 66
Jensen, P., 9, 47
Jerome, L., 74
Jersild, A.T., 83
Johnson, B.A., 102
Johnson, C.R., 119
Johnson, J., 97
Johnson, S., 139
Johnson, S.B., 48
Jones, A., 159
Jones, D.J., 106
Jones, K.L., 123
Jones, M.B., 142
Jones, R., 113
Jones, R.L., 88, 127
Jones, W., 131
Jouriles, E.N., 57, 58

Kagan, J., 68, 76
Kahn, H.S., 108
Kalat, J.W., 12

Kalikow, K., 97
Kalish-Weiss, B., 137
Kallen, R., 139, 140, 143
Kalucy, R.S., 107
Kane, M., 92
Kanner, L., 136
Karlsson, J., 72
Kasari, C., 139
Kashani, J.H., 90, 97
Kashima, K.J., 126
Kaslow, N.J., 48, 97, 99, 101
Kates, W., 122
Katz, M., 119
Katz-Garris, L., 126
Kavanaugh, L., 54
Kawashima, K., 141
Kazdin, A.E., 9, 33, 41, 47, 48, 54, 60, 63, 98
Keel, P.K., 112
Keenen, K., 55
Keller, M.B., 83
Kelly, J., 37
Kelly, K.L., 77, 78
Kelly, M.M., 98
Kendall, P.C., 21, 22, 23, 41, 44, 47, 48, 56, 60, 63, 79, 84, 87, 91, 92, 93, 94, 97, 98, 99, 102
Kendler, K.S., 90
Kennedy, C.R., 92
Keogh, B., 127
Kerig, P., 37
Kernberg, O.F., 27
Kerrick, J., 151
Kessler, R.C., 90
Kieffer, J., 71
Kiely, K., 70
Kiernan, K., 38
Kihlstrom, J.F., 28
Kimberling, W.J., 130
Kinder, B., 106
King, A.C., 71
King, M., 106
King, N., 9, 48, 84, 92
Kingerlee, P., 143

Kinsbourne, M., 72
Kirschenbaum, D.S., 111
Kistner, J.A., 119, 128, 131
Klein, D., 100
Klein, D.F., 90
Klein, R.G., 76, 81
Klerman, G.L., 97
Klin, A., 153
Klinger, L.G., 143
Klorman, R., 77
Knee, D., 71
Kneedler, R.D., 132
Knight, F., 85
Knisley, H., 84
Koby, E., 93
Koch, C., 13
Koch, M., 100
Koegal, L., 145, 149
Koegel, R.L., 138, 145, 148, 149
Kohler, F., 145
Kohut, H., 27
Kolko, D., 102
Koller, H., 119
Kolvin, I., 67
Konstantareas, M.M., 68, 71
Kortlander, E., 93
Kovacs, M., 40, 100
Kowatch, R., 101
Kozel, S., 71
Kraemer, H.C, 139, 140, 143.
Krager, J.M., 78
Krasowski, M.D, 71.
Kratochwill, T.R., 47, 125
Kriss, M.R., 100
Kroll, L., 102
Kronenberger, W., 130
Kuboki, T., 106
Kuo-Tai, T., 141
Kurland, L., 106

Lachiewicz, A., 122
LaGreca, A.M., 84
Lahey, B.B., 60, 129
Lambert, M.C., 85
Lambert, N., 116

Lambert, N.M., 76
Lampron, L.B., 61
Landau, S., 67
Landen, S.J., 126
Lapey, K., 77
Lapouse, R., 84
Larivee, S., 63
Last, C.G., 33, 74, 88, 90
Lavori, P., 83
Law, T., 57, 59
Le Couteur, A., 142, 143
Leaf, P., 33
LeBlanc, M, 63.
Leboyer, M., 140
Leckman, J.F., 13, 122, 155, 156, 157
Lee, E., 137
Lee, S., 106
Leiderman, H., 37
Leiman, A.L., 12
Leitenberg, H., 107
Leland, O., 116
Lenane, M., 86, 93
Lennon, S., 145
Leon, A.C., 70
Leon, G.R., 106
Leonard, H., 92, 93
Leonard, J., 86
Lerner, J., 129
Lerner, R.M., 35
Leslie, A., 139
Leung, P.W., 21, 70
Leventhal, B., 71
Levine, W.R., 151
Levitt, E.E., 145
Lewinsohn, P.M., 97, 99, 100, 101
Lewis, J.M., 36, 37
Lewy, A., 143
Liebenauer, L.L., 71
Liebenstein, N.L., 130
Liebowitz, M.R., 90
Lilly, R.S., 90
Lindholm, L., 100
Linnoila, M., 70

Linowitz, J., 108
Lipovsky, J., 98
Lips, H.M., 28
Litrownik, A.J., 138
Lloyd, J.W., 132
Lobascher, M., 143
Lochman, J.E., 61, 62
Loeber, M., 53
Loeber, R., 55, 58, 60
Loehlin, J.C., 120, 123
Logan, G., 66
Lombroso, P.J., 13
Loney, J., 67, 68
Long, J.S., 148
Long, N., 48
Lonigan, C., 48
Lord, C., 135, 139, 140, 143, 144
Lotspeich, L., 122, 142
Lott, R., 151
Lotter, V., 140
Lovaas, O.I., 138, 147, 148, 151, 152
Loveland, K., 121
Lubetsky, M.J., 119
Lucas, A.R., 106
Ludlow, C., 77
Luk, S., 70
Lushene, R., 89
Lykken, D.T., 13
Lynskey, M., 74
Lyon, G.R., 129, 131

Maccini, P., 132
MacDonald, J.P., 21, 47, 94
Mace, F., 125
MacKenzie, E.P., 57
MacLean, J., 142
MacMillan, D.L., 127, 148
Madle, R., 119
Magnusson, D., 60
Mahoney, M.J., 23
Malloy, P., 76
Manchi, M., 107
Mandell, F., 126
Manicavasagar, V., 88

Mann, B.J., 57
Mann, J.J., 70
Mannuzza, S., 74, 76, 90
March, J., 89, 92
Marks, R., 128
Marriott, M., 66
Martin, B., 53
Martin, D., 123
Martin, L.Y., 90
Mash, E.J., 17, 40, 43
Mastenbrook, J., 117
Masters, J., 15
Matson, J., 119, 125
Maughan, B., 53, 59, 60
Maurer, R., 139, 140, 143
Mayer, J.A., 93
Mayron, E.L., 73
Mayron, L.M., 73
Mazur, E., 37
Mazzocco, M., 122
McAdoo, W.G., 142
McArdle, P., 67
McAuliffe, S., 127
McBride, P.A., 70
McCarthy, M., 102
McCord, J., 63
McDonald, R., 58
McEachin, J.J., 148
McFarlane, J.W., 84
McGavin, J.K., 105
McGee, R., 55, 86, 97
McGraw, T., 104
McGue, M., 13
McGuffin, P., 14
McIlvane, W.J., 139, 140, 143
McInnis, E.T., 138
McLaren, J., 116, 124
McLaren, L., 119
McLeer, S., 63
McLennan, J.M., 140
McMahon, R.C., 52, 54, 71
McMahon, R.J., 29, 62, 79
McMurray, M.B., 77, 78
Medenis, R., 80
Meehl, P., 30

Mees, H., 146
Mees, L., 99
Meichenbaum, D., 22, 23
Melda, K., 150
Melton, G., 62
Merry, S., 128
Mesibov, G.B., 146, 148
Metalsky, G., 99
Meyers, A.W., 23
Meyers, C.E., 126
Mick, E., 70
Mieczkowski, T., 70
Mietzitiz, S., 101
Mikhail, C., 110
Mikkelsen, E.J., 77
Milberger, S., 70
Milich, R., 67, 68, 80
Miller, K., 112
Miller, L.C., 84
Miller, N.E., 31
Milroy, T., 76
Minkunas, D.V., 71
Minshew, N.J., 139, 140, 143
Minuchin, S., 29, 107, 112
Miranda, J., 21
Mitchell, J., 112
Mitchell, S.A., 27
Moffit, T.E., 60
Mohr, J., 71
Monk, M.A., 84
Morgan, A., 88
Morgan, R.T.T., 159
Morris, R.D., 129
Morris, R.J., 47
Morrison, D., 38
Mortimer, H., 127
Morton, T., 47
Mudford, O.C., 152
Mulick, J., 125
Mulle, K., 92
Munir, K., 71
Murphy, J.U., 72
Murphy, T., 104
Murray, L., 21
Murray, W.J., 125

Myers, J.E., 70
Myles, B.S., 139

Nations, R., 73
Nay, S.M., 131
Neal, A.M., 84, 90
Neale, M.C., 90
Nee, L.E., 157
Neiderhiser, J., 98
Neisser, U., 120, 123
Nelles, W., 40, 43
Nelson, C.A., 14
Nelson, J.E., 145
Nelson, L., 145
Nelson, W.M.. 62
Newell, L., 135
Newsom, C., 135, 137, 139,
    140, 144, 145, 151
Niemann, J.E., 19
Nihira, K., 116
Nitz, K., 35, 57
Nolan, E.E., 77
Norcross, J.C., 23
Norton, J., 145
Norwood, W., 58
Noyes, R., 90
Nwaefuna, A., 106

O'Brien, G., 67
O'Connor, M., 113
O'Connor, N., 139
O'Connor, R., 122
O'Connor, T., 30, 57, 98, 142
O'Connor, T.J., 59
Oda, S., 141
O'Donnell, D., 77
O'Fallon, W., 106
Offord, D.R., 55, 67
O'Leary, K.D., 15, 72, 73, 79
Olivardia, R., 106
Olkon, D.M., 71
Ollendick, T.H., 9, 48, 84, 92,
    93, 137
Olson, J., 60
O'Neill, R.E., 149
Orimoto, L., 109, 112

Ort, S., 122
Orvaschel, H., 90
Osher, T., 132
Oster-Granite, D., 120
Ott, J.N., 73
Overly, K., 85

Paget, K.D., 89
Palferman, S., 142
Pallmeyer, T.P., 98
Palmer, A., 144
Panagiotides, H., 143
Panichelli-Mindel, S.M., 44, 92, 93
Parker, J.D., 68, 89
Patterson, G.R., 29, 58, 60, 1
Paul, R., 140
Paulauskas, S.L., 100
Pauls, D.L., 13, 90, 153, 157
Pavlov, I.P., 15
Paykel, E., 98
Peck, S., 126
Peláez-Nogueras, M., 17
Pelham, W.E., 66, 77, 79, 80
Pennington, B.F., 70, 130
Perlman, T., 76
Perloff, R., 120, 123
Perrin, S., 90
Pettit, G.S., 58
Peveler, R.C., 113
Pfeiffer, S.I., 145
Phelan, P.W., 106
Piacentini, J., 92
Piazza, C., 126
Pickles, A., 100, 140
Pihl, R.O., 56
Plomin, R., 57, 59, 98, 120
Polinsky, R.J., 157
Polivy, J., 111
Pollard, S., 72
Pollock, V., 58
Pope, H.G., 106
Power, M., 25, 28
Price, G.H., 79
Price, R.K., 34

Prinstein, M., 84
Prior, M., 138

Quay, H.C., 46
Quintana, H., 145
Quinton, D., 57, 59

Rabian, B., 44, 92
Rachman, S., 83
Racine, Y., 55
Raeburn, S., 113
Rancurello, M.D., 98
Randall, J., 92
Rapaport, J., 77
Rapee, R.M., 44, 86, 91, 92, 93, 94
Rapoport, J.L., 77, 86, 92, 93, 97, 145
Rapport, M.D., 77, 78
Raymond, C.L., 157
Realmuto, G.M., 61
Reber, M., 63
Reed, E., 70
Regal, R.R., 121
Rehm, L.P., 102
Reich, W., 40, 44
Reichle, N., 144
Reid, J.B., 58, 61
Reid, M., 126, 127, 128, 144
Reinecke, M.A., 102
Reiss, A., 122
Reiss, D., 59, 98
Reiter, G., 81
Remington, P.I., 108
Repp, A.C., 124
Resnick, G., 37
Resnicow, K., 46
Reynolds, C.R., 89
Reynolds, W.M., 46, 101
Richardson, M.A., 49
Richardson, S.A., 119
Richmond, B.O., 89
Rimland, B., 145
Rimm, D., 15
Rincover, A., 151, 152
Rintelmann, J., 101

Risley, T.R., 125, 146, 151, 152
Ritter, P.L., 37
Robbins, K., 78
Roberts, M., 68
Roberts, R.E., 97
Robins, L.N., 34, 58, 60
Robins, P., 38
Rohaidy, H., 156
Rohde, P., 97, 100
Rollings, J.P., 152
Romanczyk, R.G., 119, 151, 152
Ronan, K.R., 63
Roseman, B.L., 29, 107, 112
Rosenbaum, A., 73, 79
Rosenbaum, J.F., 76
Rosenzweig, M.R., 12, 123
Ross-Gaddy, D., 46
Rossiter, E., 113
Roth, C., 102
Roth, J., 83
Rothman, S., 71
Rowe, D.C., 57, 71
Rubenstein, J.L.R., 122, 142
Rubinstein, B., 119
Rubio-Stipec, M., 65
Rudolph, K.D., 102
Rush, A., 101
Russell, C.D., 125
Russell, R., 48
Russo, D.C., 126, 151, 152
Russo, M.F., 60
Ruttenberg, B.A., 137
Rutter, M., 30, 33, 35, 55, 57, 59, 60, 71, 100, 135, 138, 139, 140, 142, 143, 144, 149, 150
Ryan, N., 102
Ryan, S.M., 91

Sacco, K.A., 119
Safer, D.J., 78
Sampson, P.D., 123
Sams, S., 79, 80
Sanders, M., 71

Sandler, I., 37
Santrock, J.W., 37
Saylor, C.F., 41, 98
Scarr, S., 120
Schachar, R., 66
Scherer, D., 62
Schleser, R., 81
Schneider, J., 113
Schneider, L., 58
Schoener, E., 74
Schopler, E., 135, 139, 140, 143, 146, 148
Schreibman, L., 138, 141, 145, 149
Schroeder, S.R., 151, 152
Schuhmann, E., 61
Schwartz, C.E., 83
Schweiger, U., 108
Scott, D.W., 109
Scott, S., 117, 119
Seeley, J.R., 97, 100
Segal, A., 74
Segal, N.L., 13
Segal, Z.V., 21
Seguin, J.R., 56
Sejnowski, T.J., 13
Shaffer, D., 97, 158, 159
Shapiro, A.K., 157
Shapiro, E.S., 157
Sharp, R.N., 102
Shaywitz, B.A., 71, 132
Shaywitz, S.E., 71, 132
Shea, V., 146
Sheed, T.J., 159
Shelton, T.L., 74, 77, 79
Shenker, R., 74
Shepperdson, B., 121
Sherman, S., 71
Shields, J., 14
Shirk, S.R., 48
Shisler, L., 127
Short, A., 148
Shott, S., 145
Shulman, C., 139
Shure, M.B., 56

Sicotte, N., 109
Siegel, T.C., 63
Sienna, M., 74
Sifford, L., 113
Sigman, M., 139, 140, 143
Silberg, J., 30, 142
Silove, D., 88
Silva, P.A., 55, 86, 97
Silverman, W., 40, 43, 84
Silverman, W.K., 44, 89, 92
Simmens, S.J., 59
Simmons, J.Q., 148
Simonoff, E., 30, 142
Simpson, R.L., 139
Singh, N.N., 127
Siqueland, L., 92
Sitarenios, G., 68
Sivo, P.J., 61
Skare, S., 61
Skinner, B.F., 16
Skjeldal, O., 140
Skoog, G., 87
Skoog, I., 87
Slymen, D.J., 90
Smalley, S.L., 142
Smallish, L., 74, 75
Smith, B.W., 123
Smith, D., 23
Smith, D.W., 123
Smith, S.D., 130
Smith, T., 148
Smith, T.W., 22
Smucker, M., 41
Solnick, J.V., 151, 152
Sommers-Flanagan, J., 49, 101
Sommers-Flanagan, R., 49, 101
Sonuga-Barke, E.J., 11, 44
Southam-Gerow, M.A., 44, 60, 91, 92, 93
Spence, M.A., 139, 140, 143
Spencer, T., 76, 77
Spettell, C., 159
Spielberger, C., 89

Spiller, L., 58
Spiridigliozzi, G., 122
Spirito, A., 41
Spivack, G., 56
Sponheim, E., 140
Sprafkin, J., 77
Srouf, A., 35
Stafford, M., 102
Stallings, P., 89
Stanley, M., 70
Stanley-Hagan, M., 36
Stark, K.D., 99, 101, 102
State, R.C., 145
Stattin, H., 60
Stedge, D., 145
Steen, E., 121
Steen, J., 121
Stein, M.A., 71
Steinberg, L., 37, 92
Steinhausen, H.C., 106, 107
Sternberg, R.J., 120, 123
Stevenson, J.F., 157
Stever, C., 71
Stewart, M.A., 57
Stokes, A., 156
Stone, W., 137
Strain, P., 145
Strauss, C., 85, 86
Strauss, J., 77
Streissguth, A.P., 123
Strober, M., 99
Suematsu, H., 106
Sugiyama, T., 141
Sullivan, K., 89
Sverd, J., 77
Swank, P., 58
Swanson, J., 72
Swedo, S., 86, 92, 93
Sweet, R.D., 157
Switzky, H.N., 126
Szatmari, P., 67, 142

Tannock, R., 66
Tanoue, Y., 141
Target, M., 47
Tarnowski, K.J., 131

Taylor, E., 70
Taylor, H.G., 128, 130
Teitler, J., 38
Telch, C., 113
Tellegen, A., 13
Terdal, L.G., 40, 43
Thesiger, C., 85
Thomeer, M., 102
Thompson, M., 48
Thompson, R.J., 130
Thomson, L.E., 107
Thorndike, E.L., 16
Timmerman, M.G., 110
Tizard, J., 55
Tompson, M., 135
Toone, B., 74
Torgersen, S., 90
Torgesen, J.K., 128, 131
Toro, P.A., 130
Treadwell, K.R.H., 84, 94
Treasure, J., 109
Tremblay, R.E., 56, 63
Troughton, E., 57
Tsuang, M., 71
Tuma, J.M., 33
Turbott, S., 128
Turner, R.K., 159

Unis, A.S., 98
Urbina, S., 120, 123

Valente, E., 58
Vallano, G., 80
Van Bourgondien, M.E., 144, 146
van der Linden, G., 74

Van der Molen, M., 66
Van Kammen, W.B., 53
Vandenberg, S.G., 120, 122
Vaughan, R.D., 46
Vernberg, E.M., 84
Vitousek, K.B., 112
Volkmar, F., 140
Volkmar, F.R., 137, 153
Vuchinich, S., 61

Wadden, T., 108
Wahler, R.G., 72
Waldman, I.D., 71
Walker, D.E., 156
Wallerstein, J.S., 36, 37
Walsh, B.T., 97
Wansley, R.A., 159
Warburton, R., 70
Ware, H., 58
Warman, M.J., 44, 92, 93
Warrenburg, S., 143
Warshak, R.A., 37
Waterhouse, L., 137
Waternaux, C., 71
Watson, D., 98
Watts, F.N., 28
Wayland, K.K., 62
Webster-Stratton, C., 61
Weidenman, L., 125
Weinberg, A., 101
Weinberg, R.A., 120
Weiner, H., 109
Weingartner, H., 77
Weiss, B., 47, 137
Weiss, D., 74
Weiss, G., 74, 76

Weiss, R.S., 36
Weissberg, R.P., 61, 130
Weissman, M.M., 97
Weisz, J.R., 9, 47, 48, 85
Wells, K.C., 54
Wells, L.A., 110
Wenar, C., 137
Werle, M., 104
Werry, J., 54
West, D.J., 55, 58
Whalen, C.K., 78, 80, 81
Wherry, J.S., 145
Whitaker, A., 92, 97
White, K.J., 62
Whitehouse, W., 21
Whitmore, K., 55
Whittal, M., 113
Wicks-Nelson, R., 57, 124, 130
Widom, C.S., 58
Wilen, T., 77
Wilens, T., 76, 77
Wilfrey, D., 113
Wilhelm, K., 88
Williams, P., 106
Williams, S., 55, 86, 97
Williamson, D.F., 108
Wilsher, C., 128
Wilson, G.T., 15, 103
Wing, L., 140
Wolchik, S.A., 37
Wolf, E.G., 137
Wolf, M., 125
Wolf, M.M., 146
Wolf, M.W., 125
Wolfe, V.V., 98

Wong, B.Y.I., 131, 132
Wong, M., 21
Wood, A., 102
Wood, B., 61
Woodworth, G., 57
World Health Organisation
    (WHO), 44
Wortham, B., 104
Wunder, J., 83
Wynne, M.E., 80, 81

Yamada, F.M., 71
Yates, W.R., 57
Yeates, S., 140
Yirmiya, N., 139
Yule, W., 55, 92, 93
Yurgelun-Tudd, D., 106
Yuzda, E., 142

Zahn, T.P., 77
Zakis, S., 90

Zametkin, A.J., 71
Zeman, J., 99
Zhang, Q., 60
Zigmond, N., 146
Zill, N., 37
Zimmerman, E.H., 125
Zimmerman, J., 125
Zoccolillo, M., 55
Zollo, L.J., 92
Zupan, B., 52

Subject index

Adaptive behavior, 115
Adaptive Behavior Scale, 116
ADIS-C (Anxiety Disorders Interview Schedule-Child), 40, 43–4, 89
Adolescence
  attention-deficit hyperactivity disorder, 74, 76
  conduct disorders, 60
  divorce, adjustment to, 37–8
Adoption studies, 57
Adults
  antisocial behavior, 34, 59–60
  anxiety disorders, 33, 86
  attention-deficit hyperactivity disorder, 76
  depression, 100
  memories of childhood, 1
African-Americans
  anorexia nervosa, 106
  anxiety disorders, 90
Aggression, 34
  attention-deficit hyperactivity disorder, 67
  attributional biases, 56
  case of Matt, 17–18
  cognitive dysfunctioning, 56
  genetic factors, 57

Alcoholism
  in fathers, 58
  and fetal health, 123
Anorexia nervosa, 104–9, 114
  age of onset, 105
  biological factors, 108–9
  and bulimia, 110–11
  case of Alma, 104–5
  causes, 106–9
  cognitive dysfunctioning, 108
  cultural factors, 106, 108
  diagnosis, 105
  diathesis-stress model, 109
  family factors, 29, 107
  gender differences, 106
  genetic factors, 109
  and hypothalamus, 108
  incidence, 106
  and norepinephrine, 108–9
  outcomes, 106, 109, 112
  personality traits, 107
  prevalence, 106
  psychodynamic theory, 107
  and serotonin, 108–9
  treatment, 112
Anticonvulsants, 127
Antisocial behavior, 34, see also Conduct disorders
Anxiety disorders, 83–94
  in adults, 33, 86
  assessment, 89

avoidance response, 18–19, 91
  behavioral models, 91–2
  case of Jim, 86–7
  case of Marsha, 85
  causes, 90–92
  cognitive-behavioral therapy, 92–3, 94
  cognitive dysfunctioning, 21, 90–91
  cultural factors, 90
  and depression, 93, 98
  diagnosis, 85–8
  drug treatment, 93–4
  family factors, 92
  gender differences, 90
  generalized anxiety disorder, 85–6, 90, 92–3
  genetic factors, 90
  information processing distortions, 21
  parent training, 94
  prevalence, 86, 87, 90
  self-report scales, 89
  separation anxiety, 85, 87–8
  structured interviews, 40, 43–4, 89
  treatment, 92–4
  types of, 85–8
Anxiety Disorders Interview Schedule-Child (ADIS-C), 40, 43–4, 89
Anxious apprehension, 86
Asperger's disorder, 153

Assessment methods,
  39–44, 68, 89
Attachment, 88
Attention
  and age, 73
  deficits, 66, 69
Attention-deficit
  hyperactivity disorder,
  65–81
  in adolescents, 74, 76
  in adults, 76
  age of onset, 65, 74
  and aggression, 67
  assessment, 68–9
  brain abnormalities, 71–2
  case of Zach, 65
  causes, 70–73
  cognitive-behavioral
    therapy, 80–81
  comorbidity, 67–8
  cultural factors, 70
  diagnosis, 65–9
  and diet, 72
  drug treatment, 77–8,
    80–81
  environmental factors, 72
  family factors, 67
  gender differences, 46, 69
  genetic factors, 70–71
  and learning disabilities,
    67, 129–30
  and lighting sources, 73
  misdiagnosis, 78
  outcomes, 74–6
  parent training, 79
  peer relationships, 67
  rating scales, 68
  school-based treatment,
    79–80
  self-control training, 78,
    79
  socioeconomic status, 70
  subtypes of, 67–8
  treatment, 76–81
Attributional style, 56, 99

Autism, 135, 136–50, 154
  behavioral modification
    programs, 145–8
  brain abnormalities, 143
  case of Bernie, 5–6
  case of Chuck, 136
  case of Dicky, 146–7
  case of Nadia, 136
  causes, 36, 141–4
  cognitive deficits, 138–9
  communication, 137–8,
    147
  cultural factors, 140–41
  diagnosis, 136, 137–8, 140
  drug treatment, 145
  early signs of, 137
  education, 146
  gender differences, 140
  genetic factors, 142
  high/low functioning,
    139
  intellectual functioning,
    139
  parent training, 148–50
  prenatal health, 143
  prevalence, 140, 141
  prognosis, 144, 145
  rubella infection, 143
  self-injury, 151
  sexual activity, 144
  theory of mind
    limitations, 139
  treatment, 145–50
Aversive electrical
  stimulation, 152
Avoidance learning, 19
Avoidance response, 18–19,
  91
  case of Sue, 18
Babies, signs of autism, 137
Bed-wetting, see Enuresis
Behavioral models, 15–20,
  31–2
Behavioral observation, 40,
  43

Behavioral training
  programs, 125–6, 145–8,
  152
Beliefs, 22
"Bell and pad", 159
Binge-purge syndrome, see
  Bulimia nervosa
Biological models, 11–15, 31
Brain, 11–13
Brain abnormalities, 12
  attention-deficit
    hyperactivity disorder,
    71–2
  autism, 143
  learning disabilities,
    130–31
  "minimal brain damage",
    71
Bulimia nervosa, 109–12,
  114
  and anorexia, 110–11
  case of Jenny, 109
  case of Sheila, 5
  causes, 111–12
  cognitive strategies, 111
  diagnosis, 110
  diathesis-stress model,
    112
  drug treatment, 113
  family factors, 111
  gender differences, 110
  outcomes, 112, 113
  prevalence, 110
  treatment, 113
CBCL (Child Behavior
  Checklist), 40, 41–3, 89
CDI (Children's Depression
  Inventory), 40–41
Cerebral cortex, 12
Child abuse, 58
Child Behavior Checklist
  (CBCL), 40, 41–3, 89
Childhood disintegrative
  disorder, 153
Childhood
  experiences/memories, 1

Childrearing, see Family factors
Children's Depression Inventory (CDI), 40–41
China
    anorexia nervosa, 106
    autism, 141
    hyperactive children, 70
Chromosomal aberrations, 120–22
Chromosomes, 13
Classical conditioning, 15–16, 31
Classification systems, 44–7
Classroom-based treatment, 60, 61, 79–80
Clomipramine, 93, 145
Coercive interaction, 59
Cognitive-behavioral models, 11, 22–3, 32
Cognitive-behavioral therapy
    anxiety disorders, 92–3, 94
    attention-deficit hyperactivity disorder, 80–81
    conduct disorders, 60, 62–3
    depression, 101–2
Cognitive deficiencies, 21
Cognitive distortions, 21
Cognitive models, 20–23, 32
Comorbidity, 67–8, 93, 97, 98, 119, 129–30
Compulsions, 86
Conditioned stimulus/response, 16
Conditioning,
    classical, 15–16, 31
    operant, 16–19, 31–2
Conduct disorders, 51–64
    adult behavior problems, 34, 59–60
    age of onset, 54, 60
    alcoholism in fathers, 58
    case of Gar, 41–3

case of Jamie, 3
case of Josh, 51
causes, 55–9
cognitive processing, 55–6
diagnosis, 52–3
discipline problems, 59
divorce, 59
family factors, 57–9
gender differences, 54–5
genetic factors, 56–7
marital conflict, 57, 58
outcomes, 59–60
physical abuse, 58
prevalence, 54
socioeconomic status, 55
treatment, 60–64
urban/rural environment, 55
Conners Rating Scales, 68
Conscious, 24
Coping Cat program, 93
Coprolalia, 156
Cultural factors/differences
    anorexia nervosa, 106, 108
    anxiety disorders, 90
    attention-deficit hyperactivity disorder, 70
    autism, 140–41
    Tourette's disorder, 157
Cylert, 77
Darkness, fear of, 35
Defense mechanisms, 24–6
Denial, 25
Depression, 95–102
    in adults, 100
    and age, 97, 100
    and anxiety, 93, 98
    assessment, 97–8
    attributional style, 99
    behavioral model, 99
    case of José, 95
    case of Nora, 4
    causes, 98–100
    cognitive-behavioral therapy, 101–2

cognitive models, 21–2, 99
comorbidity, 97
diagnosis, 96–7
diathesis-stress model, 99
drug treatment, 49, 101
environmental factors, 98
family factors, 100
gender differences, 97
genetic factors, 98
information processing, 21, 99
outcomes, 100
prevalence, 97
self-report measures, 98
treatment, 49, 101–2
Deprivation, 123–4
Developmental psychopathology, 34–5
Dextroamphetamine (Dexedrine), 77
Diagnostic and Statistical Manual (DSM-IV), 44–5
Diagnostic Interview for Children and Adolescents (DICA), 40, 44
Diagnostic systems, 44–7
Diatheses, 30
Diathesis-stress model, 11, 30, 32
DICA (Diagnostic Interview for Children and Adolescents), 40, 44
Diet and hyperactivity, 72
Differential reinforcement of other behavior, 152
Discipline problems in conduct disorders, 59
Divorce, 4, 36–9
    case of Lisa, 38–9
    conduct disorders, 59
Dopamine transporter gene, 71
Down's syndrome, 120–21
Drives, 12
Driving, 74

Drug treatment, 49
  using anticonvulsants,
    127
  for anxiety disorders, 93–4
  for attention-deficit
    hyperactivity disorder,
    77–8, 80–81
  for autism, 145
  for bulimia nervosa, 113
  for depression, 49, 101
  for enuresis, 158–9
  for mental retardation,
    127–8
  for self-injury, 151
  using stimulants, 77–8,
    127, 145
  for Tourette's disorder,
    157
Dry-bed training, 159
DSM-IV (Diagnostic and
  Statistical Manual), 44–5
Dutch, anorexia nervosa in,
  106
Eating disorders, 103–14
  anorexia nervosa, 29,
    104–9, 112, 114
  bulimia nervosa, 5,
    109–12, 113, 114
  family factors, 29, 104,
    107, 111
  in infancy, 103–4
  outcomes, 106, 109, 112,
    113
  treatment, 104, 112–14
Echolalia, 137
Education
  mainstreaming, 126–7,
    146
  school-based treatment,
    60, 61, 79–80
Ego, 24
Electra dilemma, 26
Electric shock treatment,
  152
Elimination disorders,
  157–9
Emotion, brain control, 12

Emotional development,
  83–5
Empirical research, 2, 9
Encopresis, 158
Enmeshment, 29
Enuresis, 157–9
  drug treatment, 158–9
  dry-bed training, 159
  gender differences, 158
  treatment, 158–9
  urine alarm systems, 159
Environmental factors
  attention-deficit
    hyperactivity disorder,
    72
  depression, 98
  see also Socioeconomic
    status
Escape response, 19
Externalizing disorders,
  46–7
Extinction, 152
Family factors, 29, 30, 35–9
  anorexia nervosa, 29, 107
  anxiety disorders, 92
  attention-deficit
    hyperactivity disorder,
    67
  bulimia nervosa, 111
  coercive interaction, 59
  conduct disorders, 57–9
  depression, 100
  eating disorders, 29, 104,
    107, 111
  enmeshment, 29
Family therapy, 48
  conduct disorders, 61–2
  mental retardation, 126
Fathers, 57–8
Fear, 35, 84
  age-related changes in, 84
  gender differences, 84
FEAR plan, 92–3
Feeding disorder of infancy,
  103–4
Fetal alcohol syndrome, 123
Fetal health, 122–3, 143

Fixation, 26
Food allergies and
  hyperactivity, 72
Forebrain, 12
Fragile X syndrome, 121–2
Freudianism, 23–8, 32
Gender differences, 14
  anorexia nervosa, 106
  anxiety disorders, 90
  Asperger's disorder, 153
  attention-deficit
    hyperactivity disorder,
    46, 69
  autism, 140
  bulimia nervosa, 110
  childhood disintegrative
    disorder, 153
  conduct disorders, 54–5
  depression, 97
  divorce, adjustment to, 37
  eating disorders, 106, 110
  encopresis, 158
  enuresis, 158
  externalizing/
    internalizing disorders,
    46
  fear, 84
  learning disabilities, 128
  mental retardation, 119
Generalized anxiety
  disorder, 85–6, 90
  treatment, 92–3
Genetic factors, 13–14
  aggression, 57
  anorexia nervosa, 109
  anxiety disorders, 90
  attention-deficit
    hyperactivity disorder,
    70–71
  autism, 142
  conduct disorders, 56–7
  depression, 98
  intelligence, 120
  learning disabilities, 130
  panic disorder, 90

phobias, 90
schizophrenia, 13–14
Tourette's disorder, 157
Haloperidol, 157
Head Start, 127
Hindbrain, 12
Holland, anorexia nervosa in, 106
Hyperactivity, 65, 67, 69
Hypothalamus, 12
in anorexia nervosa, 108
ICD-10 (International Classification of Diseases), 44
Id, 24
Imipramine, 158–9
Impulsivity, 21, 66–7, 69, 73–4
Inattention, 66, 69
Incidence, anorexia nervosa, 106
Infant feeding problems, 103–4
Information processing deficits, 21, 99
Inheritance, see Genetic factors
Intelligence, 120
Intelligence tests, 116, 117–18
Internalizing disorders, 46–7
International Classification of Diseases (ICD-10), 44
Intervention programs
conduct disorders, 63–4
Head Start, 127
mental retardation, 126–7
Interviews, 40, 43–4, 89
IQ, 120
IQ tests, 116, 117–18
Japan
anorexia nervosa, 106
autism, 141
Law of effect, 16
Learning, 15–20

Learning disabilities, 128–32
attention-deficit hyperactivity disorder, 67, 129–30
brain abnormalities, 130–31
case of David, 5
case of Ethan, 128
causes, 130–31
cognitive processing deficits, 131
defined, 128–30
gender differences, 128
genetic factors, 130
strategy training, 131–2
treatment, 131–2
Limbic system, 12
Mainstreaming, 126–7, 146
Marital conflict
case of Sarah, 3–4
conduct disorders, 57, 58
MASC (Multidimensional Anxiety Scale for Children), 89
Matching Familiar Figures, 68
Maternal age, 121
Maternal health, 122–3, 143
Medication, see Drug treatment
Medulla, 12
Memories of childhood, 1
Mental illness and mental retardation, 119
Mental retardation, 115–28, 132
adaptive behavior deficits, 115
anticonvulsant medication, 127
assessment, 116–17
behavioral training programs, 125–6
case of Lennie, 121
case of Steve, 124
causes, 120–24

chromosomal aberrations, 120–22
comorbidity, 119
degrees of, 118–19
deprivation, 123–4
diagnosis, 116–17
drug treatment, 127–8
educational facilities, 126–7
gender differences, 119
genetic factors, 120
intervention, 126–7
living arrangements, 124–5
and mental illness, 119
placement issues, 124–5
prenatal environment, 122–3
prevalence, 116–17
socioeconomic status, 119, 123–4
treatment, 125–8
Methylphenidate (Ritalin), 77, 78
Midbrain, 12
Modeling (learning), 19–20, 32
Models of psychopathology, 11–32
behavioral, 15–20, 31–2
biological, 11–15, 31
cognitive, 20–23, 32
cognitive-behavioral, 11, 22–3, 32
diathesis-stress, 11, 30, 32
integrative, 11, 23
psychodynamic, 23–8, 32
systems, 28–30, 32
Multidimensional Anxiety Scale for Children (MASC), 89
Neo-Freudianism, 27
Neurosis, 25
Neurotransmitters, 12–13
New Zealand, conduct disorders in, 55
Nonconscious processes, 28

Norepinephrine, 108–9
Normal development, 1, 35
  case of Steve, 7–8
  of emotions, 83–5
  transient adjustment, 7
Norway, autism in, 140
Object relations theory, 27
Observational assessment, 40, 43
Observational learning, 19–20, 32
Obsessions, 86
Obsessive-compulsive disorder, 86–7
  case of Jim, 86–7
  treatment, 92, 93
Oedipal dilemma, 26
Operant conditioning, 16–19, 31–2
Oppositional defiant disorder, 53, 54
Outcomes
  anorexia nervosa, 106, 109, 112
  attention-deficit hyperactivity disorder, 74–6
  bulimia nervosa, 112, 113
  conduct disorders, 59–60
  depression, 100
Panic disorder-agoraphobia, 88, 90
Parent training, 48
  anxiety disorders, 94
  attention-deficit hyperactivity disorder, 79
  autism, 148–50
  conduct disorders, 60, 61–2
Parents, see Family factors
Peer relationships, 67
Pemoline, 77
Personality traits, 107
Pervasive developmental disorders, 135–54

Phenylketonuria (PKU), 122
Phobias
  classical conditioning, 16
  genetic factors, 90
  of school, 88, 93
  social, 19, 92
  treatment, 92–3
Physical abuse, 58
Placement issues, 124–5
Play therapy, 48–9
Pons, 12
Preconscious, 24
Prenatal environment, 122–3, 143
Prevalence
  anorexia nervosa, 106
  anxiety disorders, 86, 87, 90
  autism, 140, 141
  bulimia nervosa, 110
  conduct disorders, 54
  depression, 97
  eating disorders, 106, 110
  mental retardation, 116–17
  oppositional defiant disorder, 54
Projection, 25
Prozac, 101
Psychodynamic theory, 23–8, 32
Psychological assessment, 39–44
Psychosexual development, 26–7
Punishment, 16–17
Questions, self-administered, 162–8
Reading disabilities, 129, 132
Regression, 26–7
Reinforcement, 16, 17, 18
Reliability, 39
Repression, 25
Response Class Matrix, 40, 43

Reticular activating system, 12
Rett's disorder, 153
Revised Children's Manifest Anxiety Scale, 89
Risperidone, 151
Ritalin, 77, 78
Rituals, 86
Rubella, 143
Schizophrenia
  in childhood, 135
  diathesis-stress theory, 30
  genetic factors, 13–14
School-based treatment, 60, 61, 79–80
School phobia, 88
  treatment, 93
Self-control training, 78, 79
Self-injury, 150–52
  case of Ginger, 6
  drug treatment, 151
  treatment, 151–2
Self-reports, 1, 40–41, 89, 98
Separation anxiety, 87–8
  case of Marsha, 85
Serotonin, 108–9
Sexism, 28
Sexual activity, 144
Sexuality, Freudian theory, 26–7
Shaping, 17
Shock treatment, 152
Social context, 20
Social learning theory, 19–20
Social phobia, 19
  treatment, 92
Socioeconomic status
  attention-deficit hyperactivity disorder, 70
  conduct disorders, 55
  mental retardation, 119, 123–4
State-Trait Anxiety Inventory for Children (STAI-C), 89

Stimulant medication, 77–8, 127, 145
Stimulus-response relationship, 16–19
Strategy training, 131–2
Stress, 30
Structured interviews, 40, 43–4, 89
Superego, 24
Systems models, 28–30, 32
Teacher Rating Form, 41
Test reliability, 39
Test validity, 39–40
Thalamus, 121
Theory of mind, 139
Tic disorders, 77, 155–7, 159
Time-out, 152
Tourette's disorder, 155–6, 157
  drug treatment, 157
  genetic factors, 157
Transient adjustment, 7
Treatment, 1, 47–9
  anorexia nervosa, 112
  anxiety disorders, 92–4
  attention-deficit hyperactivity disorder, 76–81
  autism, 145–50

behavior modification/training, 125–6, 145–8, 152
bulimia nervosa, 113
cognitive-behavioral, 60, 62–3, 80–81, 92–3, 94, 101–2
conduct disorders, 60–64
depression, 49, 101–2
differential reinforcement of other behavior, 152
eating disorders, 104, 112–14
efficacy, 47–8
electric shocks, 152
enuresis, 158–9
extinction, 152
family therapy, 48, 61–2, 126
feeding disorder of infancy, 104
learning disabilities, 131–2
medication, 49, 77–8, 80–81, 93–4, 101, 113, 127–8, 145, 151, 157, 158–9
mental retardation, 125–8
obsessive-compulsive disorder, 92, 93

parent training, 48, 60, 61–2, 79, 94, 148–50
phobias, 92–3
play therapy, 48–9
school-based, 60, 61, 79–80
school phobia, 93
self-injury, 151–2
social phobia, 92
strategy training, 131–2
time-out, 152
Tourette's disorder, 157
Twin studies, 13–14, 57, 70, 71, 90, 109, 120, 142
Unconditioned stimulus/response, 15
Unconscious, 24, 25, 27, 28
United Kingdom, autism in, 140
United States of America, anorexia nervosa in, 106
Urine alarm systems, 159
Validity, 39–40
Vitamins, 145
Weapons violence, 58
Wechsler Intelligence Scale for Children (WISC), 116, 117
Zimbabwe, binge-eating in, 110